AF580151

Dr Haifaa Younis

My Dear Heart

First published in England by

Kube Publishing Ltd
Markfield Conference Centre
Ratby Lane, Markfield
Leicestershire, LE67 9SY
United Kingdom
Tel: +44 (0) 1530 249230

Website: www.kubepublishing.com
Email: info@kubepublishing.com

 Cataloguing-in-Publication Data is available from the British Library

ISBN: 978-1-84774-291-9 Hardback
eISBN: 978-1-84774-292-6

Editor: Suma Din
Proofreader: Amina Mujela-Botic
Cover Design and Internal concept Design: Afreen Fazil (Jaryah Studio)
Typesetting: Nasir Cadir

Printer: IMAK Ofset, Turkey

Contents

My Dear Heart Who are You?

All of us have a heart. The heart has been mentioned repeatedly in the Qur'an and by *Rasul Allah* ﷺ using the word *al-qalb*. Is the heart that's mentioned in the Qur'an and the *Sunnah*, the same as the one that we all know? In reality, it isn't, therefore the question is, then what is this heart?

Who are you, my dear heart?

The physical heart is the heart that pumps blood to our body. We know that if it is healthy, the body is usually healthy and the opposite is true; if our heart is sick, our body is usually sick too. When our physical heart stops, we will die, and when we go to Allah ﷻ there is nothing called a physical heart. In fact, when we are in the grave, after six months there is nothing left of us except for bones.

So, what is this heart that Allah ﷻ mentioned in the Qur'an and *Rasul Allah* ﷺ mentioned in the *Sunnah*? My dear heart, who are you? Nobody knows what you are spiritually, except for what Allah ﷻ revealed, and one thing that Allah ﷻ says, is about where it is physically:

فَإِنَّهَا لَا تَعْمَى ٱلْأَبْصَٰرُ وَلَٰكِن تَعْمَى ٱلْقُلُوبُ ٱلَّتِى فِى ٱلصُّدُورِ

For Indeed, it is not eyes that are blinded, but blinded are the hearts which are within the breasts. (al-Hajj 22: 46)

We need to pay attention to this, most importantly, to ask ourselves; do we know the heart spiritually? Do we know that we need to work on and identify my dear heart as the *latifah rabbaniyah* meaning 'a subtle creation of Allah ﷻ our Lord', that is in the chest? *Why do I need to know about it? Why is this the most important part of my body, not physically, but spiritually?*

We need to learn about it and know who we are, by knowing what kind of a heart we have and who lives in that heart. To be on the straight path to *Jannah*, the only thing that will get us there and make us successful is when we go to Allah ﷻ with a sound heart. This is what Allah ﷻ taught us in the Qur'an when *Sayyidina* Ibrahim عليه السلام made the famous *du'a*:

وَلَا تُخْزِنِي يَوْمَ يُبْعَثُونَ
يَوْمَ لَا يَنفَعُ مَالٌ وَلَا بَنُونَ
إِلَّا مَنْ أَتَى ٱللَّهَ بِقَلْبٍ سَلِيمٍ

And do not disgrace me on the Day they are [all] resurrected.
The Day when there will not benefit [anyone] wealth or children.
But only one who comes to Allah with a sound heart.
(ash-Shu'ara 26: 87-89)

Sayyidina Ibrahim ﷺ our prophet, the father of the prophets, made this supplication to Allah ﷻ affirming that we will be resurrected and all this wealth that human beings focus on, and work so hard to collect, even by disobeying Allah ﷻ; and the children we love and sometimes disobey Allah ﷻ to please them, those children that we sisters, mothers, and women, pour our hearts out for, will not be of benefit to you or I.

The day we are going to be resurrected, we can call it the private interview with Allah ﷻ, neither the wealth that we worked so hard for, or children will help us. So, what will benefit us? The heart is all that will count, but it has to be a sound heart *Qalbun Saleem*, قلبٌ سليمٌ.

So firstly, we need to remember that it is our heart that will take us to *Jannah* because that's the only thing that will benefit us.

Secondly, *Rasul Allah* ﷺ, taught us what we need to learn about our hearts. *What is it? Who is it? What does it contain?*

The Prophet ﷺ said: "Truly, in the body there is a piece of flesh. If it is sound, the whole body will be sound; but if it is corrupt, the whole body will be corrupt. Truly, it is the heart." (Muslim and Bukhari)

Thirdly, when Allah ﷻ is looking at you and I, which part of us does He ﷻ look at?:

The Messenger of Allah ﷺ said "Indeed, Allah does not look at your bodies or your appearances, but He looks at your hearts."[1]

We need to work on our heart, because that's where Allah ﷻ is looking. Our spiritual heart, that subtle place, is where it lives well if there is faith, and if not, it doesn't succeed. If you ask yourself *'what lives in my heart'*, and your answer is *iman* (faith), then this is in keeping with what we are told in the Qur'an:

وَلَٰكِنَّ ٱللَّهَ حَبَّبَ إِلَيْكُمُ ٱلْإِيمَٰنَ وَزَيَّنَهُۥ فِى قُلُوبِكُمْ

... but Allah has endeared to you faith and has made it pleasing in your hearts. (al-Hujarat 49:7)

Sometimes genuine things will cause us to feel worried. The only place in our body, that will make us feel serene and live in peace is actually the heart. Allah ﷻ taught us,

أَلَا بِذِكْرِ ٱللَّهِ تَطْمَئِنُّ ٱلْقُلُوبُ

1 Muslim ibn al-Hajjaj, "Chapter: The Prohibition of wronging, forsaking, or despising a Muslim and the inviolability of his blood, honor and wealth," *Sahih Muslim*, Book 45, Hadith 41.

Unquestionably, by the remembrance of Allah hearts are assured.
(Ar-Rad 13:28)

Intention - *niyah* lives in the heart

It is in the remembrance of Allah ﷻ your dear heart will feel serenity and peace – so you need to take care of it. The other reason, the fundamental thing in our *deen* is our intention; why we do things. Where is the intention? Where does it live? As a scholar of the past said: 'The place of intention is the heart.' النِّيَّةُ مَحَلُّهَا القَلْب. So the *niyah*, the intention, why we are doing something, or why we are not doing something, resides inside the heart. When someone gives you advice, when you read something and it is hard hitting, where does it hurt? When someone says something to you and you say, *you know what, you're right*. Who's saying this? It is the heart thinking. In the Arabic language there is a saying about the heart: مَوْضِعُ العَقْلِ، وَمَوْضِعُ التَّفَكُّرِ، وَمَوْضِعُ الاِتِّعَاظِ 'It is the place where you think, you comprehend and remember, and admonition helps'. And Allah ﷻ said in *Surah Qaf*:

إِنَّ فِى ذَٰلِكَ لَذِكْرَىٰ لِمَن كَانَ لَهُۥ قَلْبٌ أَوْ أَلْقَى ٱلسَّمْعَ وَهُوَ شَهِيدٌ

Indeed in that is a reminder for whoever has a heart or who listens while he is present [in mind]. (Qaf 50:37)

Why did Allah ﷻ say this? In the previous verses, Allah ﷻ was talking about us human beings, and the moment of death, as the two angels come to us. Following this at the time of our resurrection the angel bearing witness tells Allah ﷾ what we did and didn't do. This is detailed before Allah ﷾ where He talks about *Jahannam* – the hellfire, and the heavens. Finally, at the end, He ﷾ will say, indeed all these reminders and admonitions are for the person who has a spiritually alive heart, that person is one who will understand.

So, my dear heart, I need to take care of you, so that when I go to Allah ﷾ I am satisfied, I am happy to go and know where I am going; and most importantly, I know He ﷾ is pleased with me. Allah ﷾ will be pleased with me when you, dear heart are well taken care of in the life of this world.

May Allah ﷾ grant us a heart which is cleansed from challenging what Allah ﷾ commands or disputing what He ﷾ forbids.

May Allah ﷾ safeguard our heart against the worship of anything other than Him ﷾, and seeking the judgement of anyone other than of His Messenger ﷺ.

May our heart be in total reliance, relating all matters to Him ﷾, in fear, hope, and sincere dedication. May our heart love in the way of Allah ﷾, and detest what He ﷾ detests. May it give for Allah ﷾, and withhold for Allah ﷾, and may it take as its only guide none other than His Messenger ﷺ.

Ya Rabbi Ameen.

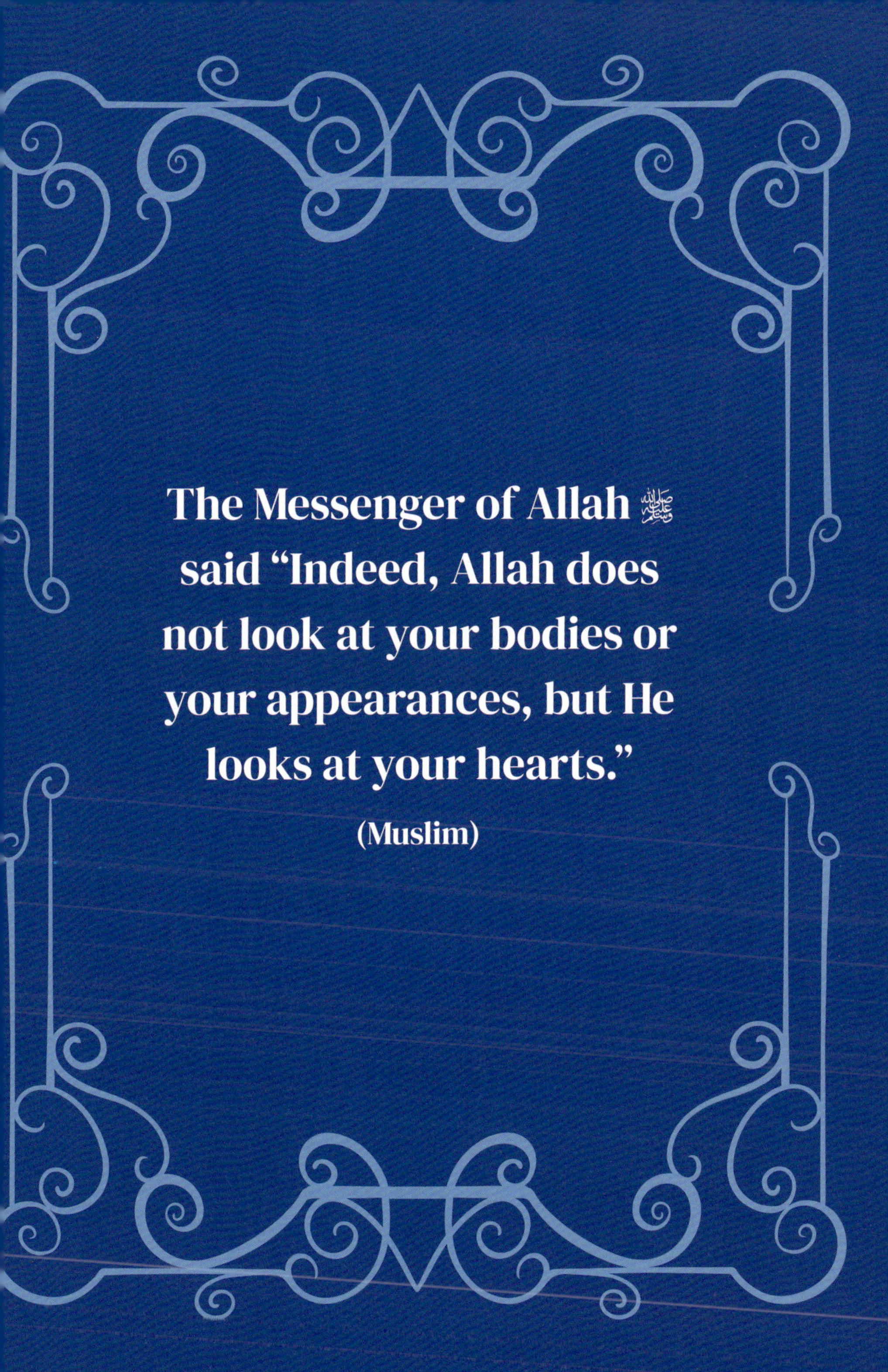
The Messenger of Allah ﷺ said “Indeed, Allah does not look at your bodies or your appearances, but He looks at your hearts.”
(Muslim)

My Dear Heart

Are you still There?

Now that we know more about our spiritual heart and its nature, we can reflect on its journey; what it started as, and how it is now. Many of you are parents or have witnessed the arrival of a baby in your family. Mothers, do you remember that moment when you delivered that beautiful baby boy or girl? When that baby was born, he or she came with the spiritual heart. We were all born with the spiritual heart, which we now know a little more about. The question I have for my heart and your dear heart is: are you still there?

The *fitrah* and our heart

That spiritual heart was born clear, just like a clear crystal – a very expensive diamond, just like that glass when we wash it and it sparkles. You see through it, reality and truth. The baby, when he or she is born, when you and I were born, our hearts were exactly like that. That's how Allah ﷻ gave us the heart and taught us. As *Rasul Allah* ﷺ taught us:

> "Every child is born upon the *fitrah* (i.e. natural disposition to worship none but Allah ﷻ Alone), and his parents convert him to Judaism, or Christianity, or Magianism."[2]

It is not just Muslims; each person is born with a natural instinct; they know who Allah ﷻ is. They know there is a Creator. Sometimes they call it a superpower; they may call it other names, but they know there is more than just what we have materially. What does this tell me? When I am born, my heart is the heart that Allah ﷻ gives to me; He ﷻ gifts it to me. Thereafter, it is my job to find out: did I keep it the way it was given to me, clean? Or did it change? My goal at the end is, if it changed, how do I bring it back to its origin? Most of us change and our heart changes too. You may wonder *What changes? Why is it not the same?*

What happens is that clear glass, the pure heart, that crystal becomes dirty and cloudy, one spot at a time, until

2 Muhammad ibn Isma'il al-Bukhari, "Chapter: The children of al-mushrikun," *Sahih Al-Bukhari*, Book 23, Hadith 137.

it changes from its original form to the descriptions we find in the Qur'an.

Our fluctuating heart

In the Qur'an, Allah ﷻ described the heart as three types: the sound, pure heart is like the clear crystal that knows its Creator. Then there is the one in between, where part of it is alive and part is dead. There is a constant fight within this second type of heart which is concerned all about this life: *should I do this, or not do this? I like it, but I shouldn't do it,* a continuous struggle goes on. Whichever of these two forces wins, the heart will take its shape; either it will stay sound or gradually get dirtier until it becomes dead. This is the third type of heart, one that is completely dead; one which doesn't know the Creator and doesn't know there is a Hereafter.

O Turner of the hearts, make my heart steadfast upon Your religion.[3]

The Prophet ﷺ frequently recited this *du'a*, emphasizing the need to seek Allah's ﷻ guidance to remain steadfast in faith.

The environment of our heart

What brings these changes? What makes the heart fluctuate is what we expose it to. Let's look at an example of twins,

3 *Jami' al-Tirmidhi* (Hadith 2140).

delivered by their mother in one country, and let's imagine at the time of delivery, these twins were separated. One twin stayed in the United States, and the other one went to Japan. Twenty years later, they are brought back together; they look the same, especially if they were identical twins. The twin who stayed in the United States speaks, acts, eats food, behaves, and has many other cultural markers like the average American, and the one who moved to Japan, will become Japanese in the way he or she speaks, behaves, food preferences, everything is influenced by Japan – their home.

What does this tell us? Our environment affects us. The same way that crystal vase is affected and changes from shiny to cloudy. It depends on what I expose my heart to, what we call external factors, what is known as the poisons of the hearts *Sumūmu al-qalb*, سُمُومُ القَلْبْ. Can I go to Allah ﷻ with the pure heart that He ﷻ wants me to have, one that will take me to *Jannah*? The answer is yes, but for that, I need to definitely take care of my heart.

The process of تَزْكِيَة *Tazkiyah* - purification, that's where I always ask my dear heart: *where are you? Are you still pure? Are you still the same as when I was born? Are you changing?*

Rasul Allah ﷺ taught us in a *hadith*,[4] القُلُوبُ أَرْبَعَةٌ what we expose our heart to, will result in four influences on it:

4 Abu Naeem al-Asbahani, *Hilyat u al-Awliya'*, Vol 1, page 276.

Four types of heart

Abu Sa'id al-Khudri reported: The Messenger of Allah ﷺ said, "There are four kinds of hearts: a polished heart as shiny as a radiant lamp, a sealed heart with a knot tied around it, a heart that is turned upside down, and a heart that is wrapped. As for the polished heart, it is the heart of the believer, and its lamp is the light of faith. The sealed heart is the heart of the unbeliever. The heart that is turned upside down is the heart of a pure hypocrite, for he had knowledge, but he denied it. As for the heart that is wrapped, it is the heart that contains both faith and hypocrisy. The parable of faith in this heart is the parable of the herb that is sustained by pure water, and the parable of the hypocrisy in it is the parable of an ulcer that thrives upon puss and blood; whichever of the two is greater will dominate."

Qalbun ajrad is the first type, a heart that is bare and pure, there is nothing in it except light. The owner of this heart tells itself *'In my life I'm going to continue to take care of it so it stays the same as when I was born: the pure heart, the only light in it is the light of faith.*

Qalbun kafir is the second heart that is sealed completely, the heart of a disbeliever.

Qalb al-Mankus. The 'upside down' heart, is one we need to be very careful about. This type of heart knew there is Allah ﷾, knew faith, and knew of the Hereafter, but then rejected it.

Qalbun Musaffah. The fourth heart is the heart that is covered, which most of us have. In this heart there is both faith, and there is hypocrisy. *I want to please Allah ﷾, but also, I like this and that*, and that's a constant struggle inside us. It depends which one has the stronger influence on us. If we work on ourselves and our environment helps to constantly feed our faith, we will be strong enough to remove the distractions which oppose faith. This requires us to keep cleansing. If not, if we succumb to our desires and do what everybody else is doing, then we are weakened, and we know this is not what Allah ﷾ wants us to do.

Gradually, that heart becomes dirtier until it dies spiritually. Allah ﷾ told us in the Qur'an about the three kinds of hearts. This *ayah* states the best heart is the sound heart, *Al-Qalb al-Saleem* اَلْقَلْبُ السَّلِيمُ:

يَوْمَ لَا يَنفَعُ مَالٌ وَلَا بَنُونَ
إِلَّا مَنْ أَتَى ٱللَّهَ بِقَلْبٍ سَلِيمٍ

The Day when there will not benefit [anyone] wealth or children.
But only one who comes to Allāh with a sound heart.
(ash-Shu'ara 26: 88-89)

This is what *Sayyidina* Ibrahim ﵇ asked Allah ﷾ for. Allah ﷾ described the second heart, *al-Qalb al-Mayyit* – a dead heart which does not know Him ﷾, in the following way:

أَوَمَن كَانَ مَيْتًا فَأَحْيَيْنَٰهُ وَجَعَلْنَا لَهُۥ نُورًا يَمْشِى بِهِۦ فِى ٱلنَّاسِ كَمَن مَّثَلُهُۥ فِى ٱلظُّلُمَٰتِ
لَيْسَ بِخَارِجٍ مِّنْهَا ۚ كَذَٰلِكَ زُيِّنَ لِلْكَٰفِرِينَ مَا كَانُوا۟ يَعْمَلُونَ

And is one who was dead and We gave him life and made for him light by which to walk among the people like one who is in darkness, never to emerge therefrom? Thus, it has been made pleasing to the disbelievers that which they were doing. (al-An'ām 6:122)

The third *al-Qalb al-Marid*, اَلْقَلْبُ الْمَرِيضُ, is the heart that is sick, that has these two forces pulling it one way or the other. In the end whichever one is stronger will win.

فِى قُلُوبِهِم مَّرَضٌ فَزَادَهُمُ ٱللَّهُ مَرَضًا ۖ وَلَهُمْ عَذَابٌ أَلِيمٌۢ بِمَا كَانُوا۟ يَكْذِبُونَ

In their hearts is disease, so Allāh has increased their disease; and for them is a painful punishment because they [habitually] used to lie. (al-Baqarah 2:10)

Ya Rabbi help us with opportunities every day, for each of us to keep this pure heart on the *fitrah. Ya Rabbi* guide our hearts to be radiant and never sealed. May Allah ﷻ strengthen our hearts during the blessed times in the year like the days and nights in *Ramadan* to cleanse and keep the crystal shining, as long as we are living. *Ya Rabbi Ameen.*

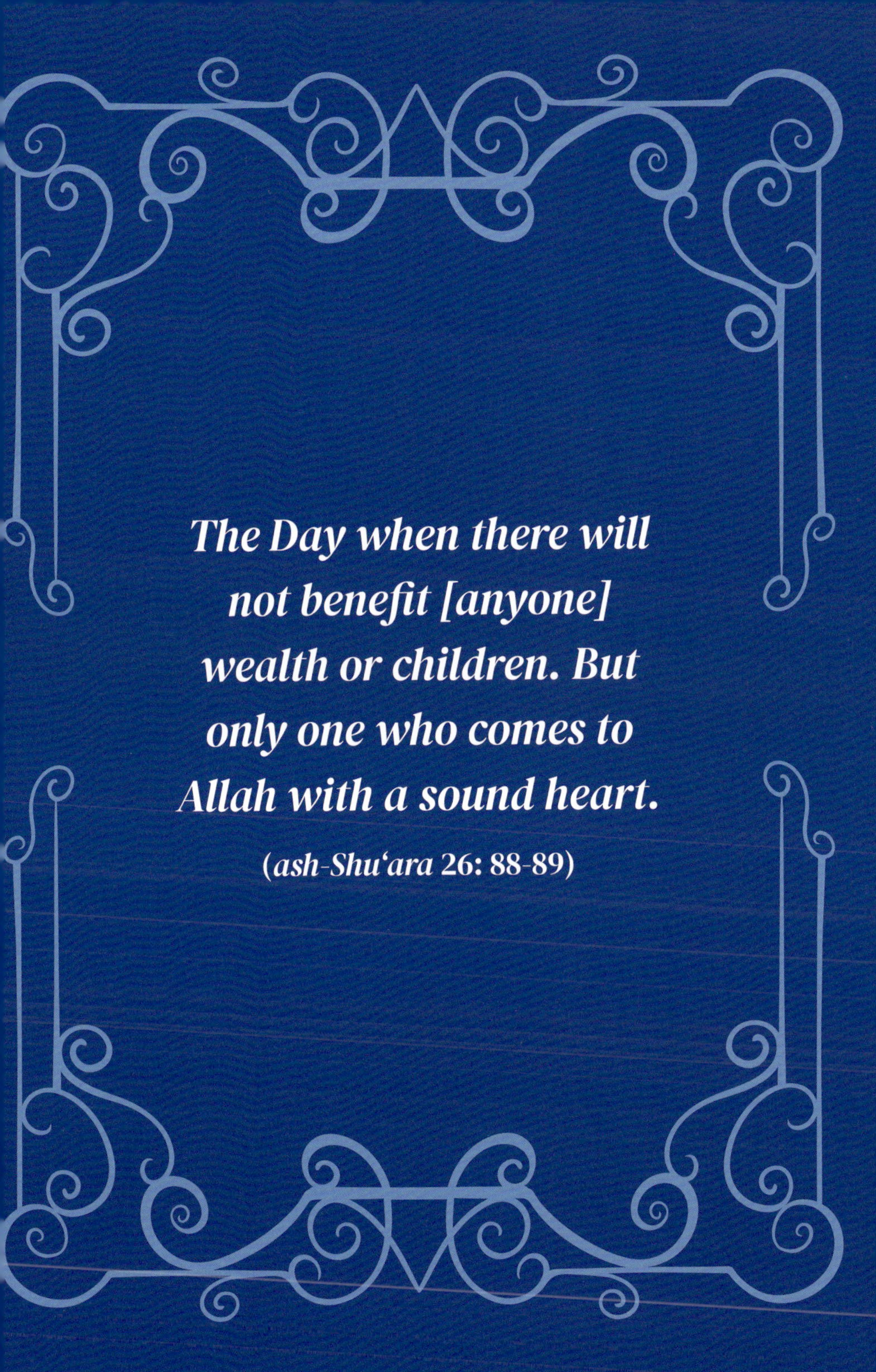
The Day when there will not benefit [anyone] wealth or children. But only one who comes to Allah with a sound heart.
(*ash-Shu'ara* 26: 88-89)

My Dear Heart

Are you Sound?

In the previous chapter we learned about the sound heart *Al-Qalb al-Saleem*, the one that *Sayyidina* Ibrahim ﵇ asked Allah ﷻ to give to him, the only one that will save us on the Day of Judgement. How do I know, my dear heart, which kind of heart you are?

More than fifteen years ago, when I was on *Hajj*, there were three of us sharing a room. Two of us were coming back from Mina to Makkah and reached the room earlier than the third one. In the room, there were two main beds and a roller bed. So, when we came in, naturally, we were going to take the two beds, and then the third person who came late would take the roller bed. However, the woman with me in the room took the roller bed, and when I asked why, she said, لَا يُؤْمِنُ أَحَدُكُمْ حَتَّى يُحِبَّ لِأَخِيهِ مَا يُحِبُّ لِنَفْسِهِ.[5]

'None of you will be a real believer unless you love for your brother or sister what you love for yourself.'

Immediately, this woman taught me the following, *Rasul Allah* ﷺ should be above my desires and what I want. If I can do that, then I am moving forward towards Allah ﷻ.

The changing state of the heart

Do you have a sound heart? Is it sick or is it dead? We don't stay in a steady state all the time. Things change, which means in the morning, I could easily have a sound heart, then during the day something happens, and I become a little bit sick. Then in the night before I go to bed, I can go back to having a sound heart. How is that?

There are two forces inside us and remembering this scenario will show us how the two forces work. Each one of us goes through this, when it's that cold night in winter and we are in bed. The *fajr* alarm for the morning *salah* goes on and then there is this debate. I call it the 'internal debate' inside you and I. One voice says *five more minutes, ten more minutes, we still have some time, I'm tired, I need a little bit more sleep, I didn't sleep well last night.* And another voice inside you

5 Muhammad ibn Isma'il al-Bukhari, "Chapter: To like for one's (Muslim's) brother what one likes for himself is a part of faith," *Sahih Al-Bukhari*, Book 2, Hadith 6.

and I will say, *come on, get up, it's Fajr, most beloved salah to Allah ﷾ described and praised for those whose backs reject the bed.* And we have this fight, this debate inside you and I. And one of them will win. One day, the one that tells you and I to wake up will win. And the other day, the other one telling you to sleep, will win.

My dear heart, are you sound? How do I know? These two forces, the desires and the thoughts inside you and I, will show us. My heart and your heart is *saleem*, if every desire inside us, throughout time, follows what Allah ﷾ wants and what the *Rasul* ﷺ wants; similarly, every thought inside us does not go against what Allah ﷾ said and what the *Rasul* ﷺ said. *Rasul Allah* ﷺ for example says, don't get angry, and immediately, although your thoughts and feelings justify being angry and losing your temper, you immediately remember that *hadith* and you change. This is exactly like the woman who was with me on *Hajj*.

Why did Allah ﷾ create this heart inside me? What does He ﷾ want from this heart and this life? There are three things: Allah ﷾ gave me this spiritual heart and gave you this spiritual heart to know Him ﷾. How do you know you know Allah ﷾? It's when you love Him ﷾, and everything He ﷾ wants you to do comes first above everything you might love and desire. When His ﷾ pleasure comes above what people want, then your heart is doing its function, doing what Allah ﷾ created it for.

Checking for a sound heart

Ask yourself, *do I think I have a sound heart?* If we think the answer is yes, then we can ask ourselves about these areas of our life.

1. The first test is to check your relationship with this life

Is your focus from morning to evening all about this world – this *dunya*; I have to do this and that and you get upset if you don't get things that you want and if you do get it, then you're happy. Or is your main focus on considering whether what you're doing in this life, takes you closer to Allah سبحانه وتعالى? Is my main focus going to bring [good in] the *akhirah* close to me? Am I building my home with Allah سبحانه وتعالى? When people see me and talk about me, do they say she or he is from the people of the *akhirah?*. Do the things that upset me align with what upsets Allah سبحانه وتعالى?

2. The second check is how you react to disobeying Allah سبحانه وتعالى?

You can reflect on this with the following questions: what happens when I don't wake up for a *salah*? The *salah* is something we do daily, and it is a good way to gauge your relationship with Allah ﷻ. When I don't wake up for *Fajr*, when I miss one *salah*, what happens inside me? Do I run to Allah ﷻ right away and say Allah ﷻ, please forgive me or do I say, you know what, I was tired? The *Al-Qalb al-Saleem* will blame itself, the owner, and keep reminding its owner to go back to Allah ﷻ. This is a good sign and gives you hope.

The person who has a *Al-Qalb al-Saleem* will disobey Allah ﷻ as any human being will, but the reaction to the disobedience is different. The one with a sound heart will feel sad, will blame themself and want to go back to Allah ﷻ, this heart is *saleem*.

3. The third check is do you miss serving Allah ﷻ?

Ask yourself the following: when I do good deeds and then I don't do them because, for example, this person or that person did something to me, do I miss this service to Allah ﷻ? The good deeds I did were done solely to please Allah ﷻ. And now I miss doing them the same way that a hungry person misses food.

4. What do you worry about?

Most of us worry about this life, my future, where will I be five years from now? What is going to happen tomorrow, am I going to be able to buy a house? All these are *halal* and necessary parts of life. But the sound spiritual heart that is focused on going to *Jannah* will focus mainly on the obedience of Allah ﷻ. Everything that a person does from the *dunya* activities - their study, getting married, having children, anything they do, if they do it in a way that pleases Allah ﷻ, externally and internally; that's obedience.

5. What do you do with your time?

The fifth check for a sound heart is about our time. This is the most important thing. How much of our time, daily do we use on social media, just scrolling? How much do we spend in *salah*, how much time in *Ramadan* do we spend in focused reading of the Qur'an, understanding and contemplating? If we are keen, then our time will not be wasted, even when we eat and sleep, we will be aware of the time we're spending.

The intention, the *niyah*, is to get closer to Him ﷻ by being stronger, more rested, so I can serve Him ﷻ. When I go and visit my mother, when I go, let's say, to take care of my neighbour, while you are doing it, that time that you are spending, you are spending it for Allah's ﷻ sake. Why? Because Allah ﷻ through our *Rasul* ﷺ told us to take care of our neighbour. That's actually a service. Therefore, the time for the *mu'min*, the believer, with a pure heart is never wasted. A believer does not say, I'm bored. 'I'm bored' – this statement does not live in the sound heart. The one with a sound heart knows there are always things we can do to get closer to Allah ﷻ, to purify our heart and keep it clean.

6. The effect of *Salah*

My dear heart, do you change before and after *salah*? Before *salah*, let's say I was very upset, something happened. I go and pray, and I come out of *salah* and I am completely different. All my worries are gone. I talked to Him ﷻ. I complained to Him ﷻ. I begged Him ﷻ to make me feel better. If you find your comfort, your happiness, the coolness of your eyes in *salah* and the heart becomes very happy, then your heart is sound. It is something we all need to work on as it's not easy, but it will happen, *bi idhnillah*.

7. The Remembrance of Allah ﷻ

This is a question for us all; What is our relationship with the remembrance of Allah ﷻ? Throughout the twenty-four-hour day, how much time do we spend remembering Him ﷻ? How much time do we spend remembering this person or that person, or my job or my plans? How many minutes or hours, were spent in the remembrance of Allah ﷻ. 'The sign that your heart and mind is pure (or healthy) is that it does not tire from the remembrance of Allah ﷻ'.[6]

---

6 Ibn Qayyim, "Chapter Ten: On the signs of the heart's sickness and its soundness," *Ighathat al-Lahfan fi Maṣayid al-Shaytan,* Vol 1, page 120.

When we see something beautiful, many of us say, oh wow, it's beautiful. Instead, if we say '*Subhan Allah*' – that's *dhikr*. When you are eating and it's very tasty or you were very thirsty and you open your fast and drink water and say, *Alhamdulillah, O Allah! I'm so grateful to You, You gave me this cold water* – that's *dhikr* of Allah. We can incorporate the *dhikr* of Allah in every part of our life if we just focus on it.

Once it becomes natural and spontaneous, my heart is sound. It may not feel easy at first, but it's not very difficult. It only feels tough because we're not used to it and because we have not thought enough about it. Yet be assured, like many of the difficult things in our life, speaking as a physician, to become a doctor we had to study and train and face so many challenges for long periods of time. Many people would say they couldn't do it, but Allah made it easy for them.

My heart, are you sound? *Insha'Allah*, by Allah's grace, by reading this book and reflecting, we would already have started the process. By Allah's Will as we work through the chapters, by the end, all our hearts will be sound.

Ya Rabb grant us the environment and right intention in all we do to move closer to You. Allow our hearts to be attached to that which pleases You and Your Messenger and be content with obedience to You. *Ya Rabbi Ameen.*

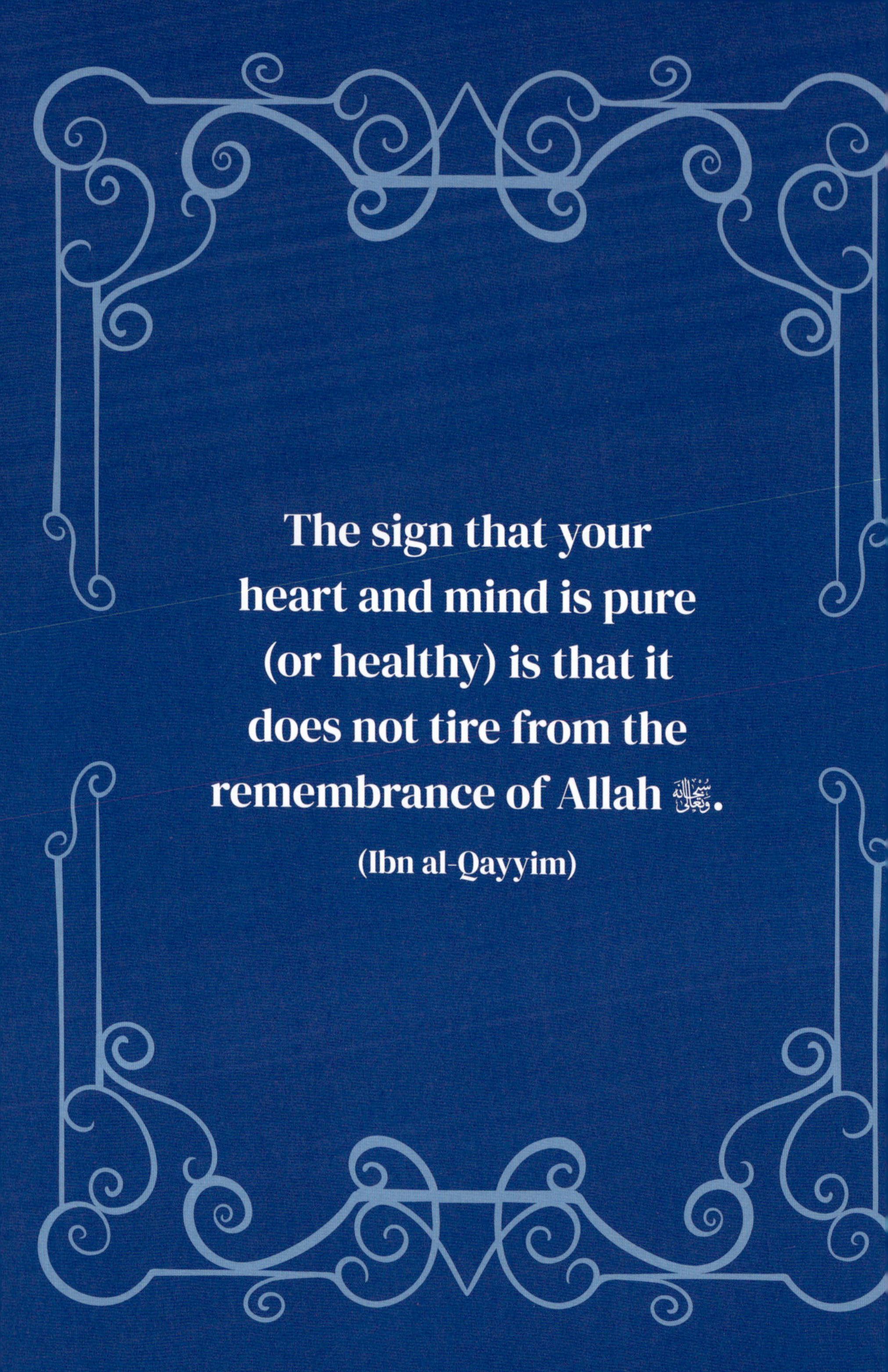
The sign that your heart and mind is pure (or healthy) is that it does not tire from the remembrance of Allah ﷻ.
(Ibn al-Qayyim)

My Dear Heart

Are you Unwell?

How many of you have had an infected wound? Whether it's a wound from surgery or a wound from a cut on your hand which was supposed to heal, but it's not healing. You may have gone to see your physician, and he says, there is pus inside the wound. Then what does he do? He says we have to open it and clean the pus completely and make sure that whatever caused that infection doesn't come back again. You keep cleaning and you keep protecting it. With time, the wound will heal. This is the state of our hearts when they become sick and unwell.

Something caused the sick heart *Al-Qalb al-Marid,* to change from the crystal which you and I were born with to become dirty, with small black dots. If no one is cleaning it, it gets infected. Allah ﷻ mentioned in the Qur'an, in *Surah al-Ahzab*, talking to the wives of *Rasul Allah* ﷺ:

يَٰنِسَآءَ ٱلنَّبِيِّ لَسْتُنَّ كَأَحَدٍ مِّنَ ٱلنِّسَآءِ ۚ إِنِ ٱتَّقَيْتُنَّ فَلَا تَخْضَعْنَ بِٱلْقَوْلِ فَيَطْمَعَ ٱلَّذِى فِى قَلْبِهِۦ مَرَضٌ وَقُلْنَ قَوْلًا مَّعْرُوفًا

O Wives of the Prophet, you are not like anyone among women. If you fear Allah, then do not be soft in speech [to men], lest he in whose heart is disease should covet, but speak with appropriate speech. (al-Ahzab 33:32)

What is the sign that the heart is sick?

The heart was created as discussed in the previous chapters, to know Allah ﷻ. A sign of knowing Allah ﷻ is that you love Allah ﷻ, and a sign that you love Allah ﷻ, is that you obey Him ﷻ. This obedience means you stay away from everything He ﷻ told you to stay away from. When the heart gets sick it doesn't do that and may not always follow what Allah ﷻ tells it to do; sometimes it follows, sometimes it may rebel.

Just like other parts of your body, like for example, your hand. Allah ﷻ created the hand to touch with, feel with, hold with and so on. What happens if your hand cannot hold or feel? Just like the heart, the hand too is sick. The same thing applies to our eyes. Allah ﷻ created and gave us eyes to see, but if our eyes suffer an infection, our vision is affected, and our eyes need treatment.

In the previous chapter we remembered the morning debate of *Fajr* that everyone experiences; *do I get up, or don't get up and delay?* Or other internal debates: when I am upset there is a debate that goes on; *do I say something that makes me feel better, or stop myself from reacting and don't say anything - because it's not pleasing to Allah ﷻ?* And then there is another voice in me saying, *Yes, say it, they deserve to hear it, you're going to feel much better, go ahead and vent.* That's the sick heart.

Again, as we said, whichever wins, the heart will change accordingly. There is beautiful hadith of *Rasul Allah* ﷺ:

> Temptations will be presented to the hearts like a mat, reed by reed. Any heart that accepts them will have a black spot marked in it, and any heart that rejects them will have a white spot marked in it. This will continue until there are two types of hearts: one white like a pure stone – no trial will harm it so long as the heavens and the earth endure – and the other black, dusty, like an upturned vessel – not recognizing what is good nor rejecting what is evil, but only following whatever desires it has absorbed. [7]

Rasul Allah ﷺ describes how temptations are presented in the way someone knits or weaves, one thread at a time,

---

7 Muslim ibn al-Hajjaj, "Chapter: Clarifying that Islam started as something strange," *Sahih Muslim,* Book 1, Hadith 276.

and how this affects the heart, whether it rejects the temptations, or accepts them and then it will be turned upside down, not knowing what is right from wrong. For example, when I'm going to check my email, for work, or to check on someone, an advert suddenly shows up on the screen. That advert is a temptation, it has things that are displeasing to Allah ﷻ, and I know it. My eyes first fell on it unintentionally, but then I liked it. This is a temptation presented to my heart. Now the choice is mine; do I keep looking? This is like the threads, one by one, every time, whether this one or next time, another thing. If this happens, as it will and then I immediately say, *Ya Allah! Please forgive me. I shouldn't watch this because it's going to affect me.* This is what *Rasul Allah* ﷺ explained, how the dark spot will be removed and the heart stays clean like the radiant vase. Instead, if I don't reject it and I say, *what did I do? Everyone is doing this; it's just a look. It's not a big deal, just ten seconds.* Then the dark spot remains, and one by one, with time, the heart becomes black.

How does your heart respond?

How do I know if my heart is sick? We can evaluate ourselves with these questions and scenarios: *When I look at haram, do I see it as haram? Or, I don't feel anything, except that it's normal, everyone is doing it.* In contrast to thinking, I immediately reject it. Like for example when I find a plate that is not clean. I immediately go to the sink and clean it before eating from it. The action of immediately cleaning the plate is similar to my heart knowing right away that this is something i shouldn't do.

There are so many viruses spiritually around us. There are too many bacteria spiritually around us and unfortunately they are free, they are available and accessible and everyone is affected. In this reality, we need to protect ourselves. The best way is by doing two things. The first thing is to identify them and know what is not good for my heart. This is simple; anything Allah سبحانه وتعالى told us not to do - don't do it, because it's not good for me.

Allah سبحانه وتعالى said this clearly in the Qur'an in *surah al-A'raf*, that He سبحانه وتعالى sent *Rasul Allah* ﷺ to guide us. Everything Allah سبحانه وتعالى made *haram*, forbidden, we can rest assured without any doubt, that it is not good for us.

ٱلَّذِينَ يَتَّبِعُونَ ٱلرَّسُولَ ٱلنَّبِىَّ ٱلْأُمِّىَّ ٱلَّذِى يَجِدُونَهُۥ مَكْتُوبًا عِندَهُمْ فِى ٱلتَّوْرَىٰةِ
وَٱلْإِنجِيلِ يَأْمُرُهُم بِٱلْمَعْرُوفِ وَيَنْهَىٰهُمْ عَنِ ٱلْمُنكَرِ وَيُحِلُّ لَهُمُ ٱلطَّيِّبَٰتِ وَيُحَرِّمُ عَلَيْهِمُ
ٱلْخَبَٰٓئِثَ وَيَضَعُ عَنْهُمْ إِصْرَهُمْ وَٱلْأَغْلَٰلَ ٱلَّتِى كَانَتْ عَلَيْهِمْ ۚ فَٱلَّذِينَ ءَامَنُوا۟ بِهِۦ
وَعَزَّرُوهُ وَنَصَرُوهُ وَٱتَّبَعُوا۟ ٱلنُّورَ ٱلَّذِىٓ أُنزِلَ مَعَهُۥٓ ۙ أُو۟لَٰٓئِكَ هُمُ ٱلْمُفْلِحُونَ

Those who follow the Messenger, the unlettered prophet, whom they find written [i.e., mentioned] in what they have of the Torah and the Gospel, who enjoins upon them what is right and forbids them what is wrong and makes lawful for them the good things and prohibits for them the evil and relieves them of their burden and the shackles which were upon them. So they who have believed in him, honoured him, supported him and followed the light which was sent down with him - it is those who will be the successful. *(al-A'raf 7:157)*

Many studies have come out which concluded that alcohol is not good for human beings. That's why Allah ﷻ makes something forbidden. We can take this example and apply it to everything; and everything Allah ﷻ said, is *halal*, and permissible, we know it's good for us.

Protecting and curing the heart

This is how we need to protect our heart; that clear, crystal vase. When we have something very valuable, we don't leave it in unsafe places, and we don't let anyone touch it. We normally protect it and keep it secure. What could be more valuable than the pure heart that will take me directly to *Jannah*? What can be more precious than the sound heart *Qalbun Saleem* that will take me directly to Allah ﷻ, compared to leaving it unprotected and exposed to everything, causing it to get sick. The sicker the heart gets, the harder it gets to cure it.

The second thing is to know what to do when we get sick? We take an antibiotic if it's bacterial and if it is virus, as we recall Covid, we covered our face and kept a safe distance from others. Spiritually this is what we need to do too; take the precautions and the medications. We identified previously that the heart doesn't stay the same and can easily get sick, especially with the viruses and bacteria outside, but with Allah's ﷻ grace we can take care of them. We can identify those viruses in our heart and in our life because each one has different remedies. At the same time we can identify: *What can I do to protect myself*? We should never forget that the One who will cure us is the one and only اَلشَّافِي, *al- Shafi*, the One who cures.

Other ways to cure our heart is through remembering Allah ﷻ in the blessed days and nights throughout the year; in *Ramadan*, in the sacred months like *Muharram* and *Dhul Hijjah*; on the day of *jumu'ah*; in *tahajjud* – the night prayer; while fasting; reading the Qur'an, and doing a lot of good deeds. We will look at these in more detail in the following chapters. Other cures are to help people, forgive people and pardon people. All these good deeds are like taking a medicine for our headache or for our infection. They will keep the heart sound and less sick. In addition, we keep asking Allah ﷻ to cure our heart.

The Prophet ﷺ used to supplicate:

"O Allah, grant our souls taqwa (piety), and purify them, for You are the best to purify them. You are their Guardian and Master."[8]

Ya Rabbi Ameen.

---

8 Muslim ibn al-Hajjaj, "Chapter: Supplications [Of the Prophet (SAW)," *Sahih Muslim*, Book 48, Hadith 99.

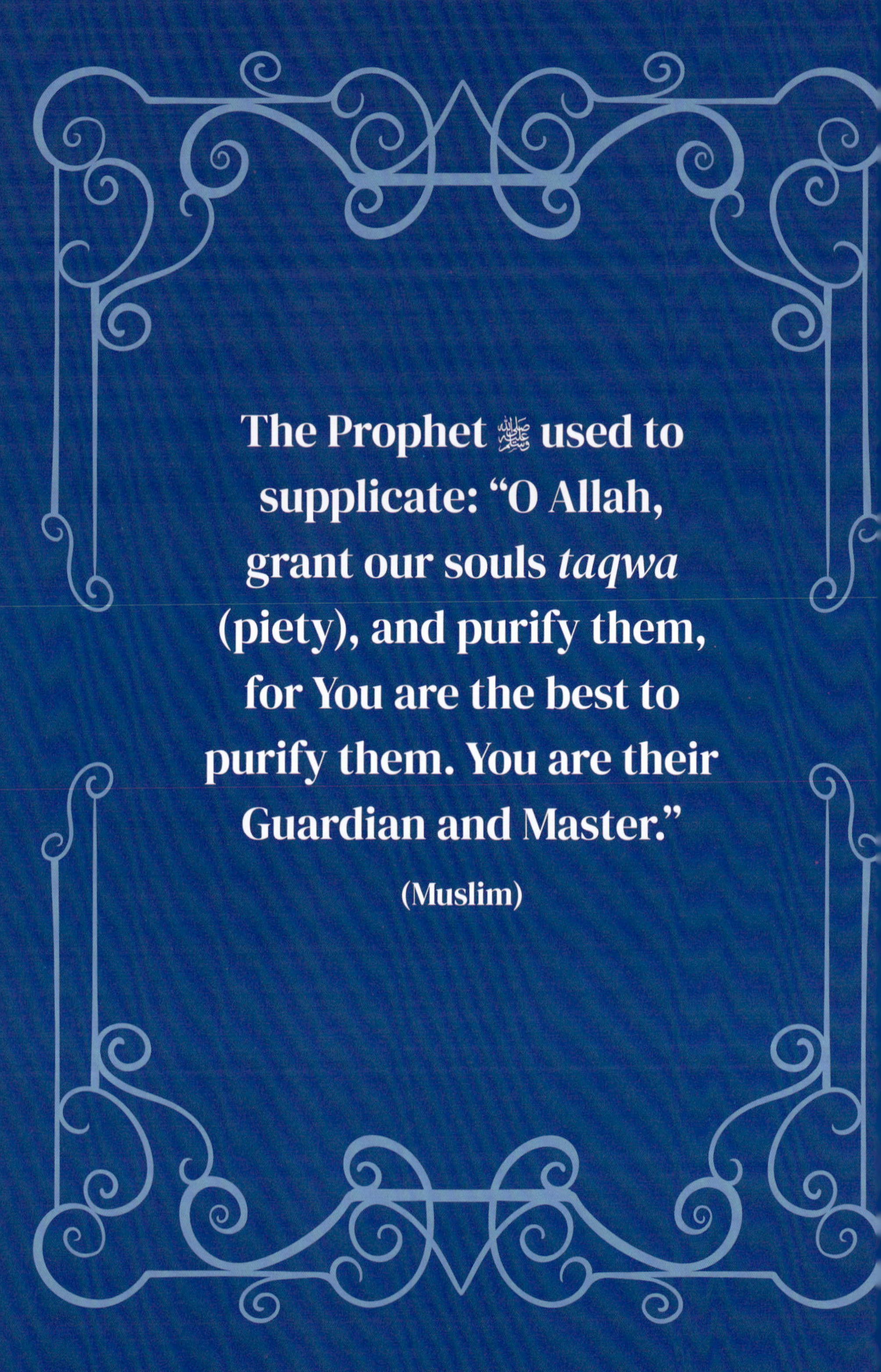
The Prophet ﷺ used to supplicate: "O Allah, grant our souls *taqwa* (piety), and purify them, for You are the best to purify them. You are their Guardian and Master."
(Muslim)

My Dear Heart

Are you Dead?

As we explored in the last chapter, our hearts can move from pure and healthy to getting sick or turning completely dead. My dear heart, how do you die? If you testify, لَا إِلٰهَ إِلَّا اللّٰهُ *La ilaha illallah* – There is no god but Allah ﷻ, your heart is not dead. If you know Allah ﷻ, your heart is not dead.

However, is it possible to go through the day for a short time, maybe ten minutes or longer, an hour or two, where the heart becomes completely dead, and then goes back? The answer is yes, as the following incident will show. Recently I visited a physically sick person in the hospital who had been very sick for two or three days before I visited. When

I came to the room, by the grace and mercy of Allah سُبْحَانَهُ وَتَعَالَىٰ, that person was much better. They still needed to improve but they were no longer very sick. Then I looked at that person and said, do you want to pray? They replied 'No. How am I going to do *wudu*?' They were asked by medical staff not to move.

I said it was not a problem, and offered to bring them water to their bed. The response was 'No, maybe I'm not able to do this'. I said, 'Okay, you can do *tayammum* because you are unwell'. And the answer was 'No. Allah knows what's in my heart.' At that moment, I fear, that heart was dead.

What is a dead heart?

This is the opposite to the sound heart. The definition in classical writings is: 'It does not know its Lord, nor does it refrain from His disobedience.' Even if this is a temporary state, for a short time, it is dead.

In this state, the heart does not control itself, or pull itself back from what Allah سُبْحَانَهُ وَتَعَالَىٰ said not to do. Rather, he or she worships their desires. The heart's answer to every temptation is yes. Even if this temptation will lead to disobedience of Allah سُبْحَانَهُ وَتَعَالَىٰ, the answer is still yes. A person in this condition, decides: *Everything I love, I'm going to do. Everything I like, I am going to do. Even if it will lead to the disobedience of Allah* سُبْحَانَهُ وَتَعَالَىٰ *and to the anger of Allah* سُبْحَانَهُ وَتَعَالَىٰ. As they say, *'Even if it displeases or angers its Lord, it does not care'*,[9] then the majority of the time the heart is not focused on Allah ﷻ and doesn't know Allah ﷻ.

If it loves, it loves because this heart loves for its own desire – *hawa*. If it hates someone, it's not for any reason other than personally not liking them. What do the thoughts of a dead heart sound like? *If I give, it's because I'm going to be praised, not because Allah ﷻ loves this. And if I don't do something and withhold, it's not because Allah ﷻ said not to do it, rather it's because I don't like it.* Or even worse, *it's because people will not like what I do, even if it is pleasing to Allah ﷻ*. I allow myself to be led by my desire. Desire becomes my guide and driver which leads my focus, which is mainly on this worldly *dunya*.

Ask yourself this question and I need to ask myself too: When someone comes to you and says, don't do this thing, it's not pleasing to Allah ﷻ, or do this thing instead, what is your response? If I don't listen, saying, *'I know, who are you to tell me this'*, is Allah ﷻ going to forgive me?

Sometimes there is a misplaced reliance that Allah ﷻ *al-Ghafur* forgives you all the time. Of course, we pray that Allah ﷻ will forgive us, but we can't choose to sin all the time and depend on forgiveness. Rather we must seek a balance so that if the spiritual heart is dead, it doesn't permanently die. As we said in the first chapter, the heart at birth is

9 Imam Ibn Qudamah Al-Maqdisi, Purification of the Soul, p.16

created pure. It is every temptation we fall into that adds a black spot after black spot until it becomes completely dead. When good advice is offered, for example, '*Why don't you fast a little bit extra? You know what, try to fast on Monday and Thursday?*' If the response is '*No, I can't because I will miss this type of food or that type of food*', that's my desires and whims – *hawa* speaking and in control.

The heart covered in stain

Allah ﷻ, describes the dead heart in the following *ayah*:

كَلَّا ۖ بَلْ ۜ رَانَ عَلَىٰ قُلُوبِهِم مَّا كَانُوا يَكْسِبُونَ
كَلَّآ إِنَّهُمْ عَن رَّبِّهِمْ يَوْمَئِذٍ لَّمَحْجُوبُونَ

No! Rather, the stain has covered their hearts of that which they were earning.

No! Indeed, from their Lord that Day, they will be partitioned. (al-Mutaffifin 83:14-15)

When we give a gift and put it in a box, and then wrap it completely, nobody knows what's inside. If the box had an eye, it too couldn't see anything outside. The dead heart is similarly completely covered and doesn't see anything. Such is the cover - the sins. In the *ayah* above, that's what Allah ﷻ tells us, that the stains are a result of what they were doing, and as a result of that they have by choice, put a seal, a divider between themselves and Allah ﷻ. The scholars say that 'That Day' in the *ayah*, could have two possible meanings; either The Day of Judgement, they are completely covered and there is a barrier between them and Allah سبحانه وتعالى. The person with the dead heart, they don't see Allah سبحانه وتعالى - May Allah سبحانه وتعالى protect us all from this. Or the other meaning is when I am doing that disobedience constantly and my heart becomes dead and black, I don't see Allah سبحانه وتعالى, and am unaware that Allah سبحانه وتعالى is seeing me. I don't have the regret inside me. If I'm asked '*How did you do that?*' Instead of running to Allah سبحانه وتعالى to ask Him سبحانه وتعالى for forgiveness, the reply is, '*What did I do? What's the big deal?*'

Nowadays, we are ready and focused on the harmless fun of taking selfies on our phones; pictures of our life and surroundings. Can we imagine if for once we try to put that camera, that selfie on the heart and ask Allah سبحانه وتعالى to show us what kind of heart we have; is it dead? Is it completely pure, sound, or sick? If it is dead, and if Allah سبحانه وتعالى showed me that, I'll be so grateful to Allah سبحانه وتعالى. Why? Because He سبحانه وتعالى showed me and at least I have time to correct it. The situation will be far worse when we are in front of Him سبحانه وتعالى and He's سبحانه وتعالى going to remind us of that moment, or that day or that year. Once we know the condition of our heart, if it's dead or going that way, we can immediately take measures. It's the same measures we normally take, but we need to put into practice more:

Remember Allah ﷾ more,

Turn and run to Him ﷾, ask for forgiveness,

Keep the tongue moist with the remembrance of Allah ﷾,

Remove the influences that will lead the heart to be dead.

In the words of the Messenger of Allah ﷺ, there are two *du'as* for protection and remedies for our heart:

نَعُوذُ بِكَ يَا مُقَلِّبَ الْقُلُوبِ، ثَبِّتْ قُلُوبَنَا عَلَىٰ دِينِكَ[10]

"We seek refuge in You, O turner of the hearts, so keep our hearts firm upon Your religion."

يَا مُصَرِّفَ الْقُلُوبِ، صَرِّفْ قُلُوبَنَا إِلَىٰ طَاعَتِكَ[11]

"O Director of the hearts, direct our hearts towards Your obedience."

May Allah ﷾ protect us from having a dead heart, *Ya Rabbi Ameen.*

O Allah ﷾ You are the One Who guides the hearts and makes them move the way You want. Make them move according to what pleases You. *Ya Rabbi Ameen.*

---

10 Abu 'Isa Muhammad al-Tirmidhi, "Chapter: The Supplication: O Changer of the hearts," *Jami' al-Tirmidhi*, Book 48, Hadith 153.

11 Muslim ibn al-Hajjaj, "Chapter: Allah directs hearts as He wills," *Sahih Muslim*, Book 46, Hadith 29.

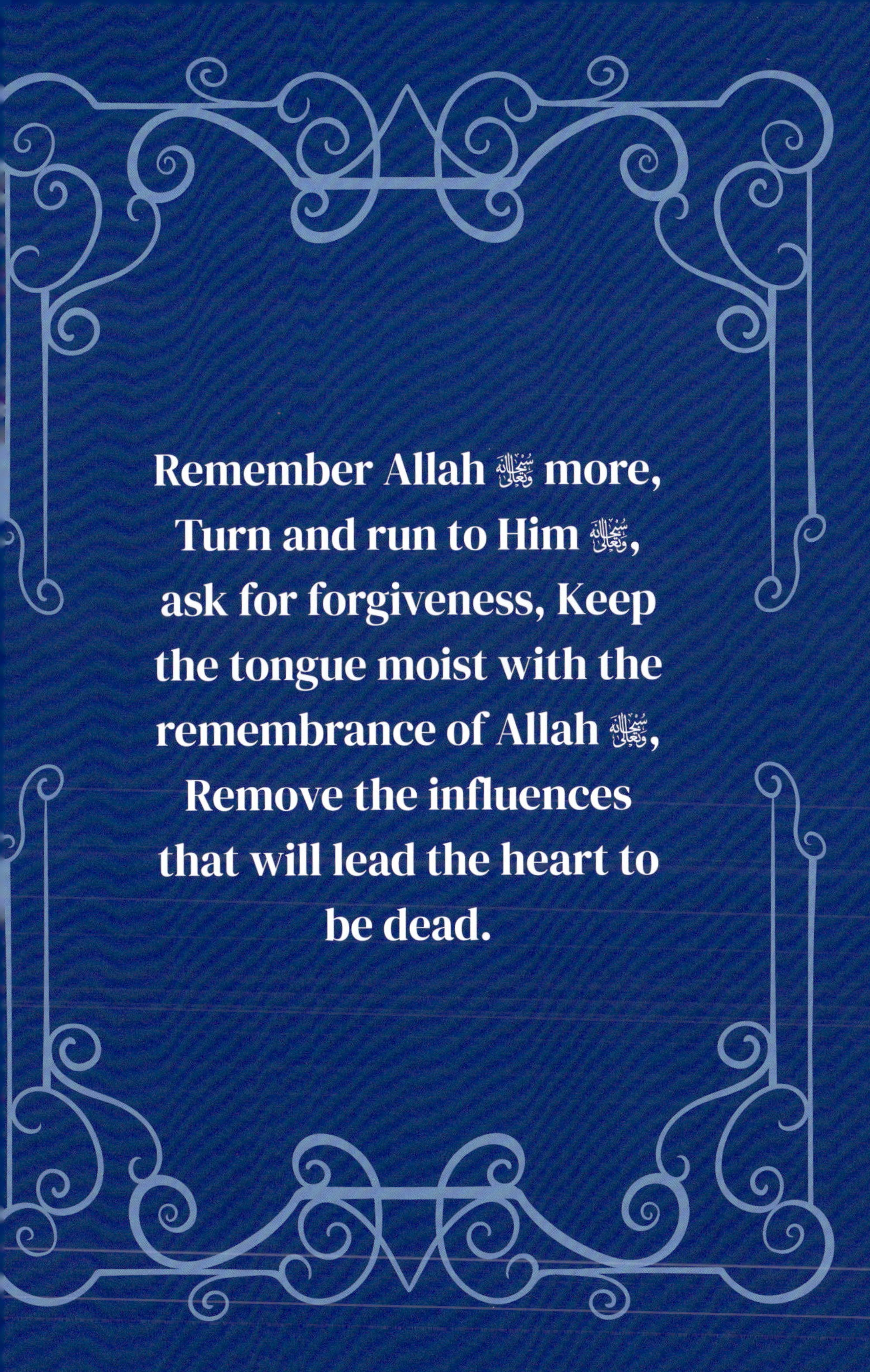
Remember Allah ﷿ more,
Turn and run to Him ﷿,
ask for forgiveness, Keep
the tongue moist with the
remembrance of Allah ﷿,
Remove the influences
that will lead the heart to
be dead.

My Dear Heart

Are you attached to this Life?

As we are taking care of our heart, this question must be asked: my dear heart, are you attached to this life, to this *dunya*? This is followed by the next question; what is the relationship between this *dunya* and the sound heart, or the lack of a sound heart?

There are several questions we have about this: *What is wrong if I love what Allah* سبحانه وتعالى *gave me? What is wrong if I get attached to what Allah* سبحانه وتعالى *gave me? What will make my heart impure? What are the temptations? These temptations Allah* سبحانه وتعالى *gave me in this dunya are there for a reason*. If we take wealth as an example, He ﷾ gave us wealth and He ﷾ gave this so we don't need to be dependent on anyone, therefore we should use this wealth as a means to reach closer to Allah ﷾. He ﷾ gave us children, a career, all these are gifts from Allah ﷾. They're not *haram* and we should enjoy and use them to get closer to Allah ﷾. For example, a father who has three daughters and he raised them well, in a way that's pleasing to Allah ﷾. These three daughters are his path to *Jannah*. *Rasul Allah* ﷺ said:

لَا حَسَدَ إِلَّا فِي اثْنَتَيْنِ: رَجُلٌ آتَاهُ اللَّهُ مَالًا، فَسَلَّطَهُ عَلَى هَلَكَتِهِ فِي الْحَقِّ، وَرَجُلٌ آتَاهُ اللَّهُ الْحِكْمَةَ، فَهُوَ يَقْضِي بِهَا وَيُعَلِّمُهَا[12]

"There is no envy except in two (cases): a man whom Allah ﷾ has given wealth, and he spends it in the cause of truth, and a man whom Allah ﷾ has given wisdom, and he judges by it and teaches it."

Wanting to be like the person who spends in the way of Allah ﷾ is a worthy feeling.

Dear heart, are you attached to the *dunya*?

Attachment to the worldly life shows when it gets to a point that it becomes a temptation which will lead me away from

12 Muhammad ibn Isma'il ibn al-Bukhari, "Chapter: The reward of judging according to al-hikmah," *Sahih Al-Bukhari*, Book 93, Hadith 5.

my path to Allah ﷾, making it easier to disobey Allah ﷾ and forget Him ﷾.

Is having *dunya haram*? The answer is no. Is getting attached to *dunya haram*? I wouldn't say it's *haram*. I would rather say it's a very dangerous road that will lead me far from Allah ﷾. Allah ﷾ said:

ٱعْلَمُوٓا۟ أَنَّمَا ٱلْحَيَوٰةُ ٱلدُّنْيَا لَعِبٌ وَلَهْوٌ وَزِينَةٌ وَتَفَاخُرٌۢ بَيْنَكُمْ وَتَكَاثُرٌ فِى ٱلْأَمْوَٰلِ وَٱلْأَوْلَٰدِ ۖ كَمَثَلِ غَيْثٍ أَعْجَبَ ٱلْكُفَّارَ نَبَاتُهُۥ ثُمَّ يَهِيجُ فَتَرَىٰهُ مُصْفَرًّا ثُمَّ يَكُونُ حُطَٰمًا ۖ وَفِى ٱلْءَاخِرَةِ عَذَابٌ شَدِيدٌ وَمَغْفِرَةٌ مِّنَ ٱللَّهِ وَرِضْوَٰنٌ ۚ وَمَا ٱلْحَيَوٰةُ ٱلدُّنْيَآ إِلَّا مَتَٰعُ ٱلْغُرُورِ

Know that the life of this world is but amusement and diversion and adornment and boasting to one another and competition in increase of wealth and children - like the example of a rain whose [resulting] plant growth pleases the tillers; then it dries and you see it turned yellow; then it becomes [scattered] debris. And in the Hereafter is severe punishment and forgiveness from Allāh and approval. And what is the worldly life except the enjoyment of delusion. (al-Hadid 57:20)

Anytime Allah ﷾ says 'know' in the Qur'an, it is for us to learn the lesson, as said in this *ayah*, that this world is a diversion. It is also a place of boastfulness between people with their wealth and children. Then Allah ﷾ gives the parable that it is like rain. The disbeliever loves what the rain assists in growing. Then that beautiful vegetation, the plants and tree become yellow and dry. Next it will become ashes. And then He ﷾ reminds us of the destination in the

Hereafter *al-akhirah*. We need to always remind ourselves that we are going to Allah ﷻ and there is both severe punishment and also forgiveness and the pleasure of Allah ﷻ, this is the beauty of this *deen*. And then He ﷻ keeps reminding us, of the value of this worldly life, it is a place of just play and amusement. In reality, if you compare this fleeting *dunya* with the *akhirah*, the enjoyment is deceiving. We are completely deceived.

Signs of being attached to the *dunya*?

What do I do, as I love the *dunya*? I need to teach myself the reality of this *dunya*. So, I need to ask my dear heart, are you attached to the *dunya* and what are the signs that I am attached?

If we look at money, we can test ourselves. Money becomes an attachment for us, what happens to us when we lose it? *Rasul Allah* ﷺ taught us, اللَّهُمَّ اجْعَلِ الدُّنْيَا فِي أَيْدِينَا وَلَا تَجْعَلِ الدُّنْيَا فِي قُلُوبِنَا

Ask Allah ﷻ to keep our blessings in our hand, not our heart.

Having money is having power and this is good. Through it we can serve this *deen*, and it can be a beautiful way for us to get closer to Allah ﷻ. But when it gets to my dear heart and we get attached to it, it will lead to all of the diseases like jealousy, hate, and anger. All the diseases of the heart stem from this love of *dunya* and being attached to it.

So, what do we do? We need to know the reality of the *dunya* first, but also remember what our beloved Prophet ﷺ said:

مَا الدُّنيا فِي الآخِرَةِ إِلَّا كمَثَلِ ما يَجعَلُ أَحدُكُمْ إِصْبَعَهُ فِي اليَمِّ، فَلْيَنظُرْ بِمَا يَرْجِعُ[13]

Rasul Allah ﷺ said, in the *hadith* of Imam Muslim, the parable of this *dunya*, this whole life, this beauty and all that we compete and spend our time on, if you compare all this life with what is in the *akhirah* waiting for us, it's like someone putting one finger in a whole ocean. What is going to come out? Maybe, the smallest drop - this is the parable of this world – the *dunya* to the hereafter - *akhirah.*

Another check for our attachment is: what happens when you lose something? What happens when you miss a *salah*? And what happens when you miss an opportunity? If you are sad, upset and angry and start blaming others, because you didn't get what you wanted, then you are attached too much to this *dunya*.

If you didn't get it and you respond and said, قَدَّرَ اللَّهُ وَمَا شَاءَ فَعَلَ 'Allah ﷻ has decreed and whatever Allah ﷻ decrees will happen', then you're not attached to it. Not attaching to *dunya*, my dear heart, doesn't mean you're going to be lazy, or that you're not going to do anything. *Rasul Allah* ﷺ taught his Companions when they questioned the Messenger of

13 Muslim ibn al-Hajjaj, "Chapter: The passing away of this world, and the gathering on the day of resurrection," *Sahih Muslim*, Book 53, Hadith 66.

Allah ﷺ about the place of doing good deeds in relation to our fate which is already decreed for us by Allah ﷻ:

ʿAlī ibn Abī Ṭālib رضي الله عنه said: "We were at a funeral in the cemetery of Baqīʿ al-Gharqad when the Messenger of Allah ﷺ came and sat down, and we sat around him. In his hand was a stick, with which he lowered his head and began to scratch the ground. Then he said: 'There is not one among you except that his place has been written in the Fire and his place has been written in Paradise.' They said: 'O Messenger of Allah, should we not rely upon what has been written for us?' He replied: 'No! Do deeds, for everyone will be facilitated towards that for which he was created. As for the one who is among the people of happiness, he will be facilitated to do the deeds of the people of happiness; and as for the one who is among the people of misery, he will be facilitated to do the deeds of the people of misery.' Then he recited:"*As for he who gives and fears Allah and affirms the best [reward], We will ease him toward ease. But as for he who withholds and considers himself free of need and denies the best [reward], We will ease him toward hardship.*" (*al-Layl* 92:5–10)

We should therefore be eager to study and work hard. We should do our best to raise our children well. Yes, we should be competitive at work and strive to be promoted. Yes, to all of this, but you are not attached to any of it. Having it or not having it, is the same. The following saying of *Sayy-*

idina Isa عليه السلام will help your heart to stay focused on this path so you don't go to the right or the left.

اَلدُّنْيَا قَنْطَرَةٌ فَاعْبُرُوهَا وَلَا تَعْمُرُوهَا[14]

"This world is a bridge, so cross it and do not settle on it." The scholars commented: 'This is a clear analogy: this world is a passageway to the hereafter, and the cradle is the first pillar at the beginning of the bridge, while the grave is the second pillar at the end of the bridge.

Some people have crossed half the bridge, some have crossed two-thirds of it, and some have only one step left but are unaware of it. Whatever the case, it is necessary to cross. Anyone who stops to build and decorate the bridge while urging others to cross is extremely ignorant and foolish.'[15]

Another wise message and beautiful reminder about this world is when this *dunya,* on the Day of Judgement, is described like an old woman who will speak and say, "Many people have wanted me and married me." Someone then asks her, and you are that ugly? She answers, 'Yes, and I killed them all. And every time I kill someone, somebody else wants me. And I kill them again.' This is *dunya.*

---

14 Abu Nuʿaym al-ʾAsbahani, *Ḥilyat al-Awliyaʾ wa Ṭabaqat al-Asfiya*, Vol 10, page 53.
15 Mukhtasar Minhaj al-Qasidin, p. 228

كُلُّ نَفْسٍ ذَآئِقَةُ ٱلْمَوْتِ ۗ وَإِنَّمَا تُوَفَّوْنَ أُجُورَكُمْ يَوْمَ ٱلْقِيَـٰمَةِ ۖ فَمَن زُحْزِحَ عَنِ ٱلنَّارِ
وَأُدْخِلَ ٱلْجَنَّةَ فَقَدْ فَازَ ۗ وَمَا ٱلْحَيَوٰةُ ٱلدُّنْيَآ إِلَّا مَتَـٰعُ ٱلْغُرُورِ

Every soul will taste death, and you will only be given your [full] compensation on the Day of Resurrection. So, he who is drawn away from the Fire and admitted to Paradise has attained [his desire]. And what is the life of this world except the enjoyment of delusion. (Āl-Imran 3:185)

We are all dying. This *dunya* for us starts from the day we are born, and it's going to get less and keep reducing until we die. Hasan al-Basri taught us something inspiring, to remind ourselves and stay focused.

'O son of Adam, your days are few. Every day that passes, part of your life has passed.' So, the more I focus at where I am going, I can use everything Allah سبحانه وتعالى gives me to build my house in the *akhirah.* I can live in a way that Allah سبحانه وتعالى loves, as He سبحانه وتعالى loves to see His سبحانه وتعالى blessings on the human being, but neither getting attached to it, nor disobeying Him سبحانه وتعالى because of it.

May Allah سبحانه وتعالى show us truth as truth, and help us to follow it, and show us falsehood as falsehood, and help us to stay away from it. *Ya Rabbi Ameen.*

اَللَّهُمَّ أَرِنَا الحَقَّ حَقًّا وَارْزُقنَا اتِّبَاعَهُ، وَأَرِنَا البَاطِلَ بَاطِلًا وَارْزُقنَا اجْتِنَابَهُ[16]

Ya Allah! Sometimes we know what is right but it's very difficult to do it. So, we ask Allah ﷻ to make it easy. Sometimes we know what falsehood is, but it is hard for us to stay away from it. So, we ask Allah ﷻ to show us falsehood, help us recognise it, and help us to stay away from it. *Ya Rabbi Ameen.*

16 Sulayman ibn Hamd al-ʿAwda, *Shuʿaʿ min al-Miḥrab*, Vol 5, page 248.

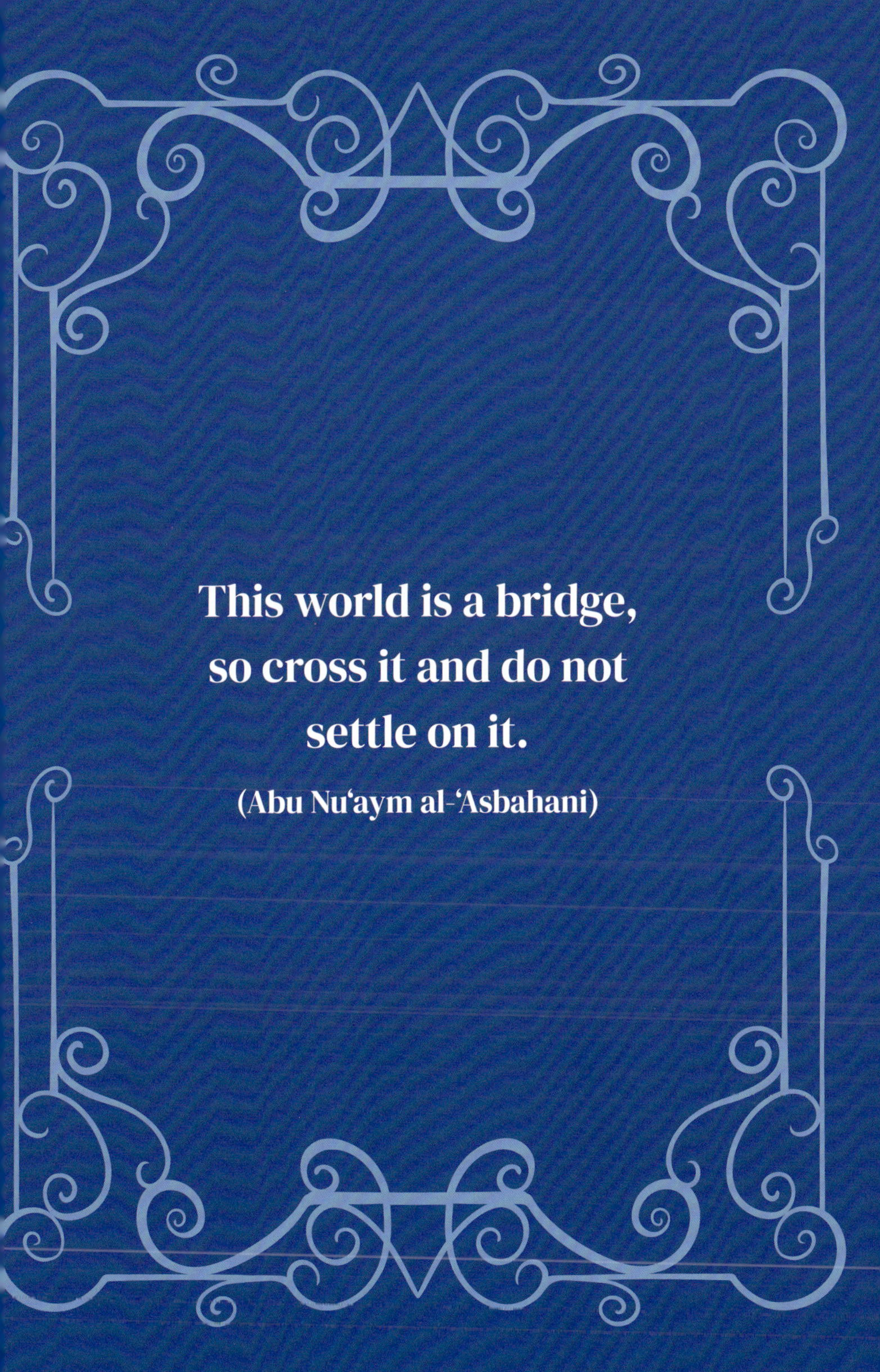
This world is a bridge,
so cross it and do not
settle on it.
(Abu Nu'aym al-'Asbahani)

My Dear Heart

Can you let go of this World?

عَنْ سَهْلِ بْنِ سَعْدٍ السَّاعِدِيِّ قَالَ: جَاءَ رَجُلٌ إِلَى النَّبِيِّ ﷺ فَقَالَ: يَا رَسُولَ اللَّهِ. فَقَالَ: دُلَّنِي عَلَى عَمَلٍ إِذَا عَمِلْتُهُ أَحَبَّنِي اَللَّهُ ,وَأَحَبَّنِي اَلنَّاسُ ازْهَدْ فِي الدُّنْيَا يُحِبُّكَ اللَّهُ، وَازْهَدْ فِيمَا عِنْدَ النَّاسِ يُحِبُّكَ النَّاسُ.

A man came to the Prophet ﷺ and asked him '*Ya Rasul Allah* ﷺ, Guide me, teach me a deed which if I do, Allah ﷻ will love me and people will love me.' He ﷺ replied: "Renounce (show detachment from) the world and Allah ﷻ will love you, and renounce what people possess, and people will love you."[17]

17 Ibn Majah, "Chapter: Indifference towards this world," *Sunan Ibn Majah*, Book 37, Hadith 3.

This man asked for the two things that we all want; do you want people to love you? Yes, of course. Do you want your spouse to love you? Do you want your children to love you? Do you want your co-worker to admire and appreciate you? Do you want your boss to respect you? Yes, for sure. Do you want Allah ﷻ to love you – this goes without saying, we all want this. So, the man asked an amazing question and the response was to let go, live with abstinence, similar to an ascetic in this *dunya* and Allah ﷻ will love you. The second advice was to let go of what people have, which includes not comparing or wanting what belongs to others, and people will love you.

Can we let go of the *dunya*?

The question to be answered is: can you let go? The answer is, it's not easy. However, if we remember that both Allah ﷻ will love us, and people will love us, then this is a motivation to try and renounce the *dunya*.

There is a beautiful *hadith* narrated by *Sayyidina* Jaber ؓ to help us. Everyone has seen a sheep at some point, and many people love to eat the meat of the sheep, lamb or goat. Now if that sheep, goat or lamb was actually defective, would you buy it? The answer is no, naturally. *Sayyidina* Jaber ؓ narrated '*Rasul Allah* ﷺ, passed through the market and people were surrounding him. As he was walking through, he passed by a small lamb which had two issues.

One problem was it was defective – something was wrong with its ears, and the second that it was actually dead. He ﷺ took it and looked at the people and asked them, 'Does any one of you want to buy this one with a few coins?' And they all said, 'No, what are we going to do with it?' And then he asked them, would they want it, if it was free? And they said, '*Wallahi ya Rasul Allah* ﷺ*!* By Allah ﷻ, if this was a live animal, but had a defect, we will not take it, and this is dead.' *Rasul Allah* ﷺ, said "By Allah ﷻ, all this *dunya,* and what it is worth, is less in the sight of Allah ﷻ than how you looked at this dead animal." [18]

How does this apply to us? Can we let go of all this attachment? Whenever we become attached to something, we get upset when we don't get it. The difficult feelings surface; *I want it but I don't have it, Allah* ﷻ *didn't give it to me but somebody else has it.* That's when we need to remember, all this *dunya*, is even less than this dead animal, which, if it is gifted for free, we would not take. Another *hadith*, which is really powerful makes a similar point about the real value of the *dunya.*

لَوْ كَانَتِ الدُّنْيَا تَعْدِلُ عِنْدَ اللَّهِ جَنَاحَ بَعُوضَةٍ مَا سَقَى كَافِرًا مِنْهَا شَرْبَةَ مَاءٍ.[19]

18 Muslim ibn Hajjaj, "The Book of *Zuhd* and Softening of Hearts," Sahih *Muslim*, Book 55, Hadith 2.

19 Abu 'Isa Muhammad *al-Tirmidhi*, "Chapter: What has been related about the insignificance of the world to Allah, the Mighty and Sublime," *Jami' al-Tirmidhi*, Book 36, Hadith 17.

'If all this *dunya* were worth in the sight of Allah ﷻ, the wing of a mosquito, He will not have given the disbeliever even a sip of water.'

So, can you let go? For most of us the answer is still – it's difficult. Yet the more we remind ourselves of the true status of this world, the more we lower the value of material things in our eyes – it helps us to detach. Let's take a car for example. Many people love cars; they are attractive and especially these days with all the technology that cars bring with them. But if we remember and keep reminding ourselves that one day we're leaving and this car will stay behind and it's not going to come with us, nor will it be of any benefit unless we used it for the sake of Allah ﷻ – then our attachment to this car will be far smaller.

There are three signs when you are ready to let go

1. The first sign is that you work on yourself to internalise the knowledge that, what Allah ﷻ has in His ﷻ hand, is far more that what you have. The sign that you've really let go of material wealth is when you have zero in the bank account, zero money, no *dirham* or dollars, and your feelings inside is exactly the same as when you have a million dollars.

Somebody blessed with wealth asked someone who was also wealthy and generous, “how much money do you have in your retirement plan?” The second person responded with a number. The one who asked said, “is that it?” He had expected much more because the person was wealthy and extremely generous. The wealthy man continued to explain “I lived all these years, I was never hungry, I was never afraid, I was never poor and Allah ﷾ gave me everything I wanted. Why at the end of my life will He ﷾ not give me?”

Likewise, someone who has let go of the *dunya* is a person who is so confident in what Allah ﷾ has and what Allah ﷾ can give, knowing it is much more than what they have or what their bank account says.

2. The second sign is how you react to the test of loss in the *dunya.* The person who has let go, it doesn’t matter to them if they have the *dunya* or if they have to leave something of it. If you have trained yourself and have this perspective, then you can easily let go, if you haven’t done so already. Whenever we are tested with something we don’t like; we lose our job or we’ve lost our wealth, or even lost someone dear to us, how do we respond? If we respond in the way that pleases Allah ﷾, meaning we don’t say anything but what pleases Allah ﷾, even though we are in pain and suffering, our tongue doesn’t say anything except what pleases Allah ﷾, then we are not attached. It will help us

to think in the following way when we lose something, *"I am going to be rewarded because of that loss"* and keep training ourselves to respond this way. Then when we lose something of the *dunya* our mind will not react with *oh God how much have I lost,* instead it responds with, what *reward will Allah ﷻ give me*? A person with this mindset can let go very easily.

It is said that on the Day of Judgement, those people who practiced patience because of what they went through in this life, when they see the reward, they will wish that during this life their skin was literally bitten by a nail clipper.[20] How painful is this? However, they wished they had that much more of a test in the *dunya* because of the reward in the hereafter. So, to let go of this attachment, especially when Allah ﷻ sometimes forces us to let go, by taking it away, then just think of the reward.

3. The third sign is that you work for Allah ﷻ, alone, with true intentions. You always say the truth and defend the truth. If people are happy with you, *alhamdulillah*, and if they are not happy, *alhamdulillah* because whether you are praised or not, it's all the same. Then you can easily let go.

The most important thing to reach this stage is to keep asking Allah ﷻ. Whenever you love something which is taking you away from Allah ﷻ, make this simple *du'a*:

20 Abu 'Isa Muhammad al-Tirmidhi, "Chapter: The Day of Judgement and the regrets of the good doer and the evil doer on that day," *Jami' al-Tirmidhi*, Book 36, Hadith 100.

'*Ya Allah!* Take it away from my heart, remove it from my heart.' When we don't love something, letting it go is much easier.

May Allah ﷻ make it easy for us to use the blessings and gifts of the *dunya* without them entering our heart. *Ya Rabbi Ameen*.

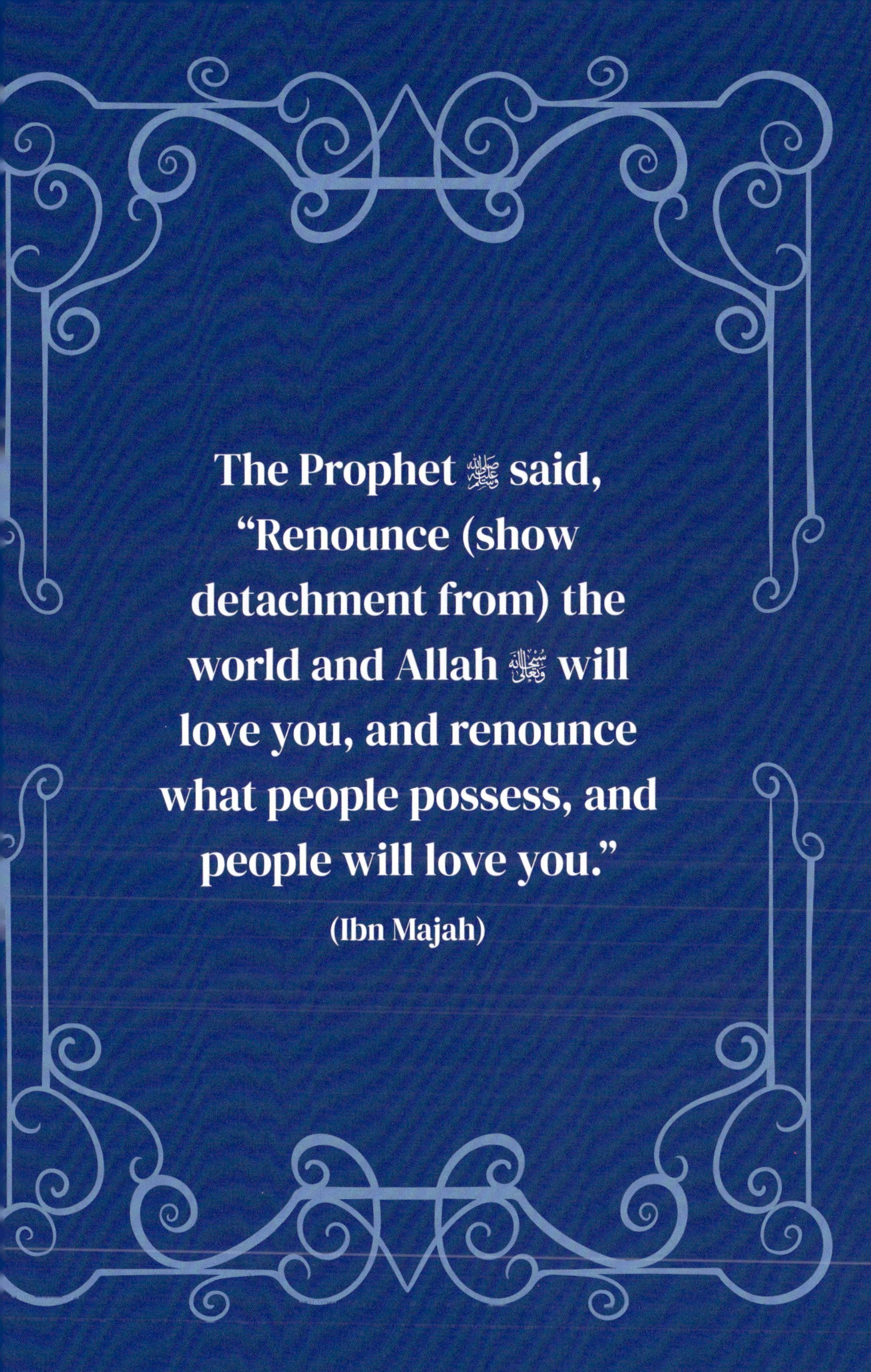
The Prophet ﷺ said,
"Renounce (show
detachment from) the
world and Allah سبحانه وتعالى will
love you, and renounce
what people possess, and
people will love you."
(Ibn Majah)

My Dear Heart

Does your Tongue affect You?

One of the things that affects you, my dear heart, is something called the tongue. You may well be surprised by this and wonder, does the tongue really affect my heart? The answer is yes! *Rasul Allah* ﷺ said,

لَا يَسْتَقِيمُ إِيمَانُ عَبْدٍ حَتَّى يَسْتَقِيمَ قَلْبُهُ، وَلَا يَسْتَقِيمُ قَلْبُهُ حَتَّى يَسْتَقِيمَ لِسَانُهُ.[21]

'The servant of Allah, his faith will not be straight and will not be sound until his heart is sound and straight. And this

---

21 Suhaib Abd al-Jabbar, *Al-Jami'; Al-Sahih Li Sunan Wa al-Masaneed*, Vol 3, page 100.

heart will not be straight and sound unless the tongue is straight and sound.'

The environment around us, directly or indirectly, influences what we hear and what we say. There is another saying of *Rasul Allah* ﷺ the meaning of which is if 'you guarantee me what is between the two jaws and the two legs I will guarantee *Jannah.'* [22] Meaning the major sins mainly come from these two parts of the body, the tongue and the private parts.

There is a beautiful *hadith* with *Sayyidina* Mu'adh ﷺ, a very well-known and loved *sahabi* where *Rasul Allah* ﷺ specifically said to him, يَا مُعَاذُ، إِنِّي أُحِبُّكَ.[23] 'I really love you.' A part of the long *hadith*, is related to the tongue when *Rasul Allah* ﷺ was talking about being careful with what we say. *Sayyidina* Mu'adh ﷺ, innocently asked.[24] *Ya Rasul Allah!* "Are we going to be taken to account for what we say?", meaning up to this point, Mu'adh thought that words were not something we give account for, they were 'just words'. *Rasul Allah* ﷺ replied:[25]

"May your mother mourn you. What else will throw the people in the hellfire on their faces [or on their nose in

22 Muhammad ibn Isma'il al-Bukhari, "Chapter: To protect one's tongue," *Sahih Al-Bukhari*, Book 81, Hadith 63.

23 Muhammad ibn 'Abd Allah Khatib Al-Tabrizi, "Chapter: The Supplication of the Tashahhud," *Mishkat Al-Masabih*, Book 4, Hadith 372.

24 Ibn Majah, "Chapter: Restraining one's tongue during times of tribulation," *Sunan Ibn Majah*, Book 36, Hadith 48.

25 Ibid.

another narration] except for, حَصَائِدُ أَلْسِنَتِهِمْ the harvest of their tongue.' What the tongues say, and the result of it, is one of the major reasons that will take the human being to *Jahannam*. In another *hadith*, *Rasul Allah* ﷺ said:

"Be fair to your ears, for you have been given two ears and one mouth." Abu Darda further explained the reason you have two ears and one tongue, is so that you listen more than you speak.[26] And it's very interesting to see that there is a reason behind everything in the way that Allah ﷻ has created us.

The best type of speech

It's natural to think *so what am I going to talk about if I'm supposed to stay silent*? We learn the answer through the Qur'an which guides us; we are told not only what we shouldn't say, but also Allah ﷻ tells us what is the best kind of speech in the following verse:

لَّا خَيْرَ فِي كَثِيرٍ مِّن نَّجْوَىٰهُمْ إِلَّا مَنْ أَمَرَ بِصَدَقَةٍ أَوْ مَعْرُوفٍ أَوْ إِصْلَٰحٍ بَيْنَ ٱلنَّاسِ ۚ
وَمَن يَفْعَلْ ذَٰلِكَ ٱبْتِغَآءَ مَرْضَاتِ ٱللَّهِ فَسَوْفَ نُؤْتِيهِ أَجْرًا عَظِيمًا

No good is there in much of the private conversation, except for those who enjoin charity or that which is right, or conciliation between people. And whoever does that seeking means to the approval of Allah – then We are going to give him a great reward. (An-Nisa 4:114)

26 Abu al-Qasim Al-Zamakhshari, "Chapter 21: Modesty and Silence," *Rabi' al-Abrar wa Nusus al-Akhyar*, Vol 2, page 121.

So, what do we say? What comes out of our mouth should be a form of charity. Charity is not only fundraising and giving money, but also something that will bring good or goodness to someone else, to a community, to a family, to the spouse or to the child. The first thing then, that's helpful and that makes someone feel good is charity because *Rasul Allah* ﷺ in another *hadith* said:

تَبَسُّمُكَ فِي وَجْهِ أَخِيكَ لَكَ صَدَقَةٌ .[27]

'Your smile in the face of your brother or sister is a form of resource' Why is it a charity? Because you make them feel good. Secondly, you could enjoin something that is well-known in the community to be a good action, like learning and teaching.

Thirdly, you can use your speech to, إِصْلَاحُ بَيْنَ النَّاسِ bring two people going through difficult times, together. It could be there is an issue between them, there's a quarrel or argument between them. What you say, could bring them back together, this is especially important between a husband and wife or between a father and a son, or parents and children, or children and parents.

We have a responsibility, which often falls on the sisters, when your friend or sister calls you, and she talks about her husband did this or that, or if the husband calls his friend and says, my wife did this or that, we should not say, *oh,*

27 Abu 'Isa Muhammad al-Tirmidhi, "Chapter: What has been related about various kinds of good deeds," *Jami' al-Tirmidhi*, Book 27, Hadith 62.

really, is that the case? Wow, don't forgive him, don't forgive her, do this or do that. On the contrary, what we should say is always *islah*, trying to rectify a relationship. We should look for reasons to either explain to the other side that maybe they didn't mean it that way. Or, calm them with reminding them it's a harmless comment, many people say it, it doesn't mean it is bad. This is one of the instances where in Islam, lying is allowed, which is when you want to bring two people together. This is what Allah ﷻ says in the above *ayah* from *Surah an-Nisa*, speaking to reconcile two people:

وَمَن يَفْعَلْ ذَٰلِكَ ابْتِغَاءَ مَرْضَاتِ ٱللَّهِ فَسَوْفَ نُؤْتِيهِ أَجْرًا عَظِيمًا .[28]

is a noble thing. It is worth reflecting on this; whomsoever does this for the sake of Allah ﷻ, not for anyone's praise, but rather to please Allah ﷻ alone, will be rewarded a great reward.

Diseases of the tongue

There are many diseases of the tongue and in this chapter we take a look at three in particular. Scholars have covered many; twenty are covered by Imam al-Ghazali. Being familiar with these encourages us to put our speech under the microscope to check what we should and shouldn't say, for the benefit of our heart.

28 An-Nisa', 4:114.

1. Speaking about something that doesn't concern you

It is a common thing we all go through, when someone asks you a question that made you feel uncomfortable, and you wonder, why did they ask me this? For example, a couple have been married for two or three years, and someone asks them, why don't you have children? Or for example, a single man or a woman, is asked why you are not married yet? Or how much did you buy your house for? These types of questions are a disease of the tongue, where a person talks about things that are not their business. In a beautiful *hadith*, *Rasul Allah* ﷺ said:

مِنْ حُسْنِ إِسْلاَمِ الْمَرْءِ تَرْكُهُ مَا لاَ يَعْنِيهِ .[29]

"Part of a person's perfection حُسْنِ *husn* of Islam is leaving that which does not concern him."

I'm being taught here that a sign of excellence in my practice of the *deen* is when I do not talk or ask about something that is not of my concern.

Another everyday example could be where let's say, I need a plumber, and my neighbour or my family friend have previously used that plumber; I'm going to ask her, 'how was the job?, how much did you pay him?' That is neces-

29 Ibn Majah, "Chapter: Restraining one's tongue during times of tribulation," *Sunan ibn Majah*, Book 36, Hadith 51.

sary because I'm thinking of hiring this person. Yet if I don't need this plumber, why do I ask these questions? It's because this is a disease of the tongue. We need to remember when the tongue is not straight, the heart is not straight. What is it we want and need? We want to go to Allah ﷻ with a straight, sound heart.

Sayyidina Luqman عليه السلام, the wise man, was asked, 'What made you so wise?' His answer is profound, as everybody wants to be wise and say the right thing. He didn't study; he didn't gain a doctorate in how to say the right things. He replied,

لَا أَسْأَلُ عَمَّا كُفِيتُ، وَلَا أَسْأَلُ عَمَّا لَا يَعْنِينِي.[30]

"I do not ask about things I don't need and have enough of, and I don't say or speak about things that are not of my concern."

2. Speaking about sin

A second disease of the tongue we need to stay away from is speaking about sins and things that are displeasing to Allah ﷻ. *Did you watch that movie? Did you watch that series? Did you see this, you should go and see it,* and then describe things that are clearly not pleasing to Allah ﷻ and are *haram*.

30 Ibn Abi Asim, *Kitab az-Zuhd*, Hadith 107, page 56.

It is enough of a problem that we all get weak sometimes and watch this or listen to that. At those times we need to ask Allah ﷻ for forgiveness, move on, and not talk about it.

3. Speaking to impress people

The third one, is called *al-taqaʿuru fī al-kalām,* اَلتَّقَعُّرُ فِي الْكَلَامِ when you speak in a way to impress people by being pretentious. This is using very sophisticated words that people don't understand, purely to show off. The Prophet ﷺ said:

"Indeed, the most beloved of you to me, and the closest of you to me on the Day of Resurrection, are those of you who have the best character. And the most detested of you to me, and the furthest of you from me on the Day of Resurrection, are the boastful, the pompous, and the arrogant in speech."

This clarifies that the beloved are those with the best manners and conduct, while the disliked are described as *al-tharthārūn* – those who are excessively talkative, *al-mutashaddiḳūn* – those who use affected, pretentious language, and *al-mutafayhiqūn* – those who speak arrogantly to impress others.

The tongue therefore affects our heart and if there was a filter to remove what displeases Allah ﷻ and replace it with what is pleasing to Allah ﷻ, it would help us.

May Allah سبحانه وتعالى teach us and help us to practice controlling our speech. May Allah سبحانه وتعالى forgive us for the sins of our tongue and protect us from falling into these diseases. *Ya Rabbi Ameen.*

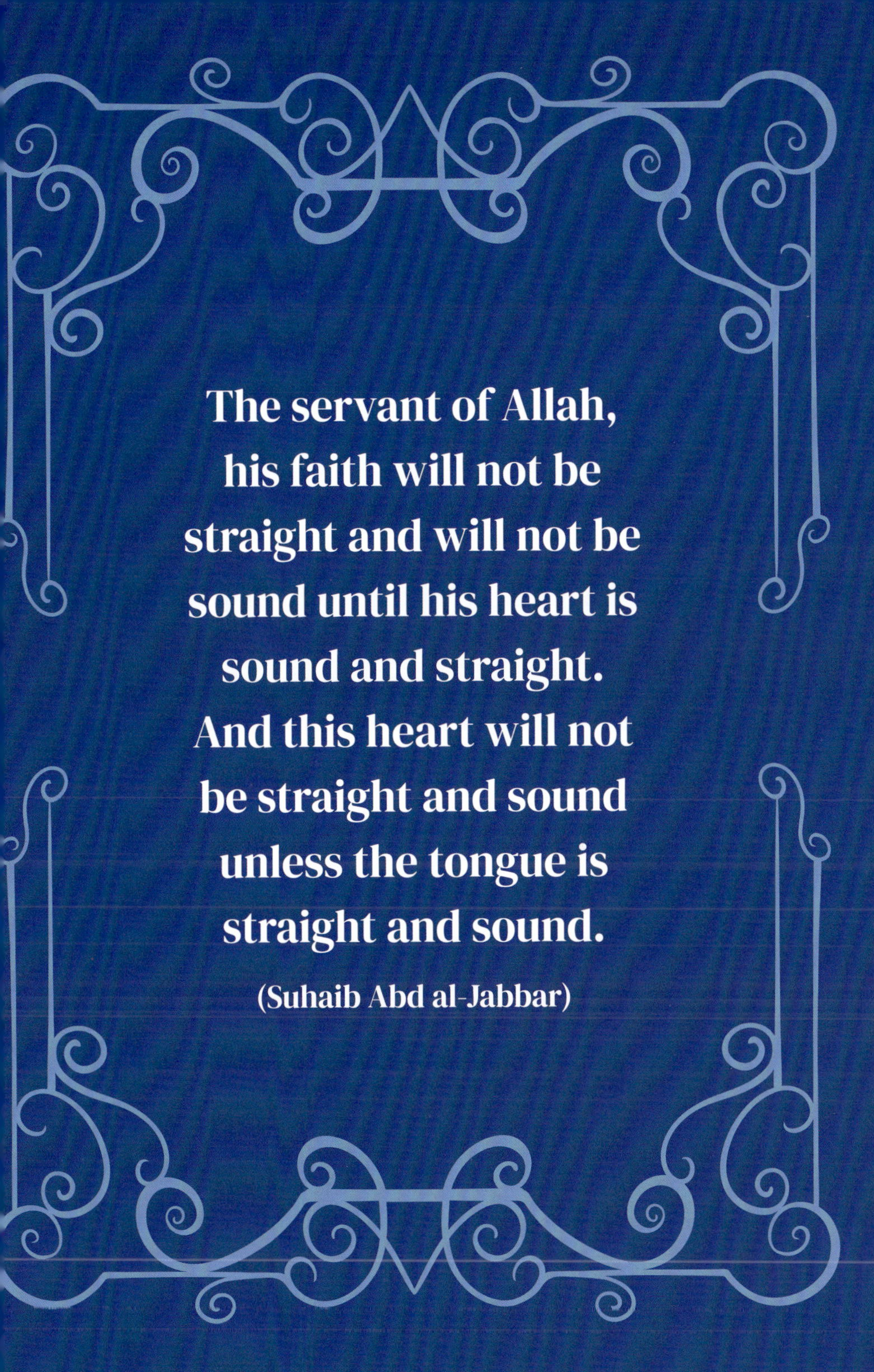
The servant of Allah,
his faith will not be
straight and will not be
sound until his heart is
sound and straight.
And this heart will not
be straight and sound
unless the tongue is
straight and sound.
(Suhaib Abd al-Jabbar)

My Dear Heart

Why isn't your Tongue Straight?

In this chapter we continue to look at more diseases of the tongue, as we said, if the tongue is not straight, the heart is not straight. The tongue needs to be sound, which means the heart is sound. This in turn means my *iman* is sound.

Disease of the tongue: *Fahisha* - foul language

Many of us have experienced at one point in our life or another, when someone talks to us in a gathering and what they said was annoying or improper, and it hurts. Using foul language is one of the diseases of the tongue called *al-fuḥsh* الْفُحْشُ, meaning obscenity. Unfortunately, it is popular, between many people including Muslims who use foul language quite often. This is a disease of the tongue which includes people saying immoral things or when they start cursing people regardless of who and where they are. There is no excuse to justify that we curse people.

Another type of foul speech is *al–badha'* الْبَذَاءُ, which is vulgarity including the common swear words that are now a part of everyday language especially in the Western world, as if it is the norm. This type of cursing or swearing, is not acceptable in Islam, and does not befit a Muslim practising Islam with excellence. This is prohibited. The Prophet ﷺ said: "Beware of obscenity, for indeed Allah ﷿ does not love those who are obscene and engage in indecency." In another narration he ﷺ said: "Paradise is forbidden for every person who is foul-mouthed and obscene."

This makes it clear that foul speech *al-fuḥsh* is strictly prohibited. The Messenger of Allah ﷺ warned us to stay away from obscenity, reminding us that Allah ﷿ does not love those who practice it, and that *Jannah* is absolutely not the place for anyone who practices obscenity.[31]

31 Muhammad ibn Isma'il al-Bukhari, "Chapter: Injustice is darkness," *Al-Adab Al-Mufrad*, Book 28, Hadith 5.

When we read these *ahadith* and reflect on them, we shouldn't think of other people, but instead we should think about ourselves. *I need to ask myself, am I that person? And if I am then I'm going to be grateful to Allah ﷻ, as He ﷻ showed me my shortcomings, which means I need to change and I have the opportunity to do so. If I'm not of those who use foul language, then I'm so grateful to Allah ﷻ that He ﷻ has saved me.* This is not self-praise, but it is the *fadl* – the grace of Allah ﷻ.

Rasul Allah ﷺ said: "The believer is not one who insults others, curses others, uses obscene language, or engages in foul speech." (al-Tirmidhi) In this, *Rasul Allah* ﷺ describes a believer not in terms of their faith and *aqeedah*, but by the excellence of their character which does not have these diseases of the tongue. In another hadith he ﷺ said "The believer is not a slanderer, a curser, an obscene person, or a vulgar person."[32]

The slanderer is the person who stabs people in the back, and is not a characteristic of an excellent believer, nor is someone cursing or speaking of vulgarities. Therefore, guarding the tongue means not only what we are saying, but how it's said and which words are being used. Our tongue is a reflection of the heart and if we expose ourselves to these words, they will affect us. Some people will say, watching something with foul language is not a problem as they don't repeat these words, but hearing these things or

32 Abu 'Isa Muhammad al-Tirmidhi, "Chapter: What has been related about the curse," *Jami' al-Tirmidhi*, Book 27, Hadith 83.

being surrounded by people who speak this way, leads to gradually getting used to it and may even start to normalise saying it. So, we need to be careful about the quality of the words that enter our ears and come from our mouth because they affect our heart.

Disease of the tongue: Excessive joking

When we remember that we want to go to Allah ﷻ with a pure heart, anything that will make this pure crystal vase dirty, needs to be cleaned. To keep it pure we need to avoid another disease of the tongue, which is excessive joking.

Joking sometimes is a pleasure, when we joke, it makes a person smile. This is good as long as it is done without excess. Did *Rasul Allah* ﷺ, joke? Yes, but the first rule was it was always the truth. There is a very famous incident when an older woman came to him and she said, 'Will I enter *Jannah*?' And he ﷺ said, 'No'. And one can imagine how the old lady felt when she heard this. Then he ﷺ said: "The believer is not one who insults others, curses others, uses obscene language, or engages in foul speech." Then immediately after he ﷺ said 'They will all enter as young and similar in age.', لَا يَدْخُلُ الْجَنَّةَ عَجُوزٌ. عُرُبًا أَتْرَابًا.[33] So, he was joking with her. We can also joke sometimes as long as it's truthful and does not mock the other person. When a 'joke' puts

33 Abu 'Isa Muhammad al-Tirmidhi, "Description of the joking of Rasul Allah," *Ash-Shama'il Al-Muhammadiyah*, Book 35, Hadith 6.

people down – that is another disease of the tongue and it's also a sign of arrogance.

Rasul Allah ﷺ used to joke with children – this softens their heart and increases love. Again, it has to be truthful.

Disease of the tongue: Disclosing secrets

There is a joke some people make which is, if you want someone to know your secrets, say your secret to someone, and tell him or her, 'don't say it to anybody', and soon everyone will know about it. Unfortunately, this isn't a joking matter, it's a disease of the tongue called إِفْشَاءُ السِّرِّ.[34] *Ifsha' al-sirr* – disclosing secrets.

When someone entrusts you with their private matters they are saying 'I trust you; I need your opinion; I need to have someone to share this with, because it's too heavy on me'. When that person tells you, please don't say this to anybody, it is a trust, an *amanah* between you and that person.

This also includes, اَلْمَجَالِسُ بِالأَمَانَةِ.[35] – when people are sitting together speaking, what is said in that gathering is a trust as well. One of the diseases of the tongue that will affect my heart is when anyone entrusts me with anything, I'll just go

34 Abu 'Isa Muhammad al-Tirmidhi, "Chapters on righteousness and maintaining good relations with relatives," *Jami' al-Tirmidhi*, Book 27, Hadith 65.

35 Abi Dawud, "Chapter: Transmitting what others have said," *Sunan Abi Dawud*, Book 43, Hadith 97.

and do that or share that. However, a point to note is that this does not include anything that may mean disobedience of Allah ﷻ.

Disease of the tongue: Speaking with two tongues

The next disease is called 'The person with two tongues' – كَلَامُ ذِيْ اللِّسَانَيْنِ as though the person literally has two tongues. This occurs when a person goes back and forth between two people who are enemies, conveying what one says to the other, speaking to each in a way that pleases them, promising to support them, or praising one to their face and criticising the other behind their backs.

Often somebody will praise you a lot in front of you, and then turn their face and go and talk to somebody else and start talking negatively about you. Literally speaking, we know nobody has two tongues, but the term two tongues means saying one thing in one place and immediately afterwards, when the circumstances change, saying something different, as if he or she has two tongues. Why does this happen? It's not honest and is in fact the complete opposite to being honest and truthful.

When you think about something that's not appropriate to say, then it's best not to say it. If it is appropriate in a nice way, as a means of advice, you should say it to that person, but then there is no need to go and share that information with anyone, as that is backbiting.

The disease of too much praise - flattery

It is common to wonder how praising someone can be wrong or a disease of the tongue. The following very insightful incident happened to *Sayyidina* Umar رضي الله عنه.

It is narrated from Al-Hasan that he said: 'Umar رضي الله عنه was sitting in a gathering when a man entered from a very well-known tribe and people there praised him as he came in – to the effect of 'this is the best man you will ever see'. When he came close, Umar رضي الله عنه struck him with his staff and the man looked at him and asked: "What is the matter with you, O Commander of the Faithful?" He said: "What is the matter with you and said, أَمَا سَمِعْتَهَا? Didn't you hear? Have you not heard what the people said?" He said: "I heard it, so what?" 'Umar رضي الله عنه said, "I was worried that the way they praised you it's going to get into your heart and you're going to act with arrogance. I want you to keep your head down."

Sometimes Allah سبحانه وتعالى makes us go through some incidents and we think that people are putting us down. In reality, Allah سبحانه وتعالى wants to protect us from being arrogant. So do not praise people too much, including children, for example saying to them, "I've never seen such a beautiful girl like you". "She's beautiful, *masha'Allah*", but we mustn't go into excesses because it will get into their heart.

There is no one who will not get affected by too much praising. There is a famous incident of *Rasul Allah* ﷺ, when he was walking and saw two people, one praising the other. He looked at that person and said, قَسَمْتَ ظَهْرَهُ, "you broke his back".[36] Why is that? This is because when we receive too much praise even if it is true, it will get into our head and heart, and we will start to become arrogant.

A common question is what if people do this to me all the time? Then learn this *du'a*, '*Ya Allah!* Make me better than what people think of me and forgive what they don't know about me.' And as one of the righteous people said, if sins had a smell, nobody would be able to sit next to me.

May Allah ﷻ protect us all from misusing our tongue. May He ﷻ grant us excellence in our character and closeness to *Rasul Allah* ﷺ on *yaum-ul-qiyama. Ya Rabbi Ameen.*

36 Muhammad ibn Isma'il al-Bukhari, "Chapter: If only one man attests the conduct of another," *Sahih Al-Bukhari*, Book 52, Hadith 26.

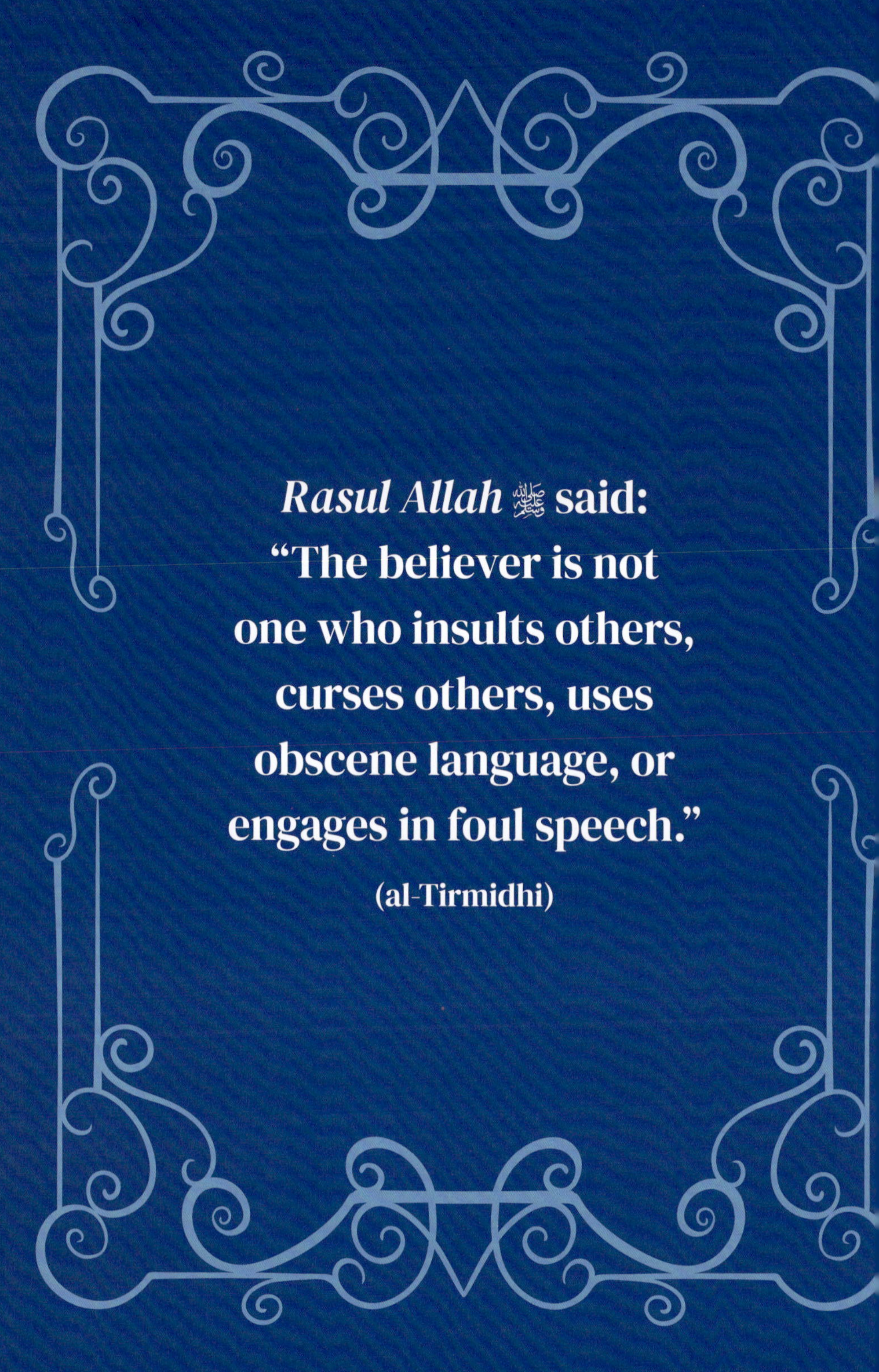
Rasul Allah ﷺ said:
"The believer is not
one who insults others,
curses others, uses
obscene language, or
engages in foul speech."
(al-Tirmidhi)

My Dear Heart

Why do we Lie?

There are questions we need to ask our heart as we strive to identify what pollutes it, and how to keep it clean. One such question we all need to ask ourselves is, my dear heart, why do you lie? Why is lying becoming so common as if it is the norm? Lying has a huge impact on our heart. What is the relationship between lying, not being truthful, and my pure heart?

Lying is a major sin as it is saying something which you know is not true. For example, someone invites you to an occasion, and you reply in the RSVP - yes, I will attend, but you know you're not going to be going; that's lying. This is in contrast to replying yes, I'm coming with the intention to go, and something unexpected happens and prevents you from going. Another example is when you say to somebody, "I don't know", when in reality you know whatever it is you're being asked about, but you don't want to tell them. Instead of being honest and saying maybe it's not the best time to say it; and instead saying I don't know, is lying.

Allah ﷻ said in the Qur'an that the result of lying is you're going to be distanced from Allah ﷻ. He's ﷻ not going to open the door for the one who lies to be guided and to get close to Him ﷻ. He ﷻ said:

إِنَّ ٱللَّهَ لَا يَهْدِى مَنْ هُوَ مُسْرِفٌ كَذَّابٌ

Indeed, Allah does not guide one who is a transgressor and a liar. *(Ghafir 40: 28)*

In a beautiful *hadith Rasul Allah* ﷺ is warning you and I about lying, he said:

إِيَّاكُمْ وَالْكَذِبَ، فَإِنَّ الْكَذِبَ يَهْدِي إِلَى الْفُجُورِ، وَإِنَّ الْفُجُورَ يَهْدِي إِلَى النَّارِ، وَمَا يَزَالُ الرَّجُلُ يَكْذِبُ وَيَتَحَرَّى الْكَذِبَ حَتَّى يُكْتَبَ عِنْدَ اللَّهِ كَذَّابًا

"Beware of lying, for lying leads to immorality, and immorality leads to the Hellfire. A person continues to lie, and seeks out opportunities to lie, until he is recorded with Allah as a liar."[37]

37 Abi Dawud, "Chapter: Stern warning regarding lying," *Sunan Abi Dawud*, Book 43, Hadith 217. Also in Bukhari and Muslim.

Why does lying lead to immorality? It's because it is not just a small slip, but it opens the door to shamelessness, leading to sins and immorality that take a person to the hellfire. Treating lying as something minor, and reacting with, What *did I say? What is the big deal?* is wrong. It is a big deal, as there are major consequences.

Lying and hypocrisy

Rasul Allah ﷺ said the following about the signs of a hypocrite:

عَنْ أَبِي هُرَيْرَةَ رَضِيَ اللَّهُ عَنْهُ، عَنِ النَّبِيِّ ﷺ قَالَ:

آيَةُ الْمُنَافِقِ ثَلَاثٌ: إِذَا حَدَّثَ كَذَبَ، وَإِذَا وَعَدَ أَخْلَفَ، وَإِذَا اؤْتُمِنَ خَانَ.

"The signs of a hypocrite are three: when he speaks, he lies; when he makes a promise, he breaks it; and when he is entrusted, he betrays that trust." [38]

This *hadith* refers to *nifāq al-'amal,* hypocrisy in actions and manners, may Allah ﷻ protect us all from being in any of these categories. The first is a person who lies when they speak. Sometimes you may warn others about such a person and say, *'don't listen to anything they say. Everything they say is not true. O, they usually lie'*. The second group are those who promise, but they do not keep their word. When they

38 Muslim ibn al-Hajjaj, "Chapter: The characteristics of the hypocrite," *Sahih Muslim*, Book 1, Hadith 119.

say they're coming, they can't be trusted, you know they will not be coming. Nobody wants to be like this. The third group are those when you give them something that they should take care of, an *amanah*, a trust, they will betray it. If they're told 'don't tell them anything', they will disclose it.

The lessons from this *hadith* are for us all; adults, teenagers, and children, that lying is absolutely *haram*.

Lying about Allah ﷾ and His Messenger ﷺ

The worst lie one can say is about Allah ﷾ and the *Rasul* ﷺ. This is something for everybody to be aware of, as we live in a time when information spreads very quickly. You may post or share a *hadith*, but before doing that, please make sure that this *hadith* is what our *Rasul* ﷺ actually said.

It is now very easy to check a *hadith* and the uninterrupted chain. So that it can be confirmed that the *hadith* is authentic. *Rasul Allah* ﷺ said, 'whomsoever lies about me intentionally, let him look or let her look at their place in the hellfire.' [39] Hence we shouldn't share anything about *Rasul Allah* ﷺ unless we are sure it is true.

39 Muslim ibn al-Hajjaj, "Chapter: Warning about lying upon the Messenger of Allah," *Sahih Muslim*, Hadith 3.

Why do people lie?

The most common problem is the everyday lying between people. The question we all have to ask ourselves is, why do we lie? This is something interesting. One time I was with a group of teenage girls and we were talking about lying. I asked the question: 'how many of you lie?' There were approximately thirty or forty girls present, and not a single hand stayed down, all were raised. So, I said, *masha'Allah*, you all are truthful, at least you're truthful in telling me you lie. Then I asked, 'why do you lie?'

Two replied about their reasons, relating the story of why they lied. The common scenario at the top of the list was 'I am worried that I will get punished from people', this was the case especially for the younger girls. 'My mom will not be happy with me, she may do this or that or punish me.' The second top reason was: 'just to make people laugh so they will like me.' The third reason was: 'so that I fit in with people, so I say things about myself that are not true.' Now look at this. There were more reasons, but the common reason was 'I'm afraid of people being upset with me.'

We need to be afraid of Allah سبحانه وتعالى being upset with us for this major sin. *Do I really want to fit in with people by lying? I shouldn't want to be part of those people. I need to fit with people who will take me to Allah سبحانه وتعالى. Do I want to make people laugh?* Making people laugh with something true is different. Sometimes people boast about themselves and say things that are not true. The lies could be about being given a raise in their salary, or about a promotion at work. What is the point? It is to impress people, it's all about people.

When we stand in front of Allah ﷻ, He will be looking at each person's book, with our name on that book. What will the title be under our name? كَذَّاب, *She's a liar, He's a liar* – nobody wants that. No one wants this title on their book of deeds.

Three instances where lying is permitted

There are only three circumstances where lying is allowed. The first is in war – *fil harb* فِي الْحَرْبِ.[40] When there is war, lying is allowed for example saying we are going to go south, when in reality we are going north.

The second instance, which is very important and rarely done enough, is for reconciliation. When there are two people who have an issue or quarrel between them and they're not talking to each other, and you want to bring them back together, then we can say something which is not true. For example, if there are two friends with some issues between them, I go to one of them and I say something not true to praise them, meaning she or he said this about you and then I say something to the other person,

40 Abi Dawud, "Chapter: Deception during war," *Sunan Abi Dawud*, Book 15, Hadith 161.

such as she or he said this good thing about you, but it's not true. My intention must be to bring them back together.

Another instance is in a marriage between a husband and a wife. The husband can say things to the wife to please her although it may not be true, and likewise the woman can say things to the husband to please him, to make them love each other more.

There is actually a *hadith:*

وزاد مسلم في رواية:

وَلَمْ أَسْمَعْهُ يُرَخِّصُ فِي شَيْءٍ مِمَّا يَقُولُ النَّاسُ إِنَّهُ كَذِبٌ إِلَّا فِي ثَلَاثٍ: الْحَرْبُ، وَالإِصْلَاحُ بَيْنَ النَّاسِ، وَحَدِيثُ الرَّجُلِ امْرَأَتَهُ، وَحَدِيثُ الْمَرْأَةِ زَوْجَهَا

"I did not hear him ﷺ permit anything of what people consider lies except in three cases: in war, in reconciling between people, and in the speech of a man to his wife, and the speech of a woman to her husband." (Muslim)

Lying and fasting

What's the relationship between lying and fasting? We fast at blessed times in the year, on certain days of the week, and of course in *Ramadan*. Imam al-Tabarani ؒ narrated this *hadith*,

عَنْ أَبِي هُرَيْرَةَ رضي الله عنه قَالَ: قَالَ رَسُولُ اللَّهِ ﷺ:

الصِّيَامُ جُنَّةٌ مَا لَمْ يَخْرِقْهَا. قِيلَ: وَبِمَ يَخْرِقُهَا يَا رَسُولَ اللَّهِ؟ قَالَ: بِكَذِبٍ أَوْ غِيبَةٍ.

Abū Hurayrah ﷺ reported that the Messenger of Allah ﷺ said: "Fasting is a shield, so long as one does not make a hole in it." He was asked: "What is going to put a hole in it, O Messenger of Allah?" He ﷺ said:"By lying or backbiting." [41]

Fasting– *siyam,* is a shield for our moral and spiritual benefit, so lies or backbiting while in a state of fasting reduces its protection and reward. The blessed month of *Ramadan* in particular is the ideal time to teach ourselves and train our tongues not to lie. A person's fasting shouldn't be belittled by our own actions. And, as it is always said when one tells the truth, you will always be safe. If not in this *dunya*, for sure one is saved in the *akhirah*. Allah ﷻ said:

يَٰٓأَيُّهَا ٱلَّذِينَ ءَامَنُوا۟ ٱتَّقُوا۟ ٱللَّهَ وَكُونُوا۟ مَعَ ٱلصَّٰدِقِينَ

O you who have believed, fear Allah and be with those who are true.
(at-Tawbah 9:119)

Each of us have a choice; either we are of the truthful or we are liars; and none of us want to be from the latter group.

41 Ibn Jarir Tabrani, "Chapter: Those whose name is Mahmood," *Al- Mo'jam al- Awsat*, Vol 8, page 15, Hadith 7814.

May Allah سبحانه وتعالى help us to practise honesty. May Allah سبحانه وتعالى show us when we are about to lie that this is something not pleasing to Him سبحانه وتعالى and remind us it is *haram*. May Allah سبحانه وتعالى protect us from hypocrisy, from speaking falsehood about Him سبحانه وتعالى and *Rasul Allah* ﷺ, *Ya Rabbi Ameen.*

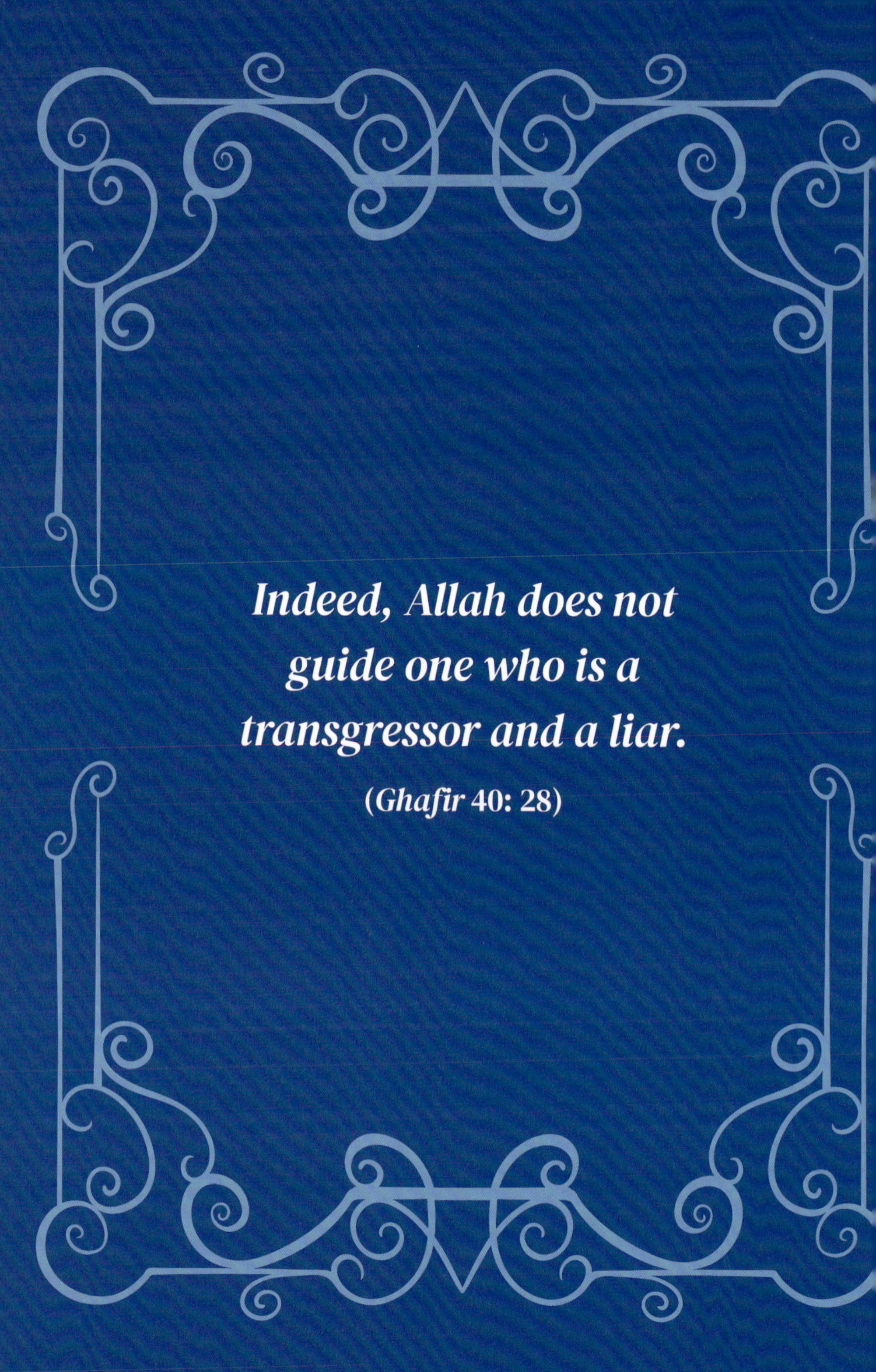
Indeed, Allah does not guide one who is a transgressor and a liar.
(*Ghafir* 40: 28)

My Dear Heart

Do you Backbite?

There are many diseases of the tongue that affect our heart. How many times have we said something about someone in their absence which was not nice? We may have heard and seen it as well as having done it ourselves. Backbiting is to mention something about your absent brother or sister that he or she dislikes, if it were to reach them. It is that simple, and it is also very serious.

It could be the absent person hears what was said about their physical appearance, or about their character, or something about their name, or even their family lineage, anything that is not praise or that is negative, is *ghiba* back-biting. A very common question arises in relation to this which is 'What about if it's true?' For example, if I said this person has a limp or this person does not have good manners, even if it is true, that's backbiting.

If what is said is false, that is even worse as that is actually slander, which has a clear punishment in the Qur'an, amounting to 80 lashes.[42] In addition, the person who slanders should not be trusted either. A second comment that is very common is '*Well, I didn't say it but I heard it.*' The problem is if you were there, whether you approved of it, or you didn't say anything when hearing it, you were also part of this *ghiba*. So, we really must be very careful.

Backbiting the living and the dead

What we say, who we sit with and what they say that we hear, has big consequences. How many of us will ever think of eating from a dead animal, or even worse, a dead human being? Nobody can even think of it, let alone do it. This *ayah* in *Surah al-Hujarat* asks us this question:

يَٰٓأَيُّهَا ٱلَّذِينَ ءَامَنُوا۟ ٱجْتَنِبُوا۟ كَثِيرًا مِّنَ ٱلظَّنِّ إِنَّ بَعْضَ ٱلظَّنِّ إِثْمٌ ۖ وَلَا تَجَسَّسُوا۟ وَلَا يَغْتَب بَّعْضُكُم بَعْضًا ۚ أَيُحِبُّ أَحَدُكُمْ أَن يَأْكُلَ لَحْمَ أَخِيهِ مَيْتًا فَكَرِهْتُمُوهُ ۚ وَٱتَّقُوا۟ ٱللَّهَ ۚ إِنَّ ٱللَّهَ تَوَّابٌ رَّحِيمٌ

O you who have believed, avoid much [negative] assumption. Indeed, some assumption is sin. And do not spy or backbite each other.

42 Al-Nur, 24:4.

Would one of you like to eat the flesh of his brother when dead? You would detest it. And fear Allāh; indeed, Allāh is Accepting of Repentance and Merciful. (al-Hujarat 49:12)

Believers are told to stay away from suspicion, as suspicion is a sin. This is followed by telling us not to spy on each other and the order, not to backbite. When there is an order in the Qur'an, it means it is an obligation, unless there is an explanation to clarify that it is not an obligation. The parable Allah ﷻ gives shows how damaging it is: would you want to eat the flesh of your dead brother? Anyone would hate this, and it raises the question of why anyone would backbite?

When *Rasul Allah* ﷺ was coming back from a funeral, two Companions were saying something negative about the person who died. He heard them and didn't say anything. As he was walking, there was a dead animal on the side and he looked at them and told them to go and eat from it. They said, '*Ya Rasulullah!*' And he said, 'you already have'.[43] If we remember this example, it will help us to be careful about the consequence of what we say about other people.

Abu Barza al-Aslami said: The Messenger of Allah ﷺ said: "O you who believe with your tongues but faith has not entered your hearts, do not backbite Muslims, and do not follow their faults, for whoever follows their faults, Allah ﷻ

43 Muhammad bin Ismail al-Bukhari, "Chapter: Backbiting and Allah's words, and backbite not one another," *Al-Adab Al-Mufrad,* Book 31, Hadith 133.

will follow his faults, and whoever Allah ﷻ follows in his faults, He ﷻ will expose him in his home.”[44]

Rasul Allah ﷺ makes it clear that true faith in the heart reflects in our actions and our speech. The order he gives to the believer in this *hadith* is, do not backbite. The second order is not to search for peoples’ shortcomings, or Allah ﷻ will expose our shortcomings even if we are inside our home.

Real bankruptcy

Everybody in this world wants some level of minimum wealth, and nobody wants to get bankrupt. What about if we get bankrupt on the Day of Judgement? Over there, there will not be any bank of money, instead it will be the bank of deeds.

أَتَدْرُونَ مَا الْمُفْلِسُ؟

قَالُوا: الْمُفْلِسُ فِينَا مَنْ لاَ دِرْهَمَ لَهُ وَلاَ مَتَاعَ.

فَقَالَ: إِنَّ الْمُفْلِسَ مِنْ أُمَّتِي يَأْتِي يَوْمَ الْقِيَامَةِ بِصَلاَةٍ وَصِيَامٍ وَزَكَاةٍ، وَيَأْتِي قَدْ شَتَمَ هَذَا، وَقَذَفَ هَذَا، وَأَكَلَ مَالَ هَذَا، وَسَفَكَ دَمَ هَذَا، وَضَرَبَ هَذَا، فَيُعْطَى هَذَا مِنْ حَسَنَاتِهِ، وَهَذَا مِنْ حَسَنَاتِهِ، فَإِنْ فَنِيَتْ حَسَنَاتُهُ قَبْلَ أَنْ يُقْضَى مَا عَلَيْهِ، أُخِذَ مِنْ خَطَايَاهُمْ فَطُرِحَتْ عَلَيْهِ، ثُمَّ طُرِحَ فِي النَّارِ.

Abu Hurayrah ؓ reported that the Messenger of Allah ﷺ said, “Do you know who is bankrupt?” They

44 Abi Dawud, “Chapter: Regarding backbiting,” *Sunan Abi Dawud*, Book 43, Hadith 108.

said, "The bankrupt among us is the one who has no dirhams and no possessions." He said, "The bankrupt among my followers is the one who comes on the Day of Resurrection with prayer, fasting, and zakat, but he has insulted this person, slandered that one, eaten this one's money, shed this one's blood, and beaten this one. Then this one will be given from his good deeds, and that one from his good deeds. If his good deeds are exhausted before his debts are paid, their sins will be taken and thrown upon him, and then he will be thrown into the Fire." (Tirmidhi)

When we think about a typical day in *Ramadan* for example, how easy or challenging was the fasting and the *salah*, the *taraweeh*, the *zakah* and the charity during the month? Many of us do this and we pray that Allah ﷻ accepts it from us during and beyond *Ramadan*. Imagine a person who, having done all this, has also then cursed this person, backbit that person, said negative things about people and their honour.

On the Day of Judgement, all the bank of the good deeds that were collected are going to start to go one by one to anybody who was transgressed against. The *hadith* says the person will reach a point, where there are no more good deeds left to give. Then how will justice be done? The bad deeds of whoever was wronged will be given to that person. Does anyone really want to be bankrupt on the Day of Judgement? Surely not, so then it's necessary to watch what we say and what we hear to make sure we are not of those people with all the good deeds being given freely to other people. One way to respond if you hear someone has back-bitten about you is, think of it in this way; Allah ﷻ wants to give you his/her good deeds. These diseases of the tongue have a direct effect of staining our heart if we let them.

Ya Rabbi protect us all from the sin of *ghiba* and all that leads to it. May we be guided away from saying and hearing what displeases You. May we not be of those who are bankrupt on the Day of Judgement. *Ya Rabbi Ameen.*

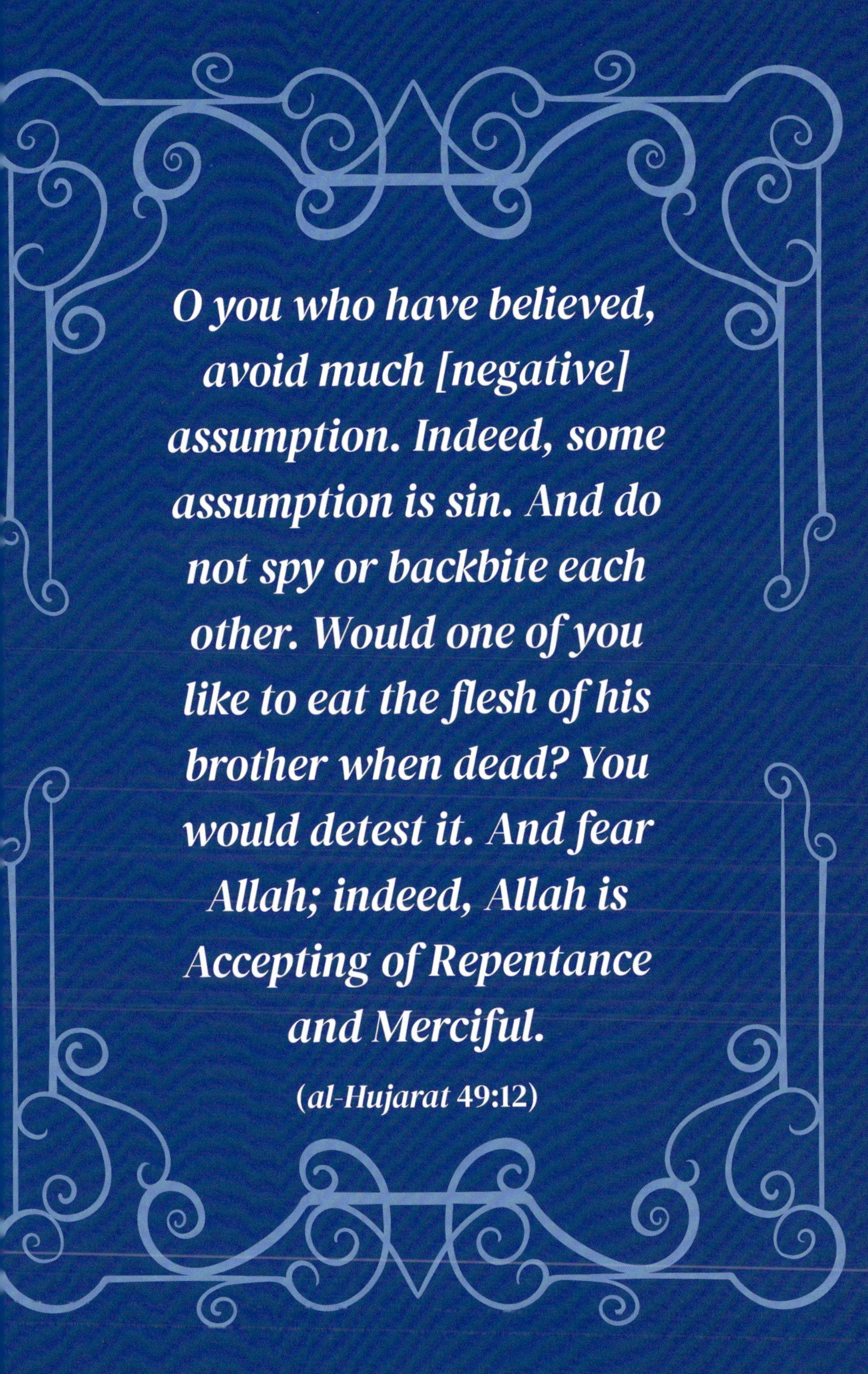

O you who have believed, avoid much [negative] assumption. Indeed, some assumption is sin. And do not spy or backbite each other. Would one of you like to eat the flesh of his brother when dead? You would detest it. And fear Allah; indeed, Allah is Accepting of Repentance and Merciful.

(*al-Hujarat* 49:12)

My Dear Heart

Why do you Backbite?

In the previous chapter we looked at the disease of the tongue – *ghiba* or backbiting. In this chapter we look deeper into why this happens and how to remedy this sickness of the heart. Every one of us needs to ask themselves '*why do I backbite? Why do I say negative things about people when they are not there, which I rarely say in front of them.* We need to analyse and look internally, and ask ourselves, *why can I not control my tongue?*

Reasons for *ghiba* – backbiting

1. Anger is the first reason. How many times did someone say or do something to you that upset you and you didn't

respond? Maybe you couldn't for whatever the reason. Then you go back home and feel angry about what they said, so you start saying negative things about them. That's backbiting and the reason was frustration.

2. Wanting to belong is the second reason. You are sitting in a gathering, especially the type where you feel you want to fit in. Some people start talking about somebody, and you just go along with them, as you want to belong. Why? Why I am not that person who changes the evil to good, or enjoin good and prohibit evil. If they are saying something unfair or unkind, I need to speak the truth and defend that person, and definitely not be a part of it.

3. Self-praise/ego is another reason. If we are honest, we know that self-praise is something we do. Sometimes this means we want to let people know that we are better than them, and this is done indirectly by putting someone else down. For example, somebody says, their children are amazingly well behaved. If a person wants to show they are superior, they will respond with relating an incident which shows the same children are badly behaved and their own children are well mannered, this way they've put the other mother down. This indirect method leads to backbiting, and its root is praising oneself.

4. Jealousy, which is a major disease of the heart. For this we need to dig deep and look into ourselves. What's the big deal if someone is praised? *Why does it upset me? Why don't I say, Alhamdulillah, may Allah ﷻ give me what He gave them?*

Instead, we want to put them down and speak about their faults, because there is jealousy in the heart.

5. Joking is another cause of backbiting, which is sadly just to have some fun. It could be, to make fun of the teacher, make fun of a neighbour or a relative, just to give others something to talk about. And soon this turns into backbiting about people, making jokes about how they spoke, dressed, or something they did.

Unfortunately, backbiting has become normal and an accepted part of conversations, to the point that if you don't backbite, people say what is wrong with you? As this damages our heart, how can we prevent and cure this disease?

Remedies for our heart

You may be thinking; what do I do about it? The first thing you need to do is work on your heart and your relationship with Allah ﷿. If you can train yourself: *remember Allah ﷿ is looking at me when I stand up and pray my daily Salah, He ﷿ is watching the fasts in Ramadan and during the year. Even when my ibadah, like long fasts or tahajjud – the pre-dawn prayer might feel difficult, I'm aware He ﷿ is looking at me and I'm hoping He ﷿ accepts it; did I do it well?* Similarly, you need to remember this that Allah ﷿ is watching when you're saying things that are not pleasing to Him ﷿ – having *taqwa* is the first remedy.

Second, remember the *hadith* of the bankrupt person from the previous chapter. Do you really want your good deeds to go to somebody else whom you are upset with? That would be doing them a favour, giving them your good deeds.

Third, remember what Allah ﷻ said in the Qur'an. Every time you want to say something, remember that dead human being or that dead animal. Do you really want to go and eat from their meat? [45]

Remedies in a gathering

In the very common scenario of a gathering where you did not say anything, but heard backbiting, you have three options. The first remedy is to remind people that we should not say these things because that's backbiting, and we don't want to disobey Allah ﷻ. Sometimes it's difficult to say that as it could be an elderly person to whom saying something directly is tough, and the other reality is in this case they may not listen to you.

Then the second option is to change the subject, by moving to another completely different topic. If you try that and it doesn't work, then you need to leave the conversation, maybe speak to another person or help out in another room, so you're not part of it.

Lastly, a general way for us to control our tongue from

45 Al-Hujarat, 49:12.

talking negatively about somebody, is to take a minute and look at ourselves and ask: *what have I done? What are my shortcomings?* And if we focus on our own shortcomings, we're not going to focus on the shortcomings of others.

The exceptional cases

We know there are no excuses to say negative things about people, except for three exceptional cases. However, we mustn't take these as an open invitation. The first instance is we can speak negatively about somebody if required regarding marriage proposals and seeking advice about the bride or groom. In a true case, a person enquiring about a prospective match asked an elderly person about a man they were considering. The elderly person answered wisely, telling them that this person has an anger issue. He did not go into detail and keep talking, rather, he said, the young man comes from a place where the people are famous for having a temper. In this case the answer was given, but not with excessive details.

Another situation would be about seeking advice, for example you want to build a house and your friend or your family used the builder you're considering. When you ask for advice, if your friend was not happy with that builder for example, or the painter, they can give a simple statement 'I will not use them again'. They've delivered the message.

The second case is if an injustice happened against you and you're going to a judge to seek your rights. The judge will have to ask you what that person did. Again, you will need to keep to the point.

The third case is to warn people about a danger. In this situation you have to say the negative thing because the outcome will be worse if you don't speak. For example, if a teacher taught your children, but he or she did not do a good job or they did something unprofessional. Even if nobody asks you for your opinion, but you hear that they are using him or her, you need to tell them.

Rasul Allah ﷺ emphasized: "Part of the responsibility of a believer is to care for others by warning them of harm, but do so with moderation and wisdom."[46] This is known as *taḥdhīr al-muslimīn* – warning fellow Muslims, showing care without unnecessary detail or exaggeration. Another teaching is *taghyīr al-munkar* – striving to correct or change something that is clearly wrong in a way that aligns with the principles of good character.

The next case where a 'negative' comment is permitted, although it is not 'intended negatively' is when describing someone. If, for example there are three Bilals in a room and you don't know their last name. Then you might say, you know, the tall Bilal, just to identify the person. And of course, it depends on the way you say it. The final situation

46 Muhammad Salih al-Munajjid, *Kitaab Mawqi 'al-Islam Su'al wa Jawab*, Vol 7, page 122.

where you can say something negative is if the person is well known, he/she is publicly doing something that is not right, and you say it, that's not backbiting because they are doing it publicly – like they drink alcohol publicly or are proudly promoting gambling.

So there are a few circumstances where Allah ﷾ allows something negative to be said. But in general, this is not the norm and should not be the majority of our speech. If we have already made these mistakes, which over the years may be many, which we may have even forgotten, we pray that Allah ﷾ forgives us all. There are a couple of things we can do to try and remedy this. If you know that person, and you know that if you ask them for forgiveness, they will accept it, and nothing worse will happen, then seek forgiveness from them. Do it to gain Allah's ﷾ forgiveness and the desire to go to *Jannah*.

If you don't know where that person is now, or they have passed away, you can actually pray for them and do good deeds for them. Finally, if it's not possible to speak to that person directly – maybe speaking to them will make matters worse, then, as well as praying for them, you can praise them. When their name is mentioned in a gathering, you can praise them. This is the opposite of the negative comments you made. When we want to go to *Jannah*, then this is what we need to do in this *dunya* before we die.

Rasul Allah ﷺ said, 'whomsoever has transgressed against another human being, let them ask for forgiveness in this *dunya*.'[47] Once they die, then it has to be done in the *akhirah* which reminds us of the *hadith* of the bankrupt person. The more we can clear of what we need to clear in this *dunya*, it will be much better for us in the *akhirah*.

May Allah ﷻ make us learn these things, help us to implement them, and may Allah ﷻ make it easy, and forgive all our shortcomings when we speak about others. *Ya Rabbi Ameen*.

47 Al-Qastallani, *Irshad al-Sari li-Sharh Sahih al-Bukhari*, Vol 10, page 56, Hadith 2449.

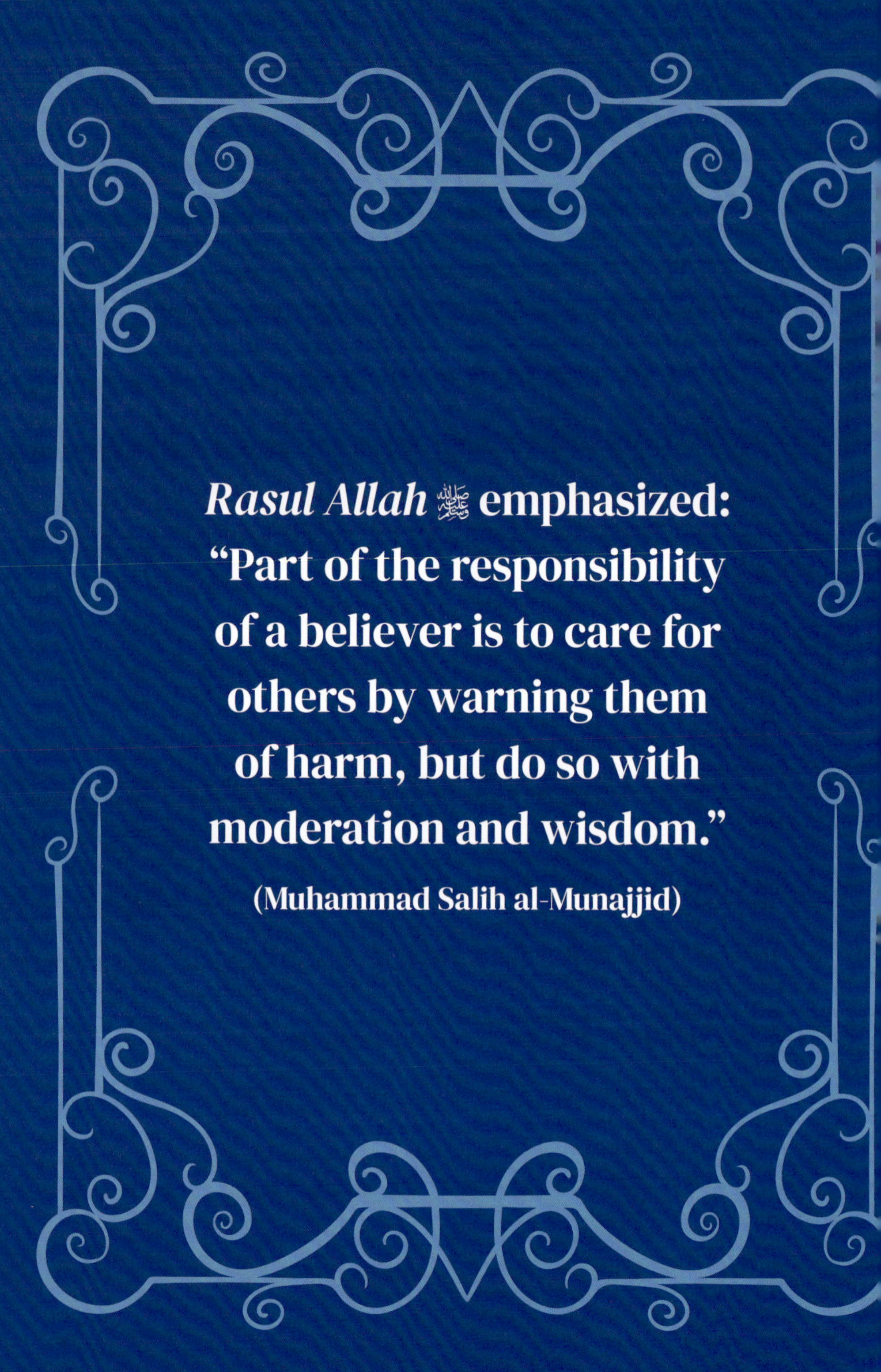
Rasul Allah ﷺ emphasized:
"Part of the responsibility of a believer is to care for others by warning them of harm, but do so with moderation and wisdom."
(Muhammad Salih al-Munajjid)

My Dear Heart

Can you Control your Tongue?

The relationship between our tongue and heart has many layers to it; both the speech we should avoid, and what we are encouraged to speak about. In this chapter, we go into further layers of what happens to our heart when the tongue is not controlled.

Rasul Allah ﷺ said in a cautionary *hadith* which should awaken us:

مَن كَانَ يُؤْمِنُ بِاللَّهِ وَالْيَوْمِ الآخِرِ فَلْيَقُلْ خَيرًا أَوْ لِيَصْمُتْ.

'Whomsoever believes in Allah and the Day of Judgement, let him or her say good or stay quiet.'[48]

As we have covered previously, 'say good' means whatever is pleasing to Allah ﷻ. It could be bringing two people together, or enjoining good, or helping people and bringing happiness to them. There is no other option, except these two; either what I'm saying is good, or what I am saying is *not* good. There is no other because he ﷺ said: 'let him be silent.'

A righteous man, Mukhalid ibn al-Husayn said 'For the last fifty years, I never said a word I need to apologise for.'[49] Whenever we need to apologise about something and say 'O, I'm sorry, I didn't mean it', that means we shouldn't have said that. It would have been better to have stayed quiet and controlled the tongue.

Tale carrying – *namimah*

Why do we have difficulty in controlling our tongue? There are many reasons. Let's look at a scenario: you're talking to someone, maybe at work, maybe at home, or in a gathering and then somebody else comes in and then they say to you, '*Did you know…?*' And then they start telling you what someone else said about you. That's actually a form

48 Muḥammad ibn 'Abd Allah at-Tabrizi, "Chapter: Hospitality," *Mishkat al-Masabih*, Book 21, Hadith 80.

49 Abu Nu'aym al-Asbahani, *Hilyat al-Awliya' wa Ṭabaqat al-Asfiya'*, Vol 8, page 266.

of backbiting called 'tale carrying' – *namimah* which is carrying words to someone about another and moving it from one person to the other with the intention to cause harm.

Conveying the words of one person to another is done most of the time voluntary. The question is, why do people do this? It could be a colleague who shares what the boss said about you; or a husband tells his wife 'My mother said this and this about you.' Or the wife reports to her husband, 'Do you know what your sister said about you?'

Responding to tale carrying

So, what do we do when we experience this? Number one, don't believe it, even if what the person tells you is true. The *namama,* the person who carrys tales to someone is publicly disobeying Allah ﷻ and is known as a *fasiq* – one who openly transgresses, and Islamically their testimony is not accepted as a witness.

Sometimes, not believing them is difficult because of our feelings. So, if I have an ill feeling towards someone and then another person tells me they said something about me, this will make me feel even more justified to believe that person. In addition, it's going to make me feel a little bit better and gives me more excuses to take revenge and to hurt that person.

The second way to deal with it, which will be a good deed, is to tell that person you don't want to hear it. Explain to them that it's not good to carry what people say like this, as it brings no benefit. Help them realise that what they are doing is even worse than backbiting.

The third method is a principle based on hating the sin, but not the person. Whenever we see someone disobeying Allah ﷻ, it could even be someone walking in the street dressed improperly, or someone speaking with bad language, we need to remember this principle: hate the word or action, but not the person.

All of us are servants of Allah ﷻ, we are His ﷻ creation, who, at one point in our lives were not where we are today. Maybe we have disobeyed Allah ﷻ, maybe we've not had the best of character, but then we changed. So, when we see someone disobeying Allah ﷻ, we can dislike the action or words for the only reason that Allah ﷻ doesn't like it. If, for example we don't like lying it's not because of *who* is lying, but because lying in general is something Allah ﷻ doesn't like. *Allah doesn't love those who lie.*[50]

The fourth method is to control our *nafs* when we hear someone say something bad about us. A result of being told something by a 'tale carrier', is having ill feelings towards the person who backbit us. This is why the disease

50 Āl-Imran, 3:61.

of *namima* is so serious as it is related to and affects the heart. When we have ill feelings towards someone.

When we feel anger against someone because of what they said, we gain black dots on our heart and this will make the pure clear heart we were born with, dirty. So, the best thing is not to believe what we are told. Even if we believe it, we can tell ourselves they didn't mean it. To do this needs a lot of internal work, but the result is beneficial and brings us peace.

The fifth thing, which is also very important is that we're not supposed to start spying on that person to see if they really said this and wondering *what else did they say about me*. Allah ﷻ described the person who carries the tales in a negative way in the Qur'an, in the following verses:

وَلَا تُطِعْ كُلَّ حَلَّافٍ مَّهِينٍ
هَمَّازٍ مَّشَّآءٍ بِنَمِيمٍ
مَّنَّاعٍ لِّلْخَيْرِ مُعْتَدٍ أَثِيمٍ

And do not obey every worthless habitual swearer. [And] scorner, going about with malicious gossip - A preventer of good, transgressing and sinful. (al-Qalam, 68:10-12)

Allah ﷻ instructed *Rasul Allah* ﷺ to not obey and follow a person who always uses the name of Allah ﷻ to make an oath. Then He ﷻ described *hammaz*, هَمَّازٍ, which means someone who walks and backbites, but not with the tongue, rather with the face and the body language, so do not obey them. Likewise, *Rasul Allah* ﷺ said, لَا يَدْخُلُ الْجَنَّةَ قَتَّاتٌ.[51] 'The backbiter will not enter *Jannah*' قَتَّاتٌ *qattat* refers to a person who engages in *namimah,* constantly tale carrying.

We can learn a valuable lesson from the story of Suleiman ibn Abdul Malik from the Umawi time, and a leader of the believers. He called a man and said to him, "Someone told me that you said this and this about me." The man said, "I didn't say anything." Suleiman ibn Abdul Malik, responded that he did, stating that the person who told him was truthful. Now the man responded and said, النَّمَّامُ لَا يَكُونُ صَادِقًا 'The person who walks with tale telling is never truthful.'[52] Then Suleiman Abdul Malik responded, "You're right. Go, I have nothing against you."

What do we learn from this? When someone comes to us and says, you don't know what they said about you, the answer is to neither listen to anything from them, nor accept they are truthful. Even if it was true and we will never know, it's not going to make any difference for us with Allah ﷻ, instead it's going to hurt our heart. It is best not to let these things get to you. Leave it and ask Allah ﷻ if it is true, to basically guide that person and keep your heart pure and sound.

---

51 Abu 'Isa Muhammad al-Tirmidhi, "Chapter: What has been related about the nammam," *Jami' al-Tirmidhi*, Book 27, Hadith 132.

52 Ibn 'Allan, "Chapter on tale-bearing (namimah)," *Al-Futuhat ar-Rabbaniyyah* 'ala *al-Adhkār an-Nawawiyyah,* Vol 7, page 36.

The benefit of silence

Have you ever seen people who speak very little? One thing you will notice and pay attention to is those people who speak less, it is very unlikely they will make mistakes. *Sayyidina* Umar ﵁ said:

مَنْ كَثُرَ كَلَامُهُ، كَثُرَ سَقْطُهُ، وَمَنْ كَثُرَ سَقْطُهُ كَثُرَتْ ذُنُوبُهُ، وَمَنْ كَثُرَتْ ذُنُوبُهُ، فَالنَّارُ أَوْلَى بِهِ.

'The person who speaks too much will make a lot of mistakes, and the person who makes a lot of mistakes will fall into a lot of sins, and the person who sins, then, *al-nar* the hellfire is a best place, a good place for him.[53]' Ibn Masʿūd ﵁ said: "There is nothing that deserves a longer imprisonment than my own tongue."

Another valuable story is that of Luqman al-Hakim – Luqman the Wise. Once he entered on *Sayyidina* Dawud ﵇ who was a blacksmith. He watched him working on a shield and he really loved what he was doing, and he didn't know why *Sayyidina* Dawud ﵇ was making the shield. *Sayyidina* Luqman ﵇, his wisdom prevented him from speaking therefore, he didn't say anything and just stayed quiet. When *Sayyidina* Dawud ﵇ finished and got up, he took the shield, looked at it and commented 'what

53 Al-Jalal as-Suyuṭi, *Al-Jamiʿ as-Saghir wa Ziyadatuhu*, page 12587.

a beautiful shield this is for war'. Luqman al-Hakim smiled and he said, الصَّمْتُ حُكْمٌ وَقَلِيلٌ فَاعِلُهُ.[54]

الصَّمْتُ is wisdom. 'Staying quiet is wisdom' and another meaning of it is staying quiet is an obligation but very few do it or are able to do it.

Sayyidina Umar ﷺ entered where *Sayyidina* Abu Bakr ﷺ was sitting and he was touching his tongue and holding it. *Sayyidina* Umar ﷺ said to *Sayyidina* Abu Bakr ﷺ 'what is this?' *Sayyidina* Umar ﷺ said to *Sayyidina* Abu Bakr ﷺ, مَا غَفَرَ اللَّهُ لَكَ, 'may Allah forgive you, what is this?' And then *Sayyidina* Abu Bakr ﷺ said, 'This is the one who took me to the wrong path' or 'This is the one who I'm so worried about on the Day of Judgement.'

The message to us is to spend more time remaining quiet than talking. We should aim to value silence. If we need to talk, and sometimes we have to, let it be something that pleases Allah ﷻ. We need an imaginary filter, so when things come out, anything that's not pleasing to Allah ﷻ, will be stopped; our filter will stop it. This way, if we start practising it and time ourselves; we can assess how much do we speak and how much we are quiet? We can make a lot of *du'a* for Allah ﷻ to make us able to practise this *hadith*, 'speak good or stay silent' قُلْ خَيْرًا أَوْ لِيَصْمُتْ.[55], by His ﷻ permission.

54 Abu al-Fadl, *Kitab Majma' al-Amthal*, Vol 1, page 402.
55 Muhammad ibn 'Abd Allah al-Tabrizi, "Chapter: Hospitality," *Mishkat al-Masabih*, Book 21, Hadith 80.

We ask Allah ﷻ to strengthen us to control our tongue. May He ﷻ forgive us for our careless speech and guide us to say what pleases Him ﷻ and protect us from hearing and joining with the ill speech of others. *Ya Rabbi Ameen*.

Rasul Allah ﷺ said:
'Whomsoever believes in Allah and the Day of Judgement, let him or her say good or stay quiet.'

(al-Tabrizi)

My Dear Heart

Do you get Angry?

Just as our heart is affected by our tongue, it is equally affected by our emotions. In this chapter we turn our attention to a common feeling: anger. When was the last time you were angry or very upset? It's a very common scenario, but the question is, why does it happen and what did you do to address it? Anger in general is something Allah سبحانه وتعالى has put inside us, so it's unlikely there's anyone out there who does not get angry at some point or another. Anger itself is not something that's going to put dark spots on the heart. The reason we have to talk about it is because *how* we react to anger is going to either put more black spots on our heart or the opposite; a pure heart that isn't harmed.

What is anger?

Have you ever seen someone who's very angry? In both the Arabic and English language, it's described in everyday language as: *my blood is boiling, literally. I feel it inside me, I'm so upset; feeling hot headed.* Often there is so much anger, it's like water boiling in a pot. What's boiling, the scholar's say it is not water, it's actually fire, which the person in a state of anger feels.

It's exactly like the *Shaytan*'s reaction, when Allah ﷻ ordered the angels to prostrate to Adam ﷺ, and he was so upset. We know this from what he said:

قَالَ ءَأَسْجُدُ لِمَنْ خَلَقْتَ طِينًا

He said, "Should I prostrate to one You created from clay?" (al-Isra 17:61)

Or in the following verse:

قَالَ مَا مَنَعَكَ أَلَّا تَسْجُدَ إِذْ أَمَرْتُكَ قَالَ أَنَا خَيْرٌ مِّنْهُ خَلَقْتَنِي مِن نَّارٍ وَخَلَقْتَهُۥ مِن طِينٍ

[Allah] said, "What prevented you from prostrating when I commanded you?" [Satan] said, "I am better than him. You created me from fire and created him from clay [i.e., earth]." (al A'raf 7:12)

So, anger comes from the fire inside us. Some will ask what is wrong with having anger? The answer is how we respond to it will affect us, and everyone around us. Most of the time, our response is not pleasing to Allah ﷻ. This is why when a Companion came to *Rasul Allah* ﷺ and said to him, 'Give me some good advice, he ﷺ replied with two words, لَا تَغْضَبْ 'Do not get angry.'[56]

Who is a strong person?

In a *hadith Rasul Allah* ﷺ sheds more light on the meaning of power and strength. Normally we call someone strong, especially men, in physical terms, when they can wrestle well or carry something heavy. *Rasul Allah* ﷺ gave a new definition when he said the following:

لَيْسَ الشَّدِيدُ بِالصُّرَعَةِ، إِنَّمَا الشَّدِيدُ الَّذِي يَمْلِكُ نَفْسَهُ عِنْدَ الْغَضَبِ [57]

'The strong person is not the person who wins in a competition. The real strong person is the one who can control himself/ herself in a state of anger.'

This applies to men and women who get angry. So, it's not who is the strongest at Jujutsu or wrestling, or who is strong because they are a champion in any sport. An incident I witnessed showed the meaning of this *hadith*. There

56 Muhammad ibn Isma'il al-Bukhari, "Chapter: To be cautious from being angry," Book 78, Hadith 143.

57 Muhammad ibn Isma'il al-Bukhari, "Chapter. To be cautious from being angry," *Sahih al-Bukhari*, Book 78, Hadith 141.

was an office meeting at which there were two heads of two companies; one was a man, the other a woman. The male head of the company publicly insulted the woman for no reason, and everyone could see this woman was clearly unhappy and likely to be angry. Yet she controlled herself and did not respond to anything, and said 'I don't want to say anything that's not pleasing to Allah ﷻ, and I don't want to have anything inside my heart that's not pleasing to Allah ﷻ, and she left the meeting which was attended by fellow Muslims. We see in her response, that the strong person is not the person who has strong muscles, rather it's the one who can control their anger.

We see this in the example when Allah ﷻ tells us about *Sayyidina* Musa ﷺ. He got angry when he came back and found the people who Allah ﷻ guided through him, were all worshiping a calf. Musa ﷺ was so upset he even threw the Tablets that Allah ﷻ gave him. But then Allah ﷻ said:

وَلَمَّا سَكَتَ عَن مُّوسَى ٱلْغَضَبُ أَخَذَ ٱلْأَلْوَاحَ ۖ وَفِى نُسْخَتِهَا هُدًى وَرَحْمَةٌ لِّلَّذِينَ هُمْ لِرَبِّهِمْ يَرْهَبُونَ

'And when the anger subsided in Moses, he took up the tablets; and in their inscription was guidance and mercy for those who are fearful of their Lord.' (al-A'raf 7:154)

Let us not confuse being calm and not responding, with being weak. People may make these comments to suggest calmness is weakness, but you should never let this confuse you. On the contrary, it is much easier to lose control, to lose your temper and start saying things displeasing to Allah ﷻ, than it is to stay calm and composed, and say only what pleases Allah ﷻ.

Less anger means stronger faith-*Iman*

Dhul Qarnain, a king with power, who Allah ﷻ mentioned in *Surah al-Kahf*,[58] met an angel. He asked the angel to teach him something that will make his faith stronger and to become a strong believer. The angel replied 'Do not get angry' and then he explained 'the *Shaytan* will have full control on the son of Adam when he is angry.' And then he said, فَرُدَّ الغضَبَ بِالْكَظْمِ meaning 'learn to control your anger.'[59]

We recall that the pure heart is the heart that is full of faith. Therefore, if we want to make our faith stronger, it's not only that we fast, pray and give charity, all of which are honourable. There are other things in daily life outside the acts of worship which will increase our *Iman* and one of them, as we see in this narration is – controlling our anger.

We are all human and it's not that we are not going to feel angry. Actually, there are certain times and places where we should be angry. For example, when I see Allah ﷻ being disobeyed, internally I shouldn't be indifferent and think

---

58 Al-Kahf, 18:83-98.

59 Abu Hamid al-Ghazali, "The book on condemning anger, resentment, and envy," *Ihya' 'Ulum ad-Din*, Vol 3, page 165.

it's okay, everyone is doing it, there's no problem. On the contrary, I need to feel angry because that's something that will make Allah ﷻ also angry. The way I respond is what is taken account of. He ﷻ praises by saying:

ٱلَّذِينَ يُنفِقُونَ فِى ٱلسَّرَّآءِ وَٱلضَّرَّآءِ وَٱلْكَـٰظِمِينَ ٱلْغَيْظَ وَٱلْعَافِينَ عَنِ ٱلنَّاسِ ۗ وَٱللَّهُ يُحِبُّ ٱلْمُحْسِنِينَ

Who spend [in the cause of Allah] during ease and hardship and who restrain anger and who pardon the people - and Allah loves the doers of good. (Āl-Imran 3:134)

Those who can control their anger and forgive people – these two criteria – controlling anger and forgiveness, qualifies a person to be from the *muhsineen*, people of excellence.

Iblis himself said to *Sayyidina* Musa عليه السلام 'beware of being angry, because I play with the human being in a state of anger, a man or a woman.' The *Shaytan* plays with the angry human being the same way a child plays with a ball, and nobody would want to be that person.

The causes of anger

Why do some people not get as angry as others? What are the reasons people get angry? The first reason, which is another disease of the heart, is self-admiration or *'ujb* ٱلْعُجْبُ. It's the attitude of: *I am better than everybody. I think I know more, I think I look more beautiful. And then when someone does not treat me as superior as I expect to be treated, I get upset.* The second reason we discussed about the diseases of the tongue is sometimes joking too much. When this gets excessive and crosses a boundary, many people get upset.

There was a young, handsome man who repeatedly made jokes which were decent, but very frequent. One day he mentioned to me that he has a hard time keeping friends. I asked, "Is this the way you deal with your friends?" He said, "Yes it is." I said, "Then this is it; don't joke too much because people will get upset with you. And those people, may Allah ﷾ reward them, did not respond to you with anger. They just pulled themselves away." So, joking can be a good thing, but we need to make sure it is within the framework and limits that please Allah ﷾.

The third reason is very common, and that is getting upset when we argue and we want to make sure we are right. There's no need to do that. Both people in an argument have their own points and opinions. Present your point, and the other person presents theirs. If your view is correct, especially if it's in the *deen*, and they didn't listen to you, then it's better to leave it. Allah ﷾ doesn't take us to account by the result. He ﷾ takes us to account by the effort we made and tried to explain our points, especially if it's about our *deen*.

We also get upset when someone has more than we have, which is basically saying *'O Allah it's not fair, why did You give them and You didn't give me as much?'* We need to take a step back and remember Who owns everything in the universe, Who decides our *rizq*? This will help to avoid becoming annoyed with envying what someone else has.

So anytime we get upset, for example when our child throws something on the kitchen floor. How will we respond? If you're going to hit that child, that's not pleasing to Allah ﷻ. If you're going to use foul language at that child, that's not pleasing to Allah ﷻ. Instead, we are going to tell the child that this is not right and it is displeasing to Allah ﷻ. Your tone has to change, otherwise you're going to take away something from that child. Discipline is necessary, but one should never use foul language, harshness or physical abuse because that is not pleasing to Allah ﷻ.

May Allah ﷻ increase our *iman* and strengthen us to control our anger and be of those who are *muhsineen,* who control themselves and pardon others. *Ameen Ya Rabb.*

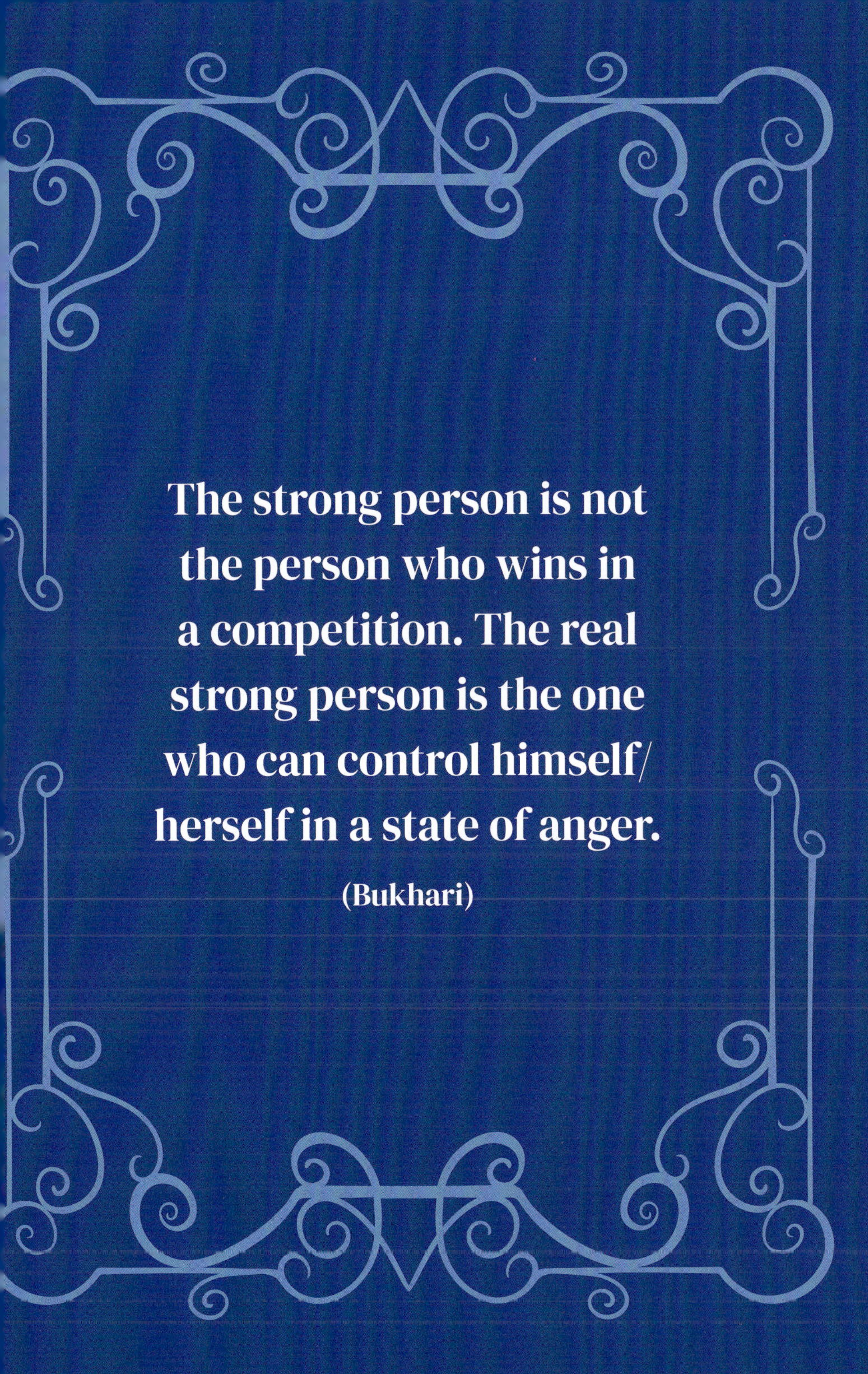
The strong person is not the person who wins in a competition. The real strong person is the one who can control himself/ herself in a state of anger.
(Bukhari)

My Dear Heart

Do you Control your Anger?

We know from the previous chapter how harmful anger is for our heart. As this is such a common emotion, we need to learn how to handle it effectively and be honest with our heart. How many of us have anger issues? The answer is probably most of us. The question is how many of us are able to control that anger? Anger is a universal problem which is why it is mentioned in this *hadith*:

A man said to the Prophet ﷺ, "Advise me! "The Prophet ﷺ said, "Do not become angry and furious." The man asked (the same) again and again, and the Prophet ﷺ said in each case, "Do not become angry and furious." (Bukhari 6166)

The Qur'anic response to anger

I witnessed a true story which I will share with you. Road rage is a popular topic all over the world, when people are either driving or parking, they get very upset. A woman, who parked her car, not blocking anyone, went to do something and came back to her car. Somebody was waiting for her and started attacking her. This woman had some young people with her and she was teaching them how to behave in a way that pleases Allah ﷾ and He ﷾ tested her on the spot. The person waiting for her, starting attacking her unjustly, shouting about how she parked her car badly, although the car was parked absolutely correctly.

The woman looked at her and said, "I'm sorry", although there was nothing she had done wrong. Still, she said I'm sorry and the agitated person kept saying 'you are not sorry.' Finally, the woman turned to her and said, "Listen, I told you I'm sorry" and then she drove away. The young people with her asked why did this happen, as they witnessed the scenario and it was annoying to watch as the woman did not do anything wrong. She replied, I remembered two verses in the Qur'an, that's when the words of Allah ﷾ come to help and shape us.

She said, the first one is:

خُذِ ٱلْعَفْوَ وَأْمُرْ بِٱلْعُرْفِ وَأَعْرِضْ عَنِ ٱلْجَٰهِلِينَ

وَإِمَّا يَنزَغَنَّكَ مِنَ ٱلشَّيْطَٰنِ نَزْغٌ فَٱسْتَعِذْ بِٱللَّهِ ۚ إِنَّهُۥ سَمِيعٌ عَلِيمٌ

إِنَّ ٱلَّذِينَ ٱتَّقَوْا۟ إِذَا مَسَّهُمْ طَٰٓئِفٌ مِّنَ ٱلشَّيْطَٰنِ تَذَكَّرُوا۟ فَإِذَا هُم مُّبْصِرُونَ

Take what is given freely, enjoin what is good, and turn away from the ignorant. And if an evil suggestion comes to you from Satan, then seek refuge in Allah. Indeed, He is Hearing and Knowing. Indeed, those who fear Allah – when an impulse touches them from Satan, they remember [Him] and at once they have insight.
(al-A'raf 7:199 -201)

When this came to her, she immediately said to herself, *This woman shouting at me is ignorant, I should turn my back to the ignorant.* Then the woman continued "The other verse I remembered was from *Surah Āl-Imran.*" This verse is striking, if we all learn this verse and practise it as much as we can, a lot of the anger issues will disappear. Allah ﷻ tells us who the righteous are:

وَسَارِعُوٓاْ إِلَىٰ مَغۡفِرَةٖ مِّن رَّبِّكُمۡ وَجَنَّةٍ عَرۡضُهَا ٱلسَّمَٰوَٰتُ وَٱلۡأَرۡضُ أُعِدَّتۡ لِلۡمُتَّقِينَ ٱلَّذِينَ يُنفِقُونَ فِي ٱلسَّرَّآءِ وَٱلضَّرَّآءِ وَٱلۡكَٰظِمِينَ ٱلۡغَيۡظَ وَٱلۡعَافِينَ عَنِ ٱلنَّاسِۗ وَٱللَّهُ يُحِبُّ ٱلۡمُحۡسِنِينَ

And hasten to forgiveness from your Lord and a garden [i.e., Paradise] as wide as the heavens and earth, prepared for the righteous. Who spend [in the cause of Allah] during ease and hardship and who restrain anger and who pardon the people – and Allah loves the doers of good. (Āl-Imran 3: 133-134)

He ﷻ describes those people who spend when they have and when they don't; this is one characteristic. Then the verse says that among the other qualities of the righteous is that, they don't get angry, they control their anger, and forgive and pardon people.

What will happen to those people? وَاللَّهُ يُحِبُّ الْمُحْسِنِينَ. Allah ﷻ loves those who act in a way of excellence and *ihsan* is the highest level with Allah ﷻ. If I can control my anger, and if I pardon people, then I am of that level.

Mu'adh ibn Anas ؓ, narrated that the Prophet ﷺ, said: "Whoever suppresses his anger when he is able to act upon it, Allah ﷻ will call him on the Day of Resurrection before all creatures and give him the choice of the *houris* of his right hand." (Ibn Majah)

These are inspiring examples and true stories. Once *Sayyidina* Umar ؓ was in his *majlis* where he normally sat surrounded by a lot of the *sahaba*. One of the people who normally attended, brought his uncle with him and asked permission from *Sayyidina* Umar ؓ, "Can I bring my uncle?". He was given permission. So, the uncle came in front of everybody, looked at *Sayyidina* Umar ؓ and said to him, "*Wallahi*, by Allah ﷻ, you don't give us anything, but a little and you do not judge between us with justice."

The nephew of that old man looked at *Sayyidina* Umar ؓ and he could see that he ؓ looked very angry. Allah ﷻ sent the following verse in relation to this type of scenario, خُذِ الْعَفْوَ وَأْمُرْ بِالْعُرْفِ وَأَعْرِضْ عَنِ الْجَاهِلِينَ. *Be gracious, enjoin what is right, and turn away from those who act ignorantly.*[60] (*al-A'raf* 7:199)

This is the same advice from the Qur'an the woman took in the parking lot. If you have an anger issue, these verses are

60 Al-Shatibi, "Chapter Ten: On the explanation of the meaning of the straight path," *Al-Itisaam*, Vol 3, page 334.

highly recommended. If you can memorize them, that's beneficial. But even if you can't, learning and using the concept is essential.

Reminders on controlling anger

The first thing to recall and think about, is how much we will be rewarded in the hereafter for controlling our anger. Secondly, which I try to remind myself of is; how many times each one of us disobeyed Allah ﷻ and made Allah ﷻ angry? How many times did Allah ﷻ continuously forgive us, pardon us, keep giving us what we don't deserve? If Allah ﷻ can do this and grants us His ﷻ favours, why can't we do it with another person?

The third is to remember, anger is from the *Shaytan* and we don't want the *Shaytan* to be happy. On the Day of Judgement, we don't want the *Shaytan* to say, I didn't do anything; I just told you to be upset and respond - and you responded.

وَقَالَ ٱلشَّيْطَٰنُ لَمَّا قُضِىَ ٱلْأَمْرُ إِنَّ ٱللَّهَ وَعَدَكُمْ وَعْدَ ٱلْحَقِّ وَوَعَدتُّكُمْ فَأَخْلَفْتُكُمْ
ۖ وَمَا كَانَ لِىَ عَلَيْكُم مِّن سُلْطَٰنٍ إِلَّآ أَن دَعَوْتُكُمْ فَٱسْتَجَبْتُمْ لِى ۖ فَلَا تَلُومُونِى وَلُومُوٓا۟
أَنفُسَكُم ۖ مَّآ أَنَا۠ بِمُصْرِخِكُمْ وَمَآ أَنتُم بِمُصْرِخِىَّ ۖ إِنِّى كَفَرْتُ بِمَآ أَشْرَكْتُمُونِ مِن قَبْلُ
ۗ إِنَّ ٱلظَّٰلِمِينَ لَهُمْ عَذَابٌ أَلِيمٌ

And Satan will say when the matter has been concluded, "Indeed, Allah had promised you the promise of truth. And I promised you, but I betrayed you. But I had no authority over you except that I invited you, and you responded to me. So do not blame me; but blame yourselves. I cannot be called to your aid, nor can you be called to my aid. Indeed, I deny your association of me [with Allah] before. Indeed, for the wrongdoers is a painful punishment. (Ibrahim 14:22)

The *Shaytan* will argue he didn't do anything. Allah سبحانه وتعالى promised you the truth, and you listened to what the *Shaytan* said, instead of listening to what Allah سبحانه وتعالى said.

Fourth, for those of us who are really worried about the way we look in a selfie or any photo, we need to see how we look when we are angry. Anger is from the *Shaytan* and a person looks their worst, when he or she is angry. From personal experience, a person I know very well, I couldn't recognise them when they got angry, their appearance completely changed. Their face was all red, there was a look in the eye that made me think *who is this person?* Remind yourself that when you are angry, you are not looking the way you normally would love to look, the way Allah سبحانه وتعالى created you.

Fifth, if we think about why we get angry, it's usually because someone said something to us that we didn't like. What they said could be true and in reality, we could be much worse. How many things are there about us that Allah سبحانه وتعالى covered for us from everyone's eyes? Or we may be arrogant and think how dare I be told this. At this point, we should reflect on how Allah سبحانه وتعالى is reminding us that we have more faults we need to address, and we need covered.

Practical steps we can take

A couple of practical things can help us control our anger.

The best advice is, when you are angry leave the situation. Don't say anything, just leave. Ask Allah ﷻ to remind you to do this. This doesn't mean you're weak, as we have covered in the previous chapter. On the contrary, the strongest person is the one who can control their anger completely, which requires being humble and pardoning others. We are reminded of this here:

Allah's Messenger ﷺ said: "Charity does not decrease wealth, no one forgives another except that Allah ﷻ increases his honour, and no one humbles himself for the sake of Allah ﷻ except that Allah ﷻ raises his status." (Muslim)

Number two, if you cannot leave and you are standing, sit down, this is the Prophetic advice.[61] If you are sitting down and angry, then lie down. And the best practical advice, may Allah ﷻ make us all remember, is go ahead immediately and do *wudu* – ablution. Why is this? As we know, anger is from the *Shaytan* and the *Shaytan* was created from fire. *Wudu* is using water, so when we are doing *wudu*, imagine a fireplace having water thrown on it and it extinguishes the fire. Doing *wudu* as soon as you feel angry therefore deals with the rising angry feelings.

---

61 Abi Dawud, "Chapter: What should be said at the time of anger," *Sunan Abi Dawud*, Book 43, Hadith 10.

Last but not the least, especially if you're someone who has a major anger issue, keep asking Allah ﷻ, "*Ya Allah*! calm me down, *Ya Allah*! calm me down." And if you are sincere and you really want to control your anger, He ﷻ will respond to your *du'a*. Anger is dangerous, and people have died for no other reason than uncontrolled anger. These days teenagers get upset and go on shooting sprees causing fatalities. Anger isn't only disobeying Allah ﷻ, but it actually creates a lot of problems, such as lives being lost due to it.

The last story which is a powerful reminder is that of *Sayyidina* Ali ﷺ. He was actually in a battle and was about to kill the enemy in front of him who was a non-believer. That person spat on his face. *Sayyidina* Ali ﷺ dropped his sword. The man asked him, "When I did not spit on you, you were about to kill me. And now that I spat at you, you didn't kill me?" *Sayyidina* Ali ﷺ replied "When I wanted to kill you in the beginning, it was for the sake of Allah ﷻ, but if I killed you after you spat in my face, then I would have been defending myself as I got upset, and I don't want to act in such a state."[62]

May Allah ﷻ teach us this self-control. Let's help each other to overcome anger. If you have someone around you with an anger issue, gently and nicely remind them. If we know we have an anger issue, we need to be open to people's advice.

---

62 Umar 'Abd al-Kafi, "Chapter: The difference between arrogance and dignity," *Durus*, Vol 17, page 7.

May Allah ﷾ help us to have self-restraint and hold back to control our anger. May Allah ﷾ make things easy for us when we feel this emotion rising by remembering His ﷾ reward for those who are pardoned. We pray Allah ﷾ cleanse our heart of this affliction and replaces anger with *sabr* – patience and perseverance. *Ya Rabbi Ameen.*

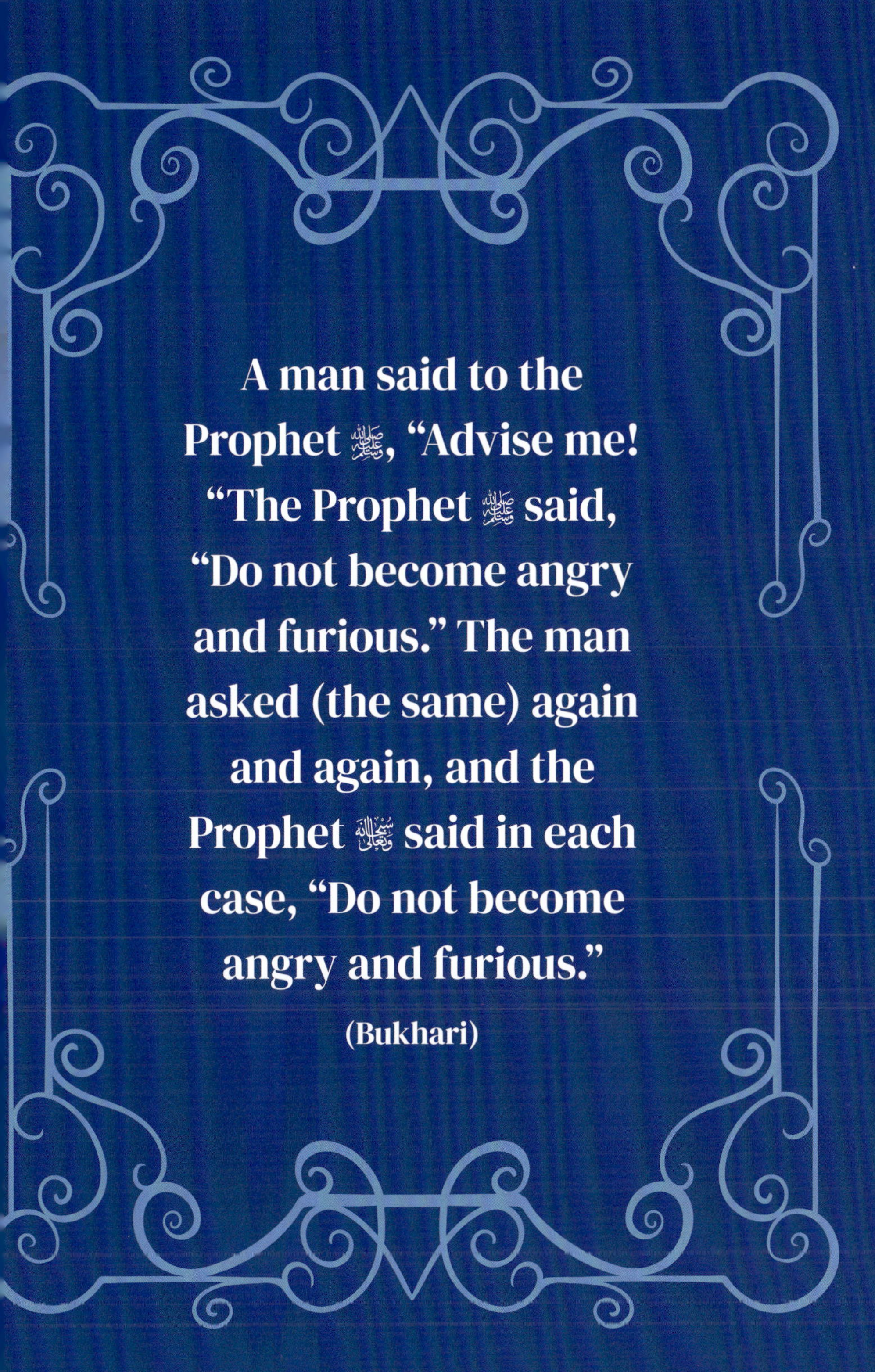

A man said to the Prophet ﷺ, “Advise me! “The Prophet ﷺ said, “Do not become angry and furious.” The man asked (the same) again and again, and the Prophet سُبْحَانَهُ وَتَعَالَىٰ said in each case, “Do not become angry and furious.”

(Bukhari)

My Dear Heart

Are you Forbearing?

In the previous chapter about anger, we recognised that it is something many of us have. Some people are quick to get angry and react, while the opposite is also true. We have to know ourselves which means asking: my dear heart, do you have forbearance?

Have you seen some people who remain calm? It is very unlikely to see them get upset, as they control themselves and take their time, responding gently. Most people will answer 'yes', as we have all seen people like this. What about us, did Allah ﷻ give us a calm temperament? Can we change if we are reactionary? Yes, everyone can change, as we learn from *Rasul Allah* ﷺ in an optimistic *hadith* narrated by *Sayyidina* Abu Hurayrah ﷺ:

"Knowledge is only gained through practicing knowledge, and forbearance is only gained through practicing forbearance. Seek knowledge and seek calmness and forbearance. Be kind to those whom you teach and to those from whom you learn, and do not be among the arrogant scholars, lest your ignorance overcomes you." [63]

There's a common saying we hear which is 'fake it till you make it.' And this is basically what this *hadith* is referring to. Practice sincerely, meaning it may not be you, but you are trying to become someone better and you keep practising the good quality, keep doing it, until it becomes your habit.

There is a Companion, may Allah ﷾ give us what He ﷾ gave him. His name is Al-Ashajj Abd al-Qa'es رضي الله عنه. The story relates that they were all on an expedition, Qa'es and some men. When they came back to Madinah, *Rasul Allah* ﷺ was waiting for them. So, everyone, as we can imagine was running to say *salam* to *Rasul Allah* ﷺ. Al-Ashajj Abd al-Qa'es رضي الله عنه however first went home, he changed, got dressed, and then came and greeted *Rasul Allah* ﷺ.

When *Rasul Allah* ﷺ looked at him, he smiled and said, "You have two characteristics that Allah ﷾ loves and your *Rasul* loves. The first is being forbearing and *al-anah* الأَنَاة (deliberation) to take your time." He responded and asked "Is this something Allah ﷾ gave me?" *Rasul Allah* ﷺ replied

63 Al-Jalal as-Suyuti, Kitab *al-Jamiʿ as-Saghir wa Ziyadatuh*, page 4093.

"yes." And Abd al-Qa'es said, "*Alhamdulillah*, Allah ﷻ gave me something He ﷻ loves."[64]

If you are blessed or know someone who Allah ﷻ gave the quality of being calm, something that is in their nature and they take their time, tell them that they are blessed and to be grateful for that blessing.

At the end of *Surah al-Furqan*, Allah ﷻ described عِبَادُ الرَّحْمٰنِ – the servants of the Most Merciful. We are all servants of Allah عِبَادُ اللهِ in the general sense, and from amongst us there are those who are special, whom Allah called عِبَادُ الرَّحْمٰنِ *ibaad-ur-Rahman* – 'the servants of the Most Merciful'. What are their qualities? The first thing He ﷻ said:

وَعِبَادُ ٱلرَّحْمَٰنِ ٱلَّذِينَ يَمْشُونَ عَلَى ٱلْأَرْضِ هَوْنًا وَإِذَا خَاطَبَهُمُ ٱلْجَٰهِلُونَ قَالُوا۟ سَلَٰمًا

And the servants of the Most Merciful are those who walk upon the earth with humbleness and ease, and when the ignorant address them [harshly], they say [words of] peace… (al-Furqan 25:63)

This comes when we have this forbearance.

Another beautiful narration demonstrates what forbearance is. *Sayyidina* Abdullah ibn Abbas ؓ, the cousin of *Rasul Allah* ﷺ was known as 'The pen of this nation' because *Rasul Allah* ﷺ made a *du'a* for him when he was young. He ﷺ prayed: "*Ya Allah*! فَقِّهْهُ فِي الدِّينِ، وَعَلِّمْهُ التَّأْوِيلَ. Teach him the

64 Abu Dawud, "Chapter: Regarding kissing the feet," *Sunan Abi Dawud*, Book 43, Hadith 453.

deeper understanding of this *deen* and teach him how to interpret the Qur'an."[65]

Since then Abdullah ibn Abbas was a high calibre man. On one occasion, it is related that a man cursed him with foul language. *Sayyidina* Abdullah ﷺ was listening. When the man finished, *Sayyidina* Abdullah ﷺ said to another Companion, "Ya 'Ikrimah! See if this man has any need from us that we can fulfil for him?' The man who cursed *Sayyidina* Abdullah ﷺ, lowered his head and felt extremely shy and ashamed because of the amazing response he received.[66]

What is the purpose of sharing these stories? The reason is to inspire each of us, and motivate us that if they can respond with forbearance, we can do it too. Allah ﷻ did not give them anything more than He ﷻ gave us. Allah ﷻ gave them *Iman*, the Qur'an and the example of *Rasul Allah* ﷺ. We too have *Iman (Alhamdulillah)*, the message of the Qur'an and the *Sunnah*, and if we apply the teachings, we too are capable of having patience and good character.' They did not have any 'superhuman' features.

In another narration, a young boy, *ghulam*, came to Abu Dhar Al-Ghaffari ﷺ, and he intentionally broke the leg of a lamb or a sheep that belonged to *Sayyidina* Abu Dhar.

65 Ibn Jarir at-Tabari, *Kitab Tahdhib al-Athar – Musnad Ibn 'Abbas*, Vol 1, page 167.
66 Najm ad Din, "Chapter: On Forbearance," *Kitab Mukhtasar Minhaj al Qasidin*, page 183.

He asked the boy, who broke the leg of this sheep, why he did it? The boy said, "I did it intentionally so you will get upset. And then you will hit me. And then you will sin and Allah ﷻ will take you to account." *Sayyidina* Abu Dharr ؓ, said, "I am going to make the person who taught you to do this upset, and I am going to let you go and do nothing to you."[67] The wisdom of these righteous *Sahabi* shows us what forbearance means.

Sayyidina Umar ibn Abdul Aziz, the fifth *khalifah* – the leader of the believers, was the great grandson of *Sayyidina* Umar ؓ. One night, he entered the *masjid*. The *masjid* was completely dark, and as he was walking, he stepped on a person who was asleep. So, the man awoke, looked up and said, "Are you blind? Are you crazy?" *Sayyidina* Omar ؓ said, "No." As he was the leader of the believers he had guards around him, who wanted to attack that man. He said, "Leave him. What's wrong with you? He asked me a question, are you crazy? Are you blind? and I said, No." [68]

The next narration is an example for all of us who have people who help us in the house, whether they come once a week or they live with us. Imam Zain al-Aabideen had a servant girl whom he asked to bring a container so that he could make *wudu*. She brought it to him, but as she was carrying it, it accidently fell from her hands and he got

67 Ibn A'sakar, "The one who was called by his kunyah: Abu Dharr al-Ghifari," *Tarikh Damishq*, Vol 66, page 211.

68 Muhammad Nasr ad-Din Muhammad Uwaydah, "The merits of 'Umar ibn 'Abd al-'Aziz," *Kitab Fasl al-Khitab fi az-Zuhd wa ar-Raqa'iq wa al-Adab*, Vol 1, page 794.

injured [or soaked]. She immediately said to him the verse we quoted previously about anger:

وَالْكَاظِمِينَ الْغَيْظَ , 'those who control anger' and he didn't say anything. Then she said, وَالْعَافِينَ عَنِ النَّاسِ ۗ, 'and those who forgive people'.

He said to her, "Go, I forgive you, you are free."

Finally she quoted: ' وَاللَّهُ يُحِبُّ الْمُحْسِنِينَ, and Allah ﷻ loves those who act with excellence.'

Amazingly, she was a *faqihah*, a young woman with a deep understanding of *deen*. [69]

The last story is a recent true incident I experienced on a plane. The flight attendant asked the man sitting in front of me if he wanted something to drink. He ordered a fizzy drink, and she said I'm sorry we don't have it. The man continued to complain for almost two hours into the flight, but the flight attendant remained calm and professional. Finally, when he was about to start becoming ruder to her, she asked calmly, "do you want me to go to the pilot and tell him we need to do an emergency landing?" Generally, if there is an issue in planes, they have the authority to land and then remove the person who's causing issues. Once she said this, the man stopped and he said, "no, that's okay." The woman showed amazing forbearance in how she dealt

69 Muhammad bin Hamud al-Wa'ili, "Chapter 2: Regarding the factors that necessitate the validity of marriage," *Bughiyat al-Muqtasid*, Vol 9, page 5634.

with the passenger. When we practice patient perseverance, we save ourselves from a lot of problems. If we don't practice forbearance, we may regret the results of losing our temper.

May Allah ﷻ teach us الْعِلْمُ بِالتَّعَلُّمِ، وَالْحِلْم بِالتَّحَلُّمِ.[70] that patience is gained by practicing forbearance and calmness, and knowledge is gained by learning. May our *Rabb* grant us to be amongst the *ibaad-ur-Rahman* – servants of The Most Merciful, who respond with humility and spread *salam*. *Ameen ya Rabbi*.

70 Al-Jalal as-Suyuti, Kitab *al-Jami' as-Saghir wa Ziyadatuh*, page 4093.

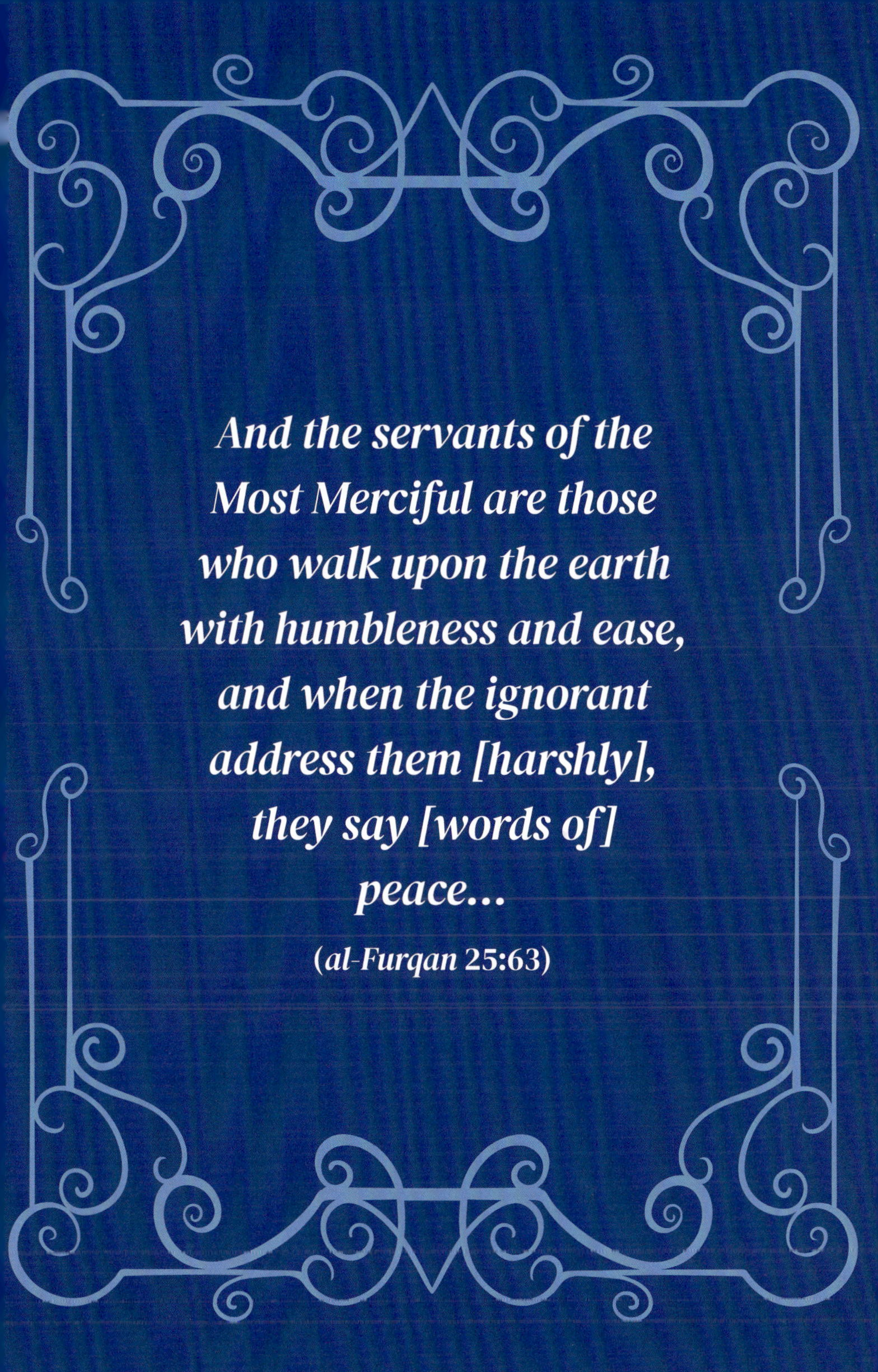
And the servants of the
Most Merciful are those
who walk upon the earth
with humbleness and ease,
and when the ignorant
address them [harshly],
they say [words of]
peace...
(al-Furqan 25:63)

My Dear Heart

Why do you Envy?

Our dear heart has many difficult feelings to deal with if we want to protect it from diseases. Some of these feelings are within us from childhood. I was watching two children play together, one of the children won the game, and the other didn't. People started praising the one who won saying *Masha Allah* and giving general praises. The other child got upset, you could see the hate in his eyes, and they were just two young boys. The one who lost, he started saying things like it's not fair, he doesn't deserve to win. While watching him, a question came to my heart: why do we get jealous of other people? It's a question that applies to us all.

Types of envy: *Ghibta, hiqd & hasad*

When you see a blessing that Allah ﷻ has given to someone, which you also want, but you don't want them to lose it, this is absolutely fine and is called غِبْطَة *ghibtah,* which is a positive envy. Someone with this will respond with good thoughts: *Ya Allah, just like you gave this woman a good husband, Ya Allah! give me one.* Or *Ya Allah! Like you gave these parents beautiful, well-behaved children, please give me the same.* In this positive form, you can pray for that family and tell them, *Masha Allah*, *Tabarak Allah*, may *Allah continue your blessing*! This envy is positive because you don't want them to lose what they received.

When Allah ﷻ gives something to another, that He ﷻ didn't give to us, it can cause feelings of anger, which can lead to hate. Hate with anger is called حِقْد *hiqd*, malice. This feeling inside grows slowly; like finding faults with that person and backbiting them. This leads to wishing that something bad happens to that person which makes the one with malice feel satisfied, telling themselves: he or she deserves it.

Envy-*hasad*, is one of the results of anger and produces internal negative thoughts, thinking the other person doesn't deserve the blessings they have. If you feel angry and feel that it's unfair, hoping that the person loses that blessing, then this is *hasad,* the negative envy.

It's as if the person who envies feels they own or are entitled to what the other has and wants the ability to give or withhold. In fact, it is all from Allah ﷾. In reality, when we look at it like this, it is equivalent to saying that Allah ﷾ is not just, because He ﷾ gave something to someone who isn't worthy of receiving it. *Rasul Allah* ﷺ, warned us about this in a beautiful *hadith* when the Companions were around him, he ﷺ said:

قَالَ رَسُولُ اللَّهِ ﷺ: دَبَّ إِلَيْكُمْ دَاءُ الْأُمَمِ قَبْلَكُمْ: الْحَسَدُ وَالْبَغْضَاءُ، وَالْبَغْضَاءُ هِيَ الْحَالِقَةُ، لَا أَقُولُ تَحْلِقُ الشَّعَرَ، وَلَكِنْ تَحْلِقُ الدِّينَ. وَالَّذِي نَفْسِي بِيَدِهِ، لَا تَدْخُلُوا الْجَنَّةَ حَتَّى تُؤْمِنُوا، وَلَا تُؤْمِنُوا حَتَّى تَحَابُّوا، أَوَلَا أُنَبِّئُكُمْ بِمَا يُثْبِتُ ذَلِكَ لَكُمْ؟ أَفْشُوا السَّلَامَ بَيْنَكُمْ.

> "The disease of the nations before you have crept into you: envy and hatred. Hatred is the shaver; I do not say it shaves hair, but it shaves away the religion. By the One in Whose Hand is my soul, you will not enter Paradise until you believe, and you will not believe until you love one another. Shall I not tell you of something which, if you do it, you will love one another? Spread salām amongst yourselves." (al-Tirmidhi)

The image we get here is that envy and malice creeps in the same way ants start walking into our home; we don't hear the sound or see how this disease comes in our heart. Envy is mentioned in the Qur'an in other places too, and Allah ﷾ teaches us to seek protection in 'The Lord of the Daybreak', from envy in *Surah al-Falaq*:

وَمِن شَرِّ حَاسِدٍ إِذَا حَسَدَ

And from the evil of an envier when he envies. (al-Falaq 113: 5)

Allah ﷻ owns everything

The first thing to recognise is that Allah ﷻ is the One who divides things between people. If you are married and you don't have children, and your friend is married with three or four children, that's Allah's ﷻ Will. He owns everything.

لِّلَّهِ مُلْكُ ٱلسَّمَٰوَٰتِ وَٱلْأَرْضِ ۚ يَخْلُقُ مَا يَشَآءُ ۚ يَهَبُ لِمَن يَشَآءُ إِنَٰثًا وَيَهَبُ لِمَن يَشَآءُ ٱلذُّكُورَ

أَوْ يُزَوِّجُهُمْ ذُكْرَانًا وَإِنَٰثًا ۖ وَيَجْعَلُ مَن يَشَآءُ عَقِيمًا ۚ إِنَّهُۥ عَلِيمٌ قَدِيرٌ

To Allah belongs the dominion of the heavens and the earth: He creates what He Wills. He gives to whom He Wills females [children], and He gives to whom He Wills males. Or He gives them [both] males and females, and He renders whom He Wills barren. Indeed, He is All Knowing and Competent. (ash-Shura 42: 49-50)

So, when someone has something, it is not in their control or my control; it's from Allah ﷻ. So why do we get jealous? And there is an order from *Rasul Allah* ﷺ not to be jealous of each other. He said 'لَا تَحَاسَدُوا Do not envy one another, وَلَا تَبَاغَضُوا, do not backbite one another وَلَا تَدَابَرُوا do not hate one another, do not turn your backs on one another, and do not sell one another's goods in order to outdo one another. Be servants of Allah, brothers to one another.'[71] Unethical practices such as undercutting one another in buying and selling creates ill feeling between people, and instead of this, the servants of Allah ﷻ are reminded to be brothers and sisters.[72]

Jealousy is when you see something, a *ni'mah*, a blessing, and you wish they didn't have it, or you wish they lose it. When we see something our heart deeply wants, given to someone else, instead of feeling, *Ya Allah why did they get it,* we need to overcome it and accept it by telling ourselves: *Ya Allah! Show me Your wisdom. Ya Allah, make my heart calm so they can enjoy your blessing. Ya Allah! Make them grateful for what You gave them. And don't let them use what You gave them, which I really want, in Your disobedience.*

Allah's Messenger ﷺ taught us to be aware and contious of jealousy when he said:

إِيَّاكُمْ وَٱلْحَسَدَ، فَإِنَّ ٱلْحَسَدَ يَأْكُلُ ٱلْحَسَنَاتِ كَمَا تَأْكُلُ ٱلنَّارُ ٱلْحَطَبَ.

'Beware of being jealous. Because jealousy will eat good deeds like the fire that eats the wood.'[73]

---

71 Muslim bin Hajjaj, "Chapter: The prohibition of wronging, forsaking, or despising a Muslim and the inviolability of his blood, honor and wealth," *Sahih Muslim*, Book 45, Hadith 40.

72 Muhammad bin Ismail al-Bukhari, "Chapter: Al-Hijra," *Sahih al-Bukhari*, Book 78, Hadith 104.

73 Abu Dawud, "Chapter: Envy (hasad)," *Sunan Abi Dawud*, Book 43, Hadith 131.

Dealing with jealousy

Imam Ibn Sirin, the famous scholar who interpreted dreams, said, مَا حَسَدْتُ أَحَدًا عَلَىٰ شَيْءٍ, 'I have never felt jealousy from anyone because they have something.[74] "I have never envied anyone for anything in this world, because if he is one of the people of Paradise, how can I envy him for something in this world when he is going to Paradise? And if he is one of the people of Hell, how can I envy him for something in this world when he is going to Hell?" This is how he talked to himself and what a wonderful method to treat the disease of jealousy.

What Ibn Sirin was saying was a man or woman who, from the way they act and conduct themselves looks like they will be from the people of *Jannah*, why be jealous of something from the *dunya* that he or she has, when they are going to *Jannah*? Instead of being jealous, I need to compete with him in goodness that will take me to *Jannah*. Likewise, if that person has something from this *dunya* that I don't have, but they will end up in the hellfire, why am I jealous of something which is going to take them to the hellfire? The point is we need to talk to ourselves and remember everything we have, Allah ﷻ has given us.

We do not own anything in this *dunya*. Allah ﷻ is the owner ٱللَّهُ ٱلْمَلِكُ وَٱلْمَالِكُ, The One Who owns everything. So, when we get upset with what someone has been given, we

74 Ibn Abi Dunya, *Kitab Al-Wara'*, page 57.

are literally getting upset with Allah ﷻ. This is when we need to pause and ask for guidance: *Ya Allah, show me the wisdom in this.*

Treating *hasad*

What is the remedy for our heart to rid it of this disease? First, we need to learn about Allah ﷻ. We need to know Allah ﷻ is Just and everything comes from Allah ﷻ. We need to train ourselves to be pleased with the decree of Allah ﷻ.

Second, remember everything in this life is going to end, nothing stays. The parable in *Surah al-Hadid*, where everything in this life, the money, the wealth, the competition, all become like ashes, is likened to a dry plant.[75] So, the more I look at the *dunya* and at this life with less attachment, with asceticism, my heart will not feel negative when I see someone has something materially more than myself.

The third practical step is if we see someone with a blessing, but they are not using it for the sake of Allah ﷻ or to please Allah ﷻ, we should be grateful Allah ﷻ didn't give it to us, because we don't want to be tested like this.

The only time we really need to envy, لَا حَسَدَ إِلَّا فِي اثْنَتَيْنِ.[76] is in two situations. The first one is when somebody who has

75 Al-Hadid, 57:20.

76 Muhammad bin Ismail al-Bukhari, "Chapter: The reward of judging according to al-hikmah," *Sahih al-Bukhari*, Book 93, Hadith 5.

more money than you and they are spending it for the sake of Allah ﷻ. The second situation is where somebody is connected to the Qur'an and they spend the night reading it by the blessing of Allah ﷻ. For these two situations we can ask Allah ﷻ to give us what He ﷻ gave them. This doesn't mean you want them to lose it.

If we have ill feelings inside us which causes the dots that will make the heart black, we need to ask ourselves where did these come from? We need to reflect: *Why do some people not have it? It's not something I can say Allah ﷻ gave me. I'm responsible and it's something inside me. I have built on these ill feelings and this is the result of it.*

Arrogance is the first reason of *hasad*: thinking we're better than other people including self-praise and feeling superior. So, when we see someone with more, or they are better than ourselves, we become jealous. Another reason is greed, wanting to own more, especially material things, which will lead to jealousy. Ill feelings towards someone is the strongest reason for jealousy and envy, and for this we should do our best not to hate people even if they have transgressed against us. The best thing to do is forgive and pardon them and clean our heart.

We ask Allah ﷻ to clean our heart from the attachment to this world, from looking down at people and from ill feelings towards people. We ask Allah ﷻ to clean our hearts completely and seek refuge in Him ﷻ from the feeling of envy and jealousy and all that leads to it. *Ya Rabbi Ameen.*

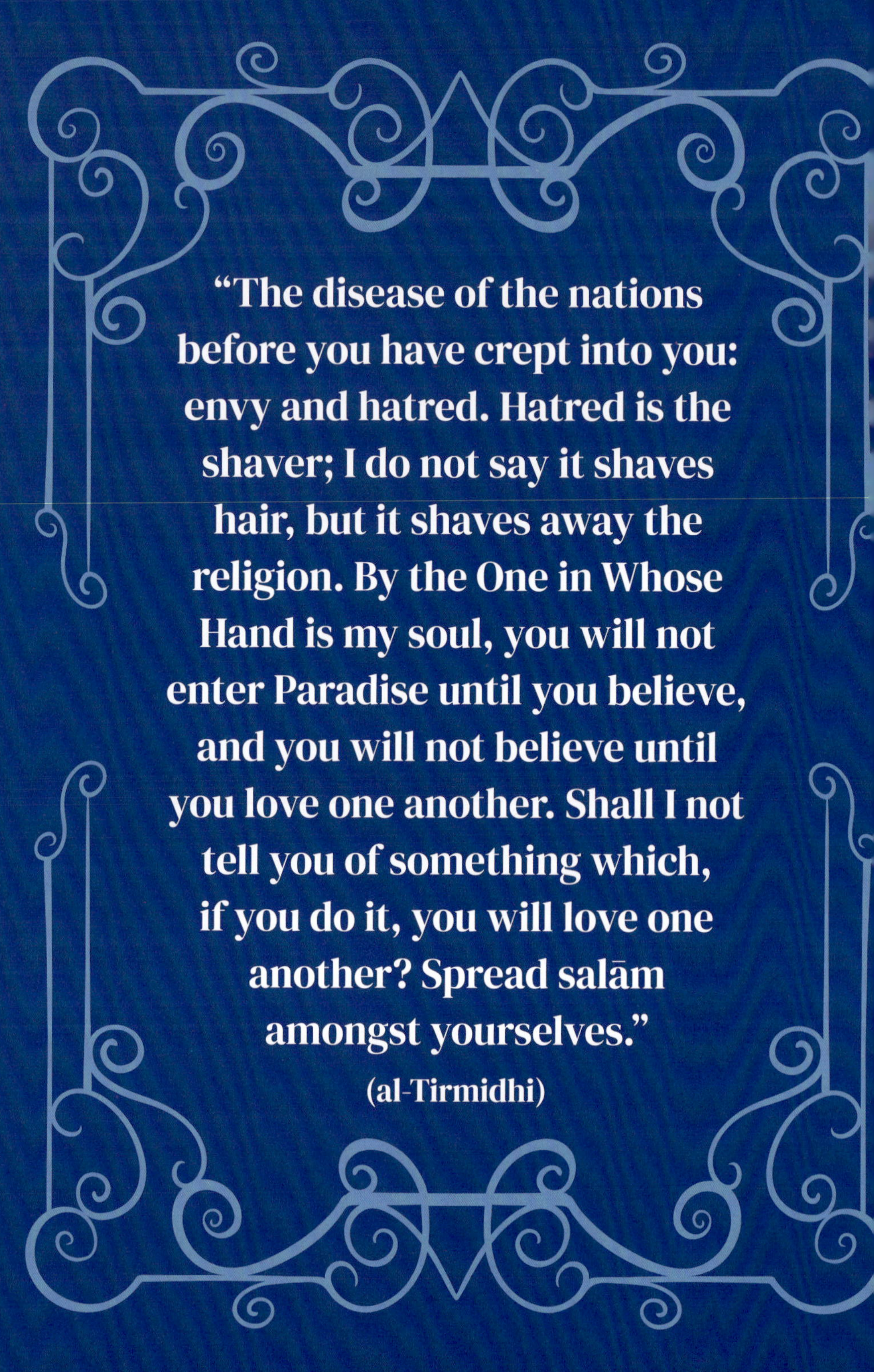

"The disease of the nations before you have crept into you: envy and hatred. Hatred is the shaver; I do not say it shaves hair, but it shaves away the religion. By the One in Whose Hand is my soul, you will not enter Paradise until you believe, and you will not believe until you love one another. Shall I not tell you of something which, if you do it, you will love one another? Spread salām amongst yourselves."

(al-Tirmidhi)

My Dear Heart

Why are you Arrogant?

A question I ask my heart, which we all need to ask our heart is; my dear heart, are you arrogant? It's a very tough question because it's very hard for us to say yes. Sometimes we don't say yes because we really don't know; sometimes we don't want to admit it, although we know that it is true. What is arrogance? We need to learn about it and understand why it is one of the biggest black dots in the heart.

Let's think about what happened when Allah ﷾ ordered all the angels to prostrate to Adam ﷷ, when *Iblis*, the devil, responded with:

وَإِذْ قُلْنَا لِلْمَلَٰٓئِكَةِ ٱسْجُدُوا۟ لِءَادَمَ فَسَجَدُوٓا۟ إِلَّآ إِبْلِيسَ أَبَىٰ وَٱسْتَكْبَرَ وَكَانَ مِنَ ٱلْكَٰفِرِينَ

And [mention] when We said to the angels, "Prostrate before Adam"; so they prostrated, except for Iblis. He refused and was arrogant and became of the disbelievers. (al-Baqarah, 2:34)

This is a characteristic that is inside us. If we are calm internally when we get upset, we will normally respond with calmness. We need to think about what's happening inside us.

Allah ﷻ said in the Qur'an, in *Surah al-A'raf*:

سَأَصْرِفُ عَنْ ءَايَٰتِيَ ٱلَّذِينَ يَتَكَبَّرُونَ فِي ٱلْأَرْضِ بِغَيْرِ ٱلْحَقِّ وَإِن يَرَوْا۟ كُلَّ ءَايَةٍ لَّا يُؤْمِنُوا۟ بِهَا وَإِن يَرَوْا۟ سَبِيلَ ٱلرُّشْدِ لَا يَتَّخِذُوهُ سَبِيلًا وَإِن يَرَوْا۟ سَبِيلَ ٱلْغَيِّ يَتَّخِذُوهُ سَبِيلًا ۚ ذَٰلِكَ بِأَنَّهُمْ كَذَّبُوا۟ بِـَٔايَٰتِنَا وَكَانُوا۟ عَنْهَا غَٰفِلِينَ

I will turn away from My signs those who are arrogant upon the earth without right; and if they should see every sign, they will not believe in it. And if they see the way of consciousness, they will not adopt it as a way; but if they see the way of error, they will adopt it as a way. That is because they have denied Our signs and they were heedless of them. (al-A'raf 7:146)

What will happen to me if I think I'm better than every-body else and act like the *Shaytan*? He said he's not going to prostrate to Adam عليه السلام, stating: 'I'm better than him, I was created from fire, he was created from clay.' If I have the same attitude, what will happen to me? Allah ﷻ will respond to me in the *dunya* by moving me away. This is the meaning of this verse. سَأَصْرِفُ عَنْ آيَاتِيَ 'I'm going to move (people) away from seeing My signs and seeing the truth.'

Consider these scenarios. When someone tells you, you need to pray, if you have arrogance in you, you're not going to listen because you feel superior and don't like being told. Pride – *Al-kibr* has many consequences. The biggest one we are warned about by *Rasul Allah* ﷺ is:

لَا يَدْخُلُ ٱلْجَنَّةَ مَنْ كَانَ فِي قَلْبِهِ مِثْقَالُ ذَرَّةٍ مِّنْ كِبْرٍ.[77]

"He will not enter Paradise who has in his heart an atom's weight of arrogance."

Turning to ourselves, we can reflect on our own state

My dear heart, make sure you don't have an atom of arrogance because if you do, then I will not be entering Jannah until it is removed. Why is that?

When I am arrogant, I don't see truth as truth, I see it from my lens. I don't see it from the lens of Allah ﷻ. I don't see that when Allah ﷻ told me to dress in a certain way it is because it is good for me. I don't want to do it because it's not what everybody else does. The arrogance inside me,

77 Muslim bin Hajjaj, "Chapter. The prohibition of pride and definition of it," *Sahih Muslim*, Book 1, Hadith 173.

makes me see it through my own lens and creates a barrier between me and *Jannah*.

Arrogance, *kibr*, is not a characteristic of a believer. In general, arrogance makes us look down at people because of the way they look, their skin colour, their accent, their background, their name, or where they come from. All of this becomes a *hijab* - a partition between me and *Jannah*.

The characteristics of the believer

1. Humility. A believer is humble, a believer loves for others what he or she loves for herself or himself.

2. A believer does not take action when angry. Their anger isn't expressed outwardly in a negative way.

3. They are not jealous of other people. They don't have this anger and hate towards people.

4. A believer is forgiving and pardons people with humility.

Together, these qualities don't come easily, they take a lot of practice. Anytime we feel arrogance, we should think of the *Shaytan*. There is only One who is worthy of pride in the positive way, that is Allah سُبْحَانَهُ وَتَعَالَىٰ, and He سُبْحَانَهُ وَتَعَالَىٰ said:

وَلَهُ ٱلْكِبْرِيَآءُ فِى ٱلسَّمَٰوَٰتِ وَٱلْأَرْضِ ۖ وَهُوَ ٱلْعَزِيزُ ٱلْحَكِيمُ

And to Him belongs [all] grandeur within the heavens and the earth, and He is the Exalted in Might, the Wise. (al-Jathiyah 45:37)

Signs of arrogance

No human being has the right to feel that he or she is better than another. Unfortunately, these days even children from a young age of seven or eight years old, say that they have been bullied and made fun of in school because one of them thinks they are better than the other, just because of the car that their mother picks them up in. Some feel superior because of their name or because of where they live. This arrogance is there at a young age and sadly these characteristics continue to develop as they grow older.

Arrogance is not the character of a believer. It causes black dots on our heart and needs to be cleaned and cleared out. What is the sign of being arrogant?

One sign is a person always wants to be in the front, and wants people to walk behind him. Another sign is not going to visit particular people because of feeling superior to them, even when they are invited. Another example may be in *Ramadan*, during *taraweeh* when we are waiting for the *salah* to start with an empty space beside us. Then someone comes into that space who we don't know, and who is not from our background. Do we wish they didn't sit next to us? If that's the feeling, then we have pride.

We need to remember, the person who has this feeling of superiority, will not enter *Jannah*.

How do I treat the disease of arrogance?

One thing we can do is remember the story of Hasan al-Basri[78]. He was sitting and the prince came in with all his entourage. Everybody, wherever they were stood up, but he didn't stand up. So, the prince looked at him, and said: 'Don't you know who I am?' Hasan al-Basri said, "Yes of course I do. You were created from a despised drop of fluid. You will one day be a decaying corpse. And in between, you are a vessel for carry stool within you. This is who we truly are."

قُتِلَ ٱلْإِنسَٰنُ مَآ أَكْفَرَهُۥ

مِنْ أَيِّ شَيْءٍ خَلَقَهُۥ

مِن نُّطْفَةٍ خَلَقَهُۥ فَقَدَّرَهُۥ

ثُمَّ ٱلسَّبِيلَ يَسَّرَهُۥ

ثُمَّ أَمَاتَهُۥ فَأَقْبَرَهُۥ

Destroyed [i.e cursed] is man; how disbelieving is he. From what thing [i.e substance] did He create him? From a sperm drop He created him and destined for him. Then He eased the way for him. Then He causes his death and provides a grave for him. (Abasa 80:17–21).

78 Muhammad bin Ahmad Al-Qurtubi, "Tafseer Surah Al-Ma'arij," *Al- Jami' li Ahkam al-Quran*, Vol 18, page 295.

Allah ﷻ uses a figure of speech in the Arabic language, meaning, 'woe on the human being', what is wrong with him, our origin is very humble. We cannot even see the egg or the sperm with our own eyes, we have to put it under the microscope. Then He ﷻ made him live this life and opened things for him.

Then anytime we have feelings of arrogance inside us because of *who we are, where we come from, the wealth we have,* we need to remember again and again what is the value of this *dunya*? Or conversely, what is the lack of value of this *dunya*, as we recalled in the beginning of this chapter. When one's background or heritage is a cause of arrogance, we are told in the words of Allah ﷻ who is really superior in *akhirah* and it is neither of these:

إِنَّ أَكْرَمَكُمْ عِندَ ٱللَّهِ أَتْقَىٰكُمْ

Indeed, the most noble of you in the sight of Allah is the most God-conscious (pious) of you. (al-Ḥujurāt 49:13)

Remembering that we are all going to our graves should prevent us from feeling pride in the things we boast about, none of which will have any value nor will they come to our help at that time. Our priority is to dig deep and look inside to see if we have any seeds of pride.

Loving beauty is not arrogance

It was narrated by Abdullah ibn 'Umar ﷺ that the Messenger of Allah ﷺ said:

"Whoever lets his garment drag on the ground out of pride, Allah ﷻ will not look at him on the Day of Resurrection." *Sayyidina* Abu Bakr ﷺ said: "O Messenger of Allah, one side of my lower garment slips down unless I take care of it." The Messenger of Allah ﷺ said: "You are not one of those who do so out of arrogance." (Bukhari)

Sayyidina Abu Bakr ﷺ was worried that he may be counted as one with arrogance. However, *Rasul Allah* ﷺ explained that it's not the length of the thobe dragging that is the problem, but if it drags out of arrogance. On the contrary *Rasul Allah* ﷺ said in the narration warning about *kibr*, "He who has in his heart an atom's weight of arrogance (*kibr*) will not enter Paradise." A man asked: "O Messenger of Allah ﷺ, a person likes his clothes and shoes to be beautiful. Is that arrogance?" The Prophet ﷺ replied: "Allah is Beautiful and loves beauty. Arrogance means rejecting the truth and looking down on people."[79]

When a person wants to look good and dress well, that doesn't mean they are arrogant. With the right intention, it can even be an act of worship. Allah ﷻ loves it. If, however,

79 Muslim bin Hajjaj, "Chapter: The prohibition of pride and definition of it," *Sahih Muslim*, Book 1, Hadith 171.

dressing well is because they want to look better than everybody else and they get upset if someone is better dressed than them, or they are annoyed when someone is more popular socially, then that is an issue. This is where we need to take account of ourselves and check for arrogance.

In dressing well, we are reminded what type of clothes are the best:

يَـٰبَنِىٓ ءَادَمَ قَدْ أَنزَلْنَا عَلَيْكُمْ لِبَاسًا يُوَٰرِى سَوْءَٰتِكُمْ وَرِيشًا ۖ وَلِبَاسُ ٱلتَّقْوَىٰ ذَٰلِكَ خَيْرٌ ۚ ذَٰلِكَ مِنْ ءَايَـٰتِ ٱللَّهِ لَعَلَّهُمْ يَذَّكَّرُونَ

O children of Adam, We have bestowed upon you clothing to conceal your private parts and as adornment. But the clothing of righteousness - that is best. That is from the signs of Allāh that perhaps they will remember. (al-Aʿraf 7:26)

If we remember to connect everything back to Allah ﷻ it helps us to be humble. After all, the best amongst us is not the person who has wealth or children or large homes. Allah ﷻ informs us:

إِنَّ أَكْرَمَكُمْ عِندَ اللَّهِ أَتْقَاكُمْ

Indeed, the most noble of you in the sight of Allah is the most righteous of you. (al-Hujurat 49:13)

May Allah سبحانه وتعالى make us among those honourable in His سبحانه وتعالى sight. We seek refuge in Allah سبحانه وتعالى from the feeling of arrogance and feeling superior to people. May Allah سبحانه وتعالى protect us and guide our hearts to humility and *taqwa*, *Ya Rabbi Ameen*.

Rasul Allah ﷺ said:
"He will not enter
Paradise who has in
his heart an atom's
weight of arrogance."
(Muslim)

My Dear Heart

Do you Love Wealth?

My dear heart, do you love wealth? If we are all honest, the answer is yes. Do we look at our bank account regularly, sometimes even more than once? Do we look at when the next salary raise will be? We think about money coming in from one place or another. Or do we get really upset when we lose some money or even in rare cases, all our money? The answer to all of this is yes. What does this have to do with our heart? The truth is we need money to live.

Allah سبحانه وتعالى said in the Qur'an:

إِنَّمَآ أَمْوَٰلُكُمْ وَأَوْلَٰدُكُمْ فِتْنَةٌۚ وَٱللَّهُ عِندَهُۥٓ أَجْرٌ عَظِيمٌ

Your wealth and your children are but a trial, and Allah has with Him a great reward. (al-Taghabun 64:15)

Money is a test and a trial, both when Allah ﷻ gives us a lot of money and when Allah ﷻ withholds money. A beautiful *hadith* of *Rasul Allah* ﷺ gives us the vital lesson that everything Allah ﷻ gives us, is useful to us as long as it is used in the right way, the way which is pleasing to Him ﷻ. Once it becomes an attachment and our core focus and leads us to disobey Allah ﷻ, then we've failed the test of wealth and it becomes something we will be asked about. *Rasul Allah* ﷺ said:

ما ذِئْبَانِ جَائِعَانِ أُرْسِلَا فِي غَنَمٍ بِأَفْسَدَ لَهَا مِنْ حِرْصِ الْمَرْءِ عَلَى الْمَالِ وَالشَّرَفِ لِدِينِهِ.[80]

"Two hungry wolves sent into a flock of sheep are not more destructive to them than a man's greed for wealth and status is to his religion."

If you've ever been in a safari, or you have watched a documentary where there's a very hungry predator, then the image of the two wolves used by *Rasul Allah* ﷺ comes to life. Imagine when they are sent into a whole herd of sheep, what damage and chaos they will do. They will go right and left and they will leave a trail of destruction. In this parable, the damage these two wolves can do, is far less than the damage of loving and being attached to wealth and status is.

80 Abu Isa Muhammad al-Tirmidhi, "Chapter: The Hadith: Two wolves free among sheep," *Jamiʿ al-Tirmidhi*, Book 36, Hadith 73.

And the result of this حِرْص, *hirs*, is that one's religion is in danger too, as the more worried we are about our wealth, the more we need, as it never feels like we have enough. It's a constant worry. We worry about, what's going to happen after five or ten years to our money; about children going to college and finances. Next, we are concerned about our retirement. It is easy to get obsessed with it, which can ruin our faith. Our faith lives in our heart. If our heart is ruined, with several dots covering it, then our final interview and meeting with Allah ﷻ will be one where there are many things to answer for.

How to handle money

Sa'eed ibn al-Musayyib said, earning and acquiring money is nothing bad, as long as that money is from *halal* sources.[81] The reason for working hard, keeping a job, investing in *halal* ways is to have enough to live on so there is no need to ask from anyone. How we define 'enough' is something else to reflect on which is a bigger discussion. In general, people want to earn enough to avoid relying on asking others for help. The more wealth we get, the more we will be questioned, but it is also a great opportunity for us to draw closer to Allah ﷻ.

81 Najm al-Din al-Ghazi, "Chapter: Imitating the Righteous," *Kitab Hasan al-Tanabbuh lima warada fi al-Tashabbuh*, Vol 3, page 438.

Rasul Allah ﷺ, said الْمُؤْمِنُ الْقَوِيُّ خَيْرٌ وَأَحَبُّ إِلَى اللَّهِ مِنَ الْمُؤْمِنِ الضَّعِيفِ، وَفِي كُلٍّ خَيْرٌ,[82] 'The strong believer is more beloved to Allah ﷻ than the weak believer. And in both there is goodness.' One part of strength or power, is wealth.

Yahya Ibn Mu'adh said: 'The dirham is a scorpion, so if you cannot handle it properly do not touch it otherwise it will sting you and its poison will kill you.' It was asked: 'How can we handle money properly?' He replied: 'Gain it lawfully and spend it rightfully.'[83] This parable warns us that the scorpion can be useful for medicinal purposes, but it can also be a killer. Likewise, we need to learn about the benefits and dangers of having money; *Why do I want money? What will I use it for?*

The first use is of course that money is needed for this *dunya* – that's the most common reason why we need it, as long as we are not disobeying Allah ﷻ. There are also a lot of benefits in the *akhirah* too, from having money. For example, if I spend it on myself to please Allah ﷻ like going for *Hajj* or *Umrah*, or giving *sadaqah*.

The second thing is charitable projects; I could build mosques or take care of many orphans or needy people; or provide education. These are all noble and beautiful uses. In this case, I don't personally need more, and I can live at a certain level without being arrogant and without feeling superior.

82 Muslim bin Hajjaj, "Chapter: Belief in the divine decree and submission to it," *Sahih Muslim*, Book 46, Hadith 52.

83 Mukhtasar Minhaj Al Qasidin, p.98

A third reason for needing money is for protection. It could be, there is a need for a lawyer, for someone to defend me and for this, money is needed and it is a blessing. Equally, it can be a distress against us, because the more we have, the more we want. The more we want, the greater likelihood that it can result in us disobeying Allah ﷻ. This is something we should be vigilant to avoid.

Sayyidina Omar ؓ used to say:

اللَّهُمَّ إِنِّي أَعُوذُ بِكَ مِنْ مَالٍ أُسْأَلُ عَنْهُ فِي قَبْرِي، وَيَنْتَفِعُ بِهِ وَرَثَتِي مِنْ وَرَائِي

'O Allah, I seek refuge in You from wealth about which I will be questioned in my grave and which will benefit my heirs after me.'[84]

Money and our time

A common response to having wealth and money is: '*everything I have is halal, so what's the problem?*' This is where we have to be very careful. Too much *halal* becomes a very easy way to slip into *haram*. And even some of the scholars and some Companions used to say, they used to leave a good amount of the *halal* so they don't fall into the *haram*.

This slip can happen in many small ways that aren't obvious at first. When, for example I was in my residency doing OB/GYN (obstetrics and gynaecology) we used to do training for twelve to sixteen hours a day. How much time

84 Umar Abd al-Kafi, "Causes that lead to the punishment of the grave," *Kitab al-Dar al-Akhirah*, Vol 5, page 21.

did this leave for remembering Allah ﷻ? We were barely able to do *salah* on time and the minimum about of remembrance. Although this was a temporary stage of my life, it easily becomes the working life and then my life is working twelve to sixteen hours, or in other professions spending just as long – going from one meeting to the other, from one deal to the other. Without a doubt this amount of time on work is going to take me away from the remembrance of Allah ﷻ. There are only twenty-four hours in the day and night and there are many needs to be fulfilled outside of work, just in order to live. So, earning and the time we spend on our work affects how focused we can be on Allah ﷻ.

Coming back to my heart, what do I need to do for it to stay clean and close to Allah ﷻ? I need to make sure the pursuit for wealth is not taking me away from Allah ﷻ. As well as taking care about where the money is coming from, I'm not going to justify doing less of what Allah ﷻ wants me to do in acts of worship, because I'm donating money to charitable causes. This equation doesn't work.

Our attitude to money must be balanced, أُمَّةً وَسَطًا.[85] – we are described as a 'just and balanced *ummah*.' Staying balanced means we earn what we need, we make sure it comes from *halal* sources and none of it is spent on *haram*, and importantly – it's not taking me away from Allah ﷻ. It's tragic

85 Al-Baqarah, 2:143.

when He ﷾ gives us wealth and we use it to move away from Him ﷾.

We seek refuge in Allah ﷾ that we never use the wealth He ﷾ gives us to disobey Him ﷾ or weaken our faith. May Allah ﷾ protect our hearts from loving and being attached to money. May He ﷾ keep us on the middle path and make us amongst those who are strong believers in closeness to Him ﷾. *Ya Rabbi Ameen.*

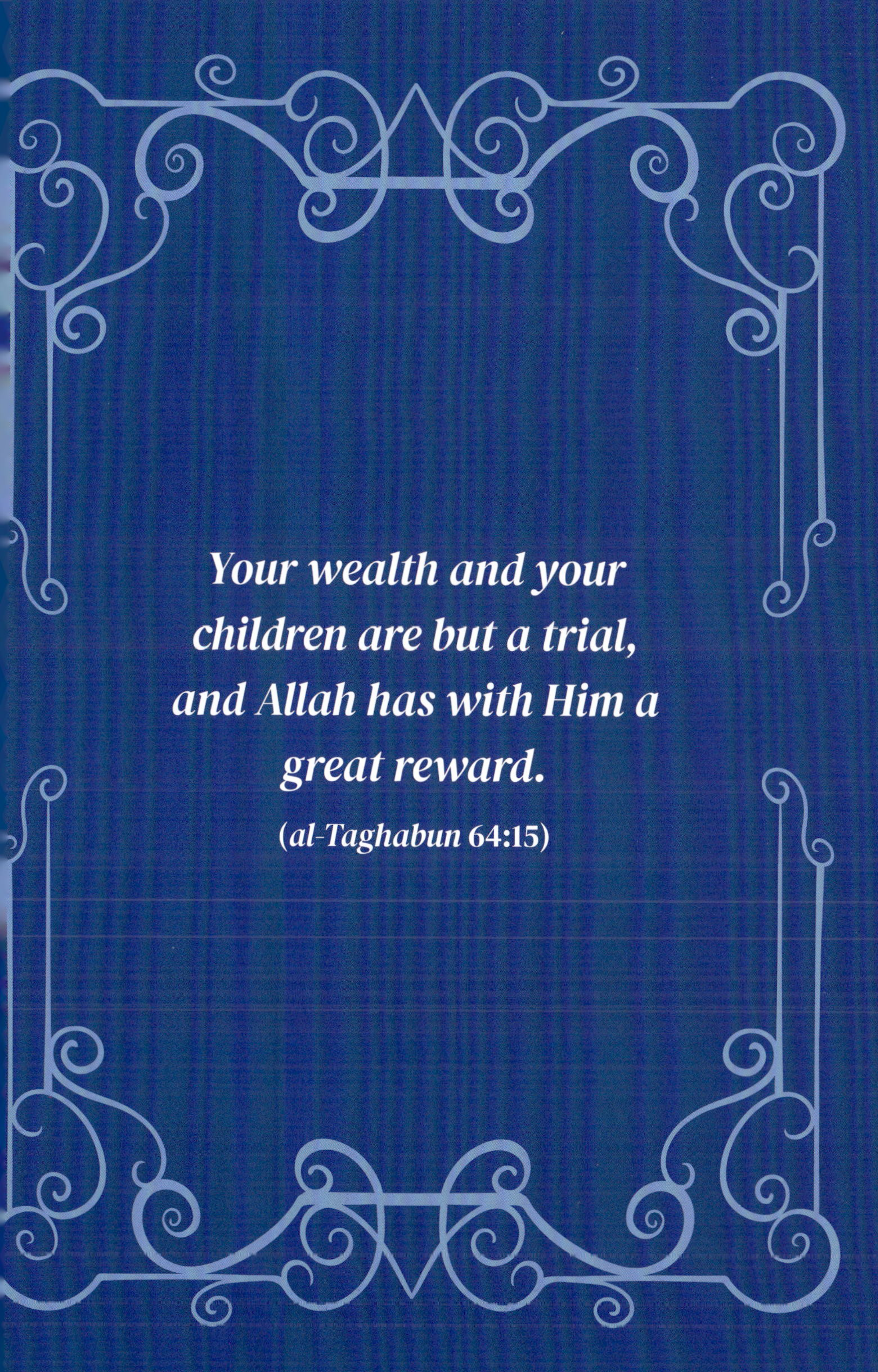
Your wealth and your children are but a trial, and Allah has with Him a great reward.
(*al-Taghabun* 64:15)

My Dear Heart

Do you Show Off?

We live in a day and age where the majority of people are focused on social media. The first thing checked when we post on social media is, whether it is reshared or how many views or likes do we have? Then we start reading the comments. There's nothing wrong with this as long as 'showing off' is not the reason you're doing this. What does this have to do with my dear heart? The answer is there's a direct relationship as we will see in this chapter. We start with asking ourselves: my dear heart, do you have ostentation?

What is ostentation?

The easiest explanation is ostentation means doing things just to be seen and praised. Within us, it sounds like: *I'll do this or that, so people know me and give me recognition.* In the Arabic language, it's called الرِّيَاءُ *riya'* and comes from the word *ru'ya* to do with seeing and being seen. السُّمْعَةُ *Sum'ah* is about being heard and about ones reputation. Ostentation, therefore is made up of both; being seen and heard. In practice this looks like a person doing something in their normal way, and as soon as someone else is present, he or she starts doing the same thing in a far better way. When they finish, they ask, 'what do you think?' If they are asking for an opinion because they need to improve themselves or to get honest feedback, then that is not a problem. However, when they need to hear a compliment and they get upset when others do not compliment them, then that is *riya'*; doing things to be seen.

Riya' and worship

In a time when displaying one's life and publicising every detail is the norm, why is *riya'* an issue? Allah ﷻ says in one of these very well-known verses in the Qur'an:

فَوَيْلٌ لِّلْمُصَلِّينَ

ٱلَّذِينَ هُمْ عَن صَلَاتِهِمْ سَاهُونَ

ٱلَّذِينَ هُمْ يُرَآءُونَ

So woe to those who pray. [But] who are heedless of their prayer - Those who make show [of their deeds] (al-Ma'un 107: 4-6)

Note how Allah ﷾ is not addressing those who are committing sins, but those who are praying with the expression 'woe to' which is linked to *Jahannam*. The warning here applies to anyone who doesn't see *salah* as a requirement and neglects their *salah*, only performing it to be seen. Generally, lessons from this can be applied to all of us, for example doing *sunnah rakah* or staying for *Taraweeh*, only for the benefit of an audience and not out of sincerity.

In *Surah al-Kahf*, which many of us read on the day of *Jumu'ah*, Allah ﷾ gives the opposite in the last verse when He ﷾ is saying to *Rasul Allah* ﷺ :

قُلْ إِنَّمَآ أَنَا۠ بَشَرٌ مِّثْلُكُمْ يُوحَىٰٓ إِلَىَّ أَنَّمَآ إِلَـٰهُكُمْ إِلَـٰهٌ وَٰحِدٌ ۖ فَمَن كَانَ يَرْجُوا۟ لِقَآءَ رَبِّهِۦ
فَلْيَعْمَلْ عَمَلًا صَـٰلِحًا وَلَا يُشْرِكْ بِعِبَادَةِ رَبِّهِۦٓ أَحَدًۢا

Say, "I am only a man like you, to whom has been revealed that your god is one God. So whoever would hope for the meeting with his Lord - let him do righteous work and not associate in the worship of his Lord anyone." (al-Kahf 18:110)

When we plan and work hard in the hope of one day meeting Allah ﷾, there are two things we should do: sincerely do righteous work, and never associate anyone with Allah ﷾.

*Riya*ʿ and minor *shirk*

What do we associate with Allah ﷻ as a result of showing off? The answer is found in these two *ahadith*. In the first, *Rasul Allah* ﷺ said:

أَخْوَفُ مَا أَخَافُ عَلَى أُمَّتِي الرِّيَاءُ

"The thing I fear most for my *Ummah* is showing off (*riyā*ʿ)."[86]

In another narration he ﷺ said:

إِنَّ أَخْوَفَ مَا أَخَافُ عَلَيْكُمُ الشِّرْكُ الْأَصْغَرُ

قَالُوا: وَمَا الشِّرْكُ الْأَصْغَرُ يَا رَسُولَ اللَّهِ؟ قَالَ: الرِّيَاءُ

"The thing I fear most for you is minor shirk." They asked: "What is minor shirk, O Messenger of Allah?" He said: "It is showing off *riyā*ʿ."[87]

The thing that worried *Rasul Allah* ﷺ and he was concerned about, was us showing off, which is the small shirk of associating partners with Allah ﷻ.

He ﷺ explained it by saying when everyone is going to come and they will be rewarded for what they have done on the Day of Judgement, Allah ﷻ will say ,إِذَا جُزِيَ النَّاسُ بِأَعْمَالِهِمْ اذْهَبُوا إِلَى الَّذِينَ كُنْتُمْ تُرَاءُونَ فِي الدُّنْيَا. 'Go to those who you used to work to impress. You were looking for praise from them. Go to them, هَلْ تَجِدُونَ عِنْدَهُمْ جَزَاءً؟. Go and see if they will reward you.[88]

86 Imām Aḥmad in *Musnad Aḥmad* (no. 23630)

87 Imām Aḥmad in Musnad Aḥmad (no. 23630),

88 Ibn Hajar al-Asqalani, *Bulugh al-Maram*, Book 16, Hadith 1527.

In another *hadith*, *Rasul Allah* ﷺ explained again that *riya'* is when people do things to be seen. So, if I want to do a good deed and want to meet Allah ﷻ and be happy with it, I should not associate a compliment, nor look to be given status so people will look up to me. Whatever I should be, should be for the reason of pleasing Allah ﷻ alone.

It can be argued, what when someone does well at something, where they didn't do it for praise or recognition, but are now getting both? For example, one may say 'I didn't study and get my PhD to be praised', or 'I didn't work hard on my children and raise them so people will praise me and them.' Yet this is what happened, people are now looking at me and praising me.' If you were never looking for that praise and are unaffected whether you are praised or not, then Allah ﷻ is gifting you this gift of being recognised in this *dunya*. So, this is not something to worry about, as long as you are not working for it.

In another *hadith* أنا أَغْنَى الشُّرَكَاءِ عَنِ الشِّرْكِ، مَنْ عَمِلَ عَمَلًا أَشْرَكَ فِيهِ مَعِي غَيْرِي تَرَكْتُهُ وَشِرْكَهُ The Messenger of Allah ﷺ said: Allah ﷻ, Blessed and Exalted, said "I am the One most free of need of any partners. Whoever does an action in which he associates someone else with Me, I will abandon him and his act of shirk."[89]

We need to be careful to do things purely for Allah ﷻ. Anytime we're doing something that will be known publicly,

89 Muslim bin Hajjaj, "Chapter: The prohibition on showing off," *Sahih Muslim*, Book 55, Hadith 58

we need to ask Allah ﷻ to make it for His ﷻ sake alone and not for any other person or recognition. If people acknowledge what we do, *Alhamdulillah*. If people praise you, *Alhamdulillah*. If it is not praised, but is done for His ﷻ sake alone, we can rest assured that Allah ﷻ has seen it and knows what you and I did, and He ﷻ will reward us. Why do we care about other people's praise or opinion? We have so many examples of the genuine and sincere righteous people who were always worried about *riya'* to inspire us.

Sayyidina Abdullah ibn Mas'ud رضي الله عنه said, he was walking and people were following him. He looked at them and said "why are you following me, if you only knew who I am when the door is closed." [90] Abdullah ibn Mas'ud رضي الله عنه was an important *sahabah*, humbling himself and fearful about having followers. Bishr al-Hafi, a very righteous and spiritual man, narrates how a man came to him and asked for advice. The advice he gave to him was, أَخْمِلْ ذِكْرَكَ وَطَيِّبْ مَطْعَمَكَ. 'Try not to be very well known publicly and make sure what you eat is pure.'[91] And then he said to him: 'The person who is so keen to be well known in public, that person will not find sweetness in the Day of Judgement.'[92]

Compare this to the advice we seek nowadays. If I come to you and get advice, the subjects given advice about would be to work hard; sleep this amount; exercise and

90 Ibn Abi Dunya, "Chapter on what has been narrated about fame," *Kitab al-Tawadu' wa al-Khumul*, page 78.

91 Ibn Abi Dunya, "Chapter on caution regarding the belly," *Al-Wara'*, page 88.

92 Abu Nu'aym al-Asbahani, *Kitab Hilyat al-Awliya wa Tabaqat al-Asfiya*, Vol 8, page 343.

take care of your body – all of which is helpful and needed. Yet where is the *akhirah* in the advice we seek and give. For this man, and Bishr al- Hafi, the *akhirah* is the focus of the advice given, as this is what will benefit the heart.

Today, we can make our advice focused around Allah ﷿ and the *akhirah* too when we have the opportunity. One such chance happened in an encounter I had with a youth. As I was leaving the *masjid* after *isha* having just given a lecture, a young boy came up to me and said “I think I know you; I’ve heard your voice before.” The person with me told him he had probably heard me on Youtube or on social media. He asked me “do you have a social media?” I said “yes, I do.” So he immediately took out his phone and looked me up, and saw the number of followers, “wow, what did you do for that? What do I need to do for that?” I replied, “I did nothing. Allah ﷿ put *barakah* in it” and I looked at him and said “Don’t do anything in order to get that number of followers. Rather do it to please Allah ﷿.” The boy asked “How can I do that?” I asked him what he likes doing. And as expected from a 15-year-old, he said he liked sports, football. I said “you know what? then post about football and what reminds people of Allah ﷿ and don’t look at how many followers and how many likes you have.”

If we want Allah ﷿ to love us, then we should reflect on the following *hadith*:

إِنَّ اللَّهَ يُحِبُّ الْعَبْدَ التَّقِيَّ النَّقِيَّ الْغَنِيَّ الْخَفِيَّ[93]

"Indeed, Allah loves the servant who is pious (*taqī)*, self-sufficient (*ghanī)*, and hidden (*khafī)*." (Muslim)

As we all want Allah ﷻ to love us, then we need to strive to be the following: Allah-conscious, الْغَنِيِّ *Al-Ghani*, which is not being rich, but self-sufficient, and if there's a need to ask, we ask only from Allah ﷻ. The last quality is being, الْخَفِيِّ, *khafi*, someone who is unknown to others. One of the best advice I was given by a sheikh is to make sure you have a private act of worship for Allah ﷻ that no one knows about. This is advice we can all think about; what is the one thing you could do that nobody will know about? Whether it is the *salah* in the night, charity or something else – there are many things we can do for the sake of Allah ﷻ. If we make sure nobody knows about it, then on the Day of Judgement, Allah ﷻ will remind us and He ﷻ will make it public to everybody.

May Allah ﷻ remind us to purify our intention and to do good only for Him ﷻ. May He ﷻ forgive our mistakes and make us from those whom He ﷻ loves. Ya Allah, protect us from the minor *shirk* of *riya'* and doing things to show others, and purify our deeds. *Ya Rabbi Ameen.*

93 Abu Nu'aym al-Asbahani, *Kitab Hilyat al-Awliya wa Tabaqat al-Asfiya*, Vol 1, page 94.

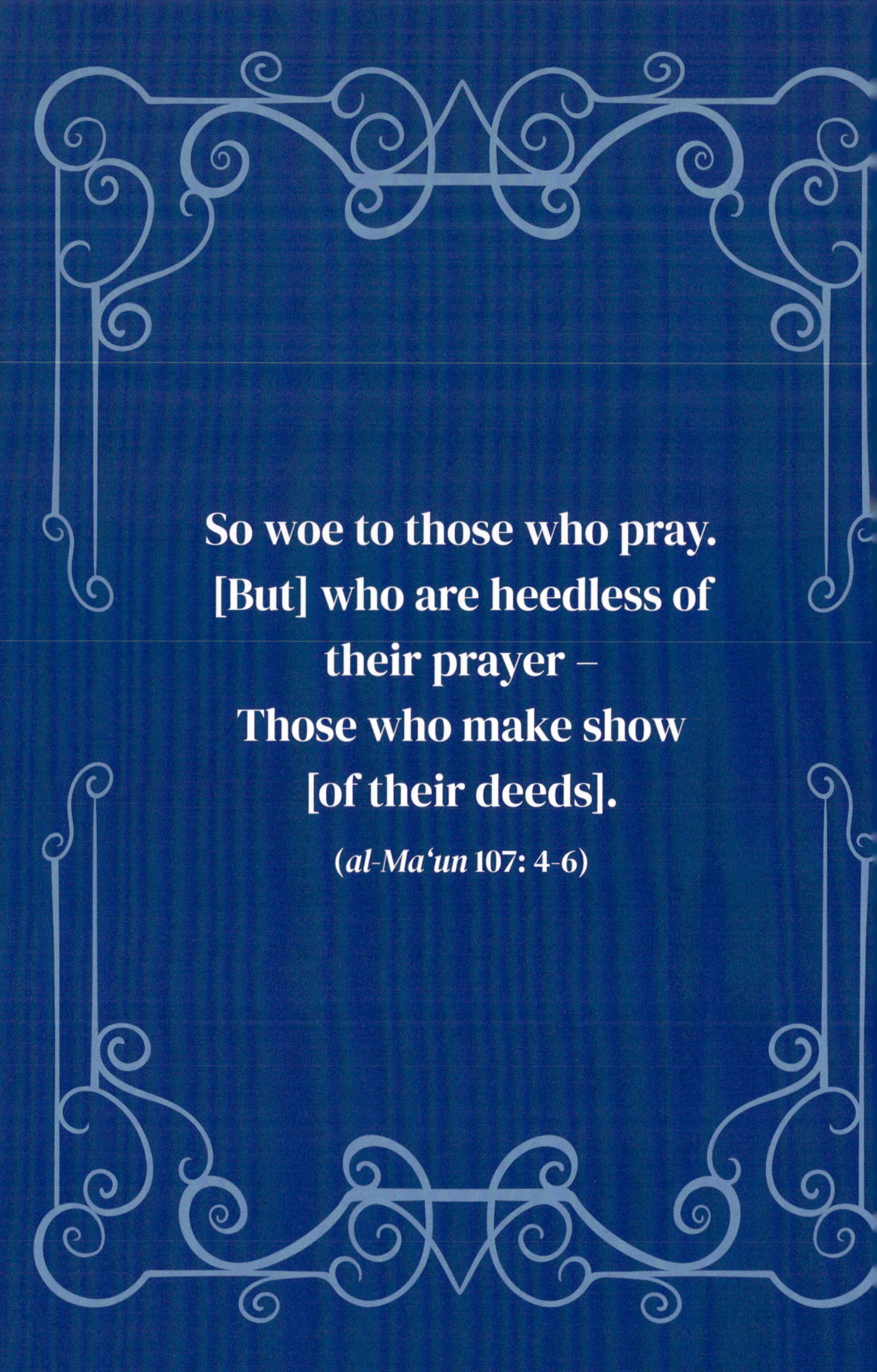
So woe to those who pray.
[But] who are heedless of
their prayer –
Those who make show
[of their deeds].
(*al-Ma'un* 107: 4-6)

My Dear Heart

When will you Repent?

In the past twenty chapters we have covered the many diseases that can put black dots on our heart, if left unchecked. Allah ﷻ alone knows how many we have. *What do we do with these?* We agreed that we want to return to Allah ﷻ in *Jannah*, with the same pure heart He ﷻ gave us. Our heart is the only thing that will benefit us there. You may be thinking: *my heart is not sound, my heart is not pure, there are so many black dots.* This doesn't mean we lose hope, as the beauty of this *deen* is that there are many ways to better our hearts, and one way is through *tawbah*, repentance.

There is a beautiful saying in Arabic:

ٱلرُّجُوعُ إِلَىٰ سَتَّارِ الْعُيُوبِ وَعَلَّامِ ٱلْغُيُوبِ

'The return is to the Concealer of faults and the Knower of the unseen.'[94]

We are told in this concise rhyming line that we will go back to the One who has concealed all the shortcomings *Sattār al-ʿUyūb* and the One who knows all the unseen and every hidden matter *ʿAllām al-Ghuyūb*. The journey of repentance is life-long; we start at the beginning with a clean heart, a beautiful dear heart, then as we grow up and into adulthood, right till the end, we need to continuously repent. *Tawbah* is not something we do once as there is always a possibility we are going to disobey Allah ﷻ, knowingly or unknowingly. This repentance, turning back to Allah ﷻ is not actually a choice, it's an order. Allah ﷻ said:

يَٰٓأَيُّهَا ٱلَّذِينَ ءَامَنُوا۟ تُوبُوٓا۟ إِلَى ٱللَّهِ تَوْبَةً نَّصُوحًا عَسَىٰ رَبُّكُمْ أَن يُكَفِّرَ عَنكُمْ سَيِّـَٔاتِكُمْ وَيُدْخِلَكُمْ جَنَّٰتٍ تَجْرِى مِن تَحْتِهَا ٱلْأَنْهَٰرُ يَوْمَ لَا يُخْزِى ٱللَّهُ ٱلنَّبِىَّ وَٱلَّذِينَ ءَامَنُوا۟ مَعَهُۥ ۖ نُورُهُمْ يَسْعَىٰ بَيْنَ أَيْدِيهِمْ وَبِأَيْمَٰنِهِمْ يَقُولُونَ رَبَّنَآ أَتْمِمْ لَنَا نُورَنَا وَٱغْفِرْ لَنَآ ۖ إِنَّكَ عَلَىٰ كُلِّ شَىْءٍ قَدِيرٌ

O you who have believed, repent to Allah with sincere repentance. Perhaps your Lord will remove from you your misdeeds and admit you into gardens beneath which rivers flow [on] the Day when Allah will not disgrace the Prophet and those who believed with him. Their light will proceed before them and on their right; they will say,

94 Imam Ghazali, Ihya ulum -al din

"Our Lord, perfect for us our light and forgive us. Indeed, You are over all things competent." (al-Tahrim 66:8)

Tawbah is not for those who don't believe, it's actually for us all, because we sin. *Rasul Allah* ﷺ reminded us that we are all sinners, كُلُّ بَنِي آدَمَ خَطَّاءٌ all the children of Adam are sinners. We will fall into sin, but we strive to be وَخَيْرُ الْخَطَّائِينَ التَّوَّابُونَ 'The best among them as those who practice tawbah,' *repentance, [as they will] go back to Allah.'*[95]

What is *tawbah*?

In the Arabic language *tawbah* means to return. A return to what? You can think of it like this: *When I disobey Allah* ﷻ, *I was not with Him at that moment. Nobody remembers Allah* ﷻ *and disobeys Allah* ﷻ *at the same time. No, it's usually a time, a moment of,* غَفْلَة, *heedlessness - ghaflah. Where I just forgot, I didn't think, I didn't remember He's looking at me, and I did this, whatever this is. Looked at haram, listened to haram, said haram. But then by doing tawbah, I'm going to go back to Allah* ﷻ.

And this is an order in *Surah al-Nur*:

وَتُوبُوٓاْ إِلَى ٱللَّهِ جَمِيعًا أَيُّهَ ٱلْمُؤْمِنُونَ لَعَلَّكُمْ تُفْلِحُونَ

And turn to Allāh in repentance, all of you, O believers, that you might succeed. (al-Nur 24: 31)

In another verse in *Surah al-Hujurat*, we are told:

95 Abu Abdullah al-Khatib, "Chapter: Prayer for pardon, and repentance," *Mishkat al-Masabih,* Book 9, Hadith 114.

وَمَن لَّمْ يَتُبْ فَأُوْلَٰٓئِكَ هُمُ ٱلظَّٰلِمُونَ

And whoever does not repent (go back to Allah) – then it is those who are the wrongdoers. (al-Hujurat 49:11)

So *tawbah* is actually the eraser! As a human being, either I am a person who responds to Allah ﷻ in *tawbah*, I return to Him ﷻ, or I do not do *tawbah*, then I am a wrongdoer. There is nothing in between. A concept shared in a *Jumu'ah khutbah* helps to look at this another way: imagine if there was no *tawbah*. Imagine if Allah ﷻ did not open that door and He ﷻ says to us, if you disobey me and sin, you are done and there is no way to erase it. If that were the case, we would all be finished, but *alhamdulillah* we have *tawbah* to erase the sins and *dhikr* for cleansing the heart.

Allah ﷻ said in *Surah al-Furqan* at the end:

إِلَّا مَن تَابَ وَءَامَنَ وَعَمِلَ عَمَلًا صَٰلِحًا فَأُوْلَٰٓئِكَ يُبَدِّلُ ٱللَّهُ سَيِّـَٔاتِهِمْ حَسَنَٰتٍ ۗ وَكَانَ ٱللَّهُ غَفُورًا رَّحِيمًا

Except for those who repent, believe and do righteous work. For them Allah will replace their evil deeds with good. And ever is Allah Forgiving and Merciful. (al-Furqan, 25:70)

When a believer commits sins; and then asks for forgiveness, and does good deeds, then look at what will happen. فَأُولَٰئِكَ يُبَدِّلُ اللهُ سَيِّئَاتِهِمْ حَسَنَاتٍ. Allah ﷻ will change their bad deeds to good deeds, which is good news for everybody. We shouldn't keep thinking of what we did before, nor does it matter to anyone else, what you or I did.[96] Allah ﷻ is ٱلْغَفُورُ ٱلرَّحِيمُ – the Forgiving, the Merciful. He will forgive us, if we really want to be forgiven, turning to Him ﷻ fully with trust and belief-*yaqeen*.

The most hopeful verse in the Qur'an is when Allah ﷻ says:

قُلْ يَٰعِبَادِىَ ٱلَّذِينَ أَسْرَفُوا۟ عَلَىٰٓ أَنفُسِهِمْ لَا تَقْنَطُوا۟ مِن رَّحْمَةِ ٱللَّهِ ۚ إِنَّ ٱللَّهَ يَغْفِرُ ٱلذُّنُوبَ جَمِيعًا ۚ إِنَّهُۥ هُوَ ٱلْغَفُورُ ٱلرَّحِيمُ

He said: '*Say, O Muhammad, to my servants.*' He ﷻ called us His ﷻ servants and next we see what the description of those servants is. Are they described as those who do *qiyam al-layl* and they obey Allah ﷻ twenty-four hours a day, seven days a week? No, it's not! Instead, this is how Allah ﷻ describes His ﷻ servants:

Who have transgressed against themselves [by sinning], do not despair of the mercy of Allah. Indeed, it is He who is Forgiving, the Merciful. (al-Zumar 39:53)

Another word for *tawbah* is إنابة *inaba*, meaning when you turn completely, refocus and move away. So *tawbah*, turning to Allah ﷻ is another tool. Prophet ﷺ advised: "Fear Allah wherever you are, follow up a bad deed with a good one—it will erase it—and treat people with good character." (al-Tirmidhi) Going forward, we can remind ourselves: *I'm carrying this tool of tawbah with me all the time because as I am*

96 Al-Furqan, 25:70.

moving through my life, I am exposed to sins and I am committing sins. I need to immediately follow the sin with Astaghfirullah and do a good deed.[97]

Three steps of *tawbah*

Tawbah has the following three steps:

Firstly, you have to feel regret and question yourself: *Why did I do that? Why did I say this? Why did I hurt that person? Why did I look at that?* Say it to yourself, you don't have to say it to people. It will not be a proper *tawbah* unless you regret what you did and feel some pain inside. And how do I regret? One thing to say to yourself should be: *who did I disobey?* لَا تَنْظُرْ إِلَىٰ صِغَرِ الذَّنْبِ، وَلَكِنِ ٱنْظُرْ إِلَىٰ مَنْ عَصَيْتَ. Don't look at what you did, but look at Who you disobeyed.[98] If I know who Allah ﷻ is, then I'm going to question my actions.

Second, I have this firm resolution that I am not going to go back to that sin. Just as people make New Year resolutions they intend to keep, we have to take some action with our intention. This resolution means you're going to remove the things from your life and surroundings that make you disobey Allah ﷻ. If you keep watching *haram*, then you need to remove those channels that bring *haram* and make it easy for yourself to stay away. It's similar to if

97 Abu Isa Muhammad al-Tirmidhi, "Chapter: What has been related about having amicable relations with people," *Jami' al-Tirmidhi*, Book 27, Hadith 93.

98 Ali bin Umar, "Scrupulousness and precaution (al-wara' wal-ihtiyat)," *Duroos*, Vol 108, page 17.

you want to lose weight, then the advice is don't put the wrong foods in front of yourself. If you have weight gaining food in front of you and you think you won't eat it, then you will be wrong. So, removing the cause of the problem is a necessary step in *tawbah.*

The third step, after the first two are put into practice properly, is making a commitment that you will not go back to the sin again. Most of the time, we will slip, and it will happen again. However, if you've gone back, don't despair. Go back to Allah ﷾. The beauty of Allah ﷾ is He ﷾ is All-Generous. We aren't the same, if someone hurts us, we'll forgive them once, possibly a second time, but the third time we'll say 'I'm done: three strikes and you're out'. It's not the same with Allah ﷾ because He ﷾ is All-Generous. If we disobey Allah ﷾, return back to Him ﷾, He ﷾ is the All-Forgiving.

The following are practical steps we can do to help us with *tawbah*:

- Write down the sins that come to your mind. Ask Allah ﷾ to remind you of what you did.
- Look at the list and think about how they happened. Ask Allah ﷾ to help you, and to forgive each one of those sins.
- Make time to do this regularly and ask Allah ﷾ to forgive you, as the more we ask Allah ﷾ to forgive us, He ﷾ will open ways to return back to Him ﷾.

There is a famous story of the three *Sahabi* who stayed in Madinah, and did not go out with *Rasul Allah* ﷺ on an expedition. By doing so, the Companions even disobeyed Allah ﷻ, but they felt very guilty. When Allah ﷻ saw inside their heart and knew how bad they felt about not going with the *Rasul* ﷺ,[99] He ﷻ facilitated their *tawbah* and made it easy for them. When there is sincerity inside us, He ﷻ will send people to us to remind us. Whenever we truly repent to Allah ﷻ, He ﷻ will open the doors for us. At the point when we do sin, we just need to take a minute, pause and think: *who did I disobey? I need to acknowledge this and turn to Allah ﷻ for forgiveness.*

After that we shouldn't feel stressed and worried. He ﷻ will forgive and He ﷻ forgives all sins, so we shouldn't despair. Nor should we allow anyone to make us feel like despairing because the One we are asking to forgive us is Himself, ٱلْغَفُورُ ٱلرَّحِيمُ – The All-Forgiving and the All-Merciful.

May Allah ﷻ forgive all our sins. May Allah ﷻ wipe away our wrongdoings whenever we turn sincerely to Him ﷻ in *du'a*. May we have our sins completely wiped away and may our hearts and tongues be guided to regularly seeking forgiveness. *Ya Rabbi Ameen.*

99 At-Tawbah, 9:118.

Except for those who
repent, believe and do
righteous work. For them
Allah will replace their
evil deeds with good. And
ever is Allah Forgiving
and Merciful.
(al-Furqan 25:70)

My Dear Heart

Why don't you seek Forgiveness?

On our journey of cleansing the heart and striving to meet Allah ﷾ with a pure one, the most important step is turning to Him ﷾ and asking for that purification. The question to ask our heart is: why don't you seek forgiveness from Allah ﷾? Do we not ask Him ﷾, because we think Allah ﷾ will not forgive us? If that's the case, then we don't know Allah ﷾ well because He ﷾ has told us in *Surah Nuh*, when *Sayyidina* Nuh ﵇ went to his people:

فَقُلْتُ ٱسْتَغْفِرُوا۟ رَبَّكُمْ إِنَّهُۥ كَانَ غَفَّارًا

يُرْسِلِ ٱلسَّمَآءَ عَلَيْكُم مِّدْرَارًا
وَيُمْدِدْكُم بِأَمْوَٰلٍ وَبَنِينَ وَيَجْعَل لَّكُمْ جَنَّٰتٍ وَيَجْعَل لَّكُمْ أَنْهَٰرًا

And said, 'Ask forgiveness of your Lord. Indeed, He is ever a Perpetual Forgiver. He will send [rain from] the sky upon you in [continuing] showers. And give you increase in wealth and children and provide for you gardens and provide for you rivers.'
(Nuh 71:10-12)

Allah ﷻ is telling us through the account of Prophet Nuh ﷺ that He ﷻ is غَفَّارًا *ghaffara* – a hyperbole, an exaggeration, meaning every time you ask Allah ﷻ for forgiveness, He ﷻ will forgive you. Then why we are not doing it, what is stopping us?

What is *istighfar*?

It is the act of asking Allah ﷻ to forgive you or forgive me? We continue to sin in this world. When you reflect, there are many things that come to mind; *I delayed my salah. I backbit. I felt arrogant*. These are all sins, and when we ask Allah ﷻ for forgiveness sincerely, two things happen. Allah ﷻ will remove the sin and will also protect me from doing it again. In addition, Allah ﷻ sometimes will conceal it, which is an even better outcome; no one will know what we did. It's a beautiful tool Allah ﷻ gave us, knowing we are weak. خُلِقَ الإنسانُ ضَعِيفًا, *the human being is weak*,[100] knowing we

100 An-Nisa, 4:28.

are going to disobey Allah ﷻ. And then He's ﷻ telling us, try not to disobey Me, but when it happens, part of the *tawbah* – repentance of the feelings and actions discussed in the previous chapter, is *al-istighfar* by itself. And it is repeatedly mentioned in the Qur'an.

In surah *al-Muzzamil* we find another order:

وَٱسْتَغْفِرُوا۟ ٱللَّهَ ۖ إِنَّ ٱللَّهَ غَفُورٌ رَّحِيمٌۢ

And seek forgiveness of Allah. Indeed, Allah is all Forgiving and Merciful. (al-Muzzammil 73:20)

Allah ﷻ praises those who ask for forgiveness. Normally we're praised if we've done something good. Imagine being praised by Allah ﷻ. This is what we also find in Surah *Āl-Imran*, Allah ﷻ praises those who ask Him ﷻ for forgiveness at the time of dawn, just before *fajr*.

ٱلصَّٰبِرِينَ وَٱلصَّٰدِقِينَ وَٱلْقَٰنِتِينَ وَٱلْمُنفِقِينَ وَٱلْمُسْتَغْفِرِينَ بِٱلْأَسْحَارِ

The patient, the true, the obedient, those who spend [in the way of Allah], and those who seek forgiveness before dawn. (Āl-Imran 3: 17)

In *Surah al-Nisa* we are reassured that whomsoever commits a sin or injustice to himself or herself, then asks Allah ﷻ for forgiveness, He ﷻ will forgive them. Allah ﷻ is waiting to forgive you and I.

وَمَن يَعْمَلْ سُوٓءًا أَوْ يَظْلِمْ نَفْسَهُۥ ثُمَّ يَسْتَغْفِرِ ٱللَّهَ يَجِدِ ٱللَّهَ غَفُورًا رَّحِيمًا

And whoever does a wrong or wrongs himself but then seeks forgiveness of Allah will find Allah Forgiving and Merciful. (al-Nisa 4:110)

Istighfar is the action our tongue does to seek forgiveness, and we have been given the words to say this often:

رَبِّ اغْفِرْ لِي، يَا اللّٰهُ إِنَّكَ غَفُورٌ رَّحِيمٌ[101]

Allah, forgive me, for You are Forgiving and Merciful.

The best *du'a* for forgiveness – *istighfar*

Istighfar is a tool that has been made very easy for us, just by using our tongue to seek forgiveness. The best *du'a* for this is that of *Sayyidina* Yunus عليه السلام. *Sayyidina* Yunus عليه السلام did something that was not pleasing to Allah سبحانه وتعالى when he gave up on his people and left them. He was on a ship which was going to capsize, and somebody had to be removed, otherwise the ship would sink. *Sayyidina* Yunus عليه السلام was the one who was chosen to be thrown into the sea. After being thrown in, he was swallowed by a whale.[102] This instead put him in three layers of darknesses; the belly of the whale, the sea, and the darkness of the night.

In that situation, what did he do and what did he say?

101 Muhammad bin Ismail al-Bukhari, "Chapter: And Allah is Ever All-Hearer, All-Seer," *Sahih al Bukhari*, Book 97, Hadith 17.

102 As-Saffat, 37:139-144.

لَّآ إِلَٰهَ إِلَّآ أَنتَ سُبْحَٰنَكَ إِنِّي كُنتُ مِنَ ٱلظَّٰلِمِينَ [103]

The first thing he did was acknowledge that there is no God worthy of worship but Allah ﷻ. Then he glorified Him ﷻ سُبْحَانَكَ, followed by calling out 'Ya Allah! I have done something wrong.' He didn't specify what he did wrong when he said إِنِّي كُنْتُ مِنَ الظَّالِمِينَ. *I am from the wrongdoers.*

Rasul Allah ﷺ commented on this *du'a* by saying: "The supplication of Dhun-Nūn (Prophet Yunus ﷺ) when he called upon Allah ﷻ from the belly of the whale was: '*Lā ilāha illā anta, subḥānaka innī kuntu min al-ẓālimīn*': There is no deity except You; Glory be to You, indeed I was of the wrongdoers. No Muslim ever supplicates with it for anything, except that Allah ﷻ responds to him." (Tirmidhi)

We are told, if we say this *du'a* to ask Allah ﷻ for something, He ﷻ will give it to us, therefore say this for not only asking for forgiveness, but whatever our needs are that we call on Allah ﷻ for.

The *sayyidul istighfar*: The master of *istighfar*

This is the *du'a* I highly recommend particularly for memorisation, as it is the master of everything when you want Allah ﷻ to forgive you. *Rasul Allah* ﷺ taught this to us:

103 Al-Anbiya, 21:87.

اللَّهُمَّ أَنْتَ رَبِّي لا إِلَهَ إِلا أَنْتَ، خَلَقْتَنِي وَأَنَا عَبْدُكَ، وَأَنَا عَلَى عَهْدِكَ وَوَعْدِكَ مَا اسْتَطَعْتُ، أَعُوذُ بِكَ مِنْ شَرِّ مَا صَنَعْتُ، أَبُوءُ لَكَ بِنِعْمَتِكَ عَلَيَّ، وَأَبُوءُ بِذَنْبِي، فَاغْفِرْ لِي، فَإِنَّهُ لا يَغْفِرُ الذُّنُوبَ إِلا أَنْتَ.

"O Allah, You are my Lord, there is no deity except You. You created me and I am Your servant. I uphold Your covenant and promise as best I can. I seek refuge in You from the evil of what I have done. I acknowledge Your favour upon me, and I acknowledge my sin, so forgive me, for indeed none forgives sins except You."

The Prophet ﷺ said about this *du'a*: "Whoever says it during the day with firm faith in it and dies that day before evening, he will be one of the people of Paradise. And whoever says it at night with firm faith in it and dies before morning, he will be one of the people of Paradise." (Bukhari)

If we set a few minutes aside in our day and think about a couple of things we did today or yesterday, that were not pleasing to Allah ﷻ, this will be enough to make us feel connected to what we are saying, when we acknowledge every blessing Allah ﷻ has given us and all the sins we commit. This beautiful *du'a* is a private talk between you and Allah ﷻ فَاغْفِرْ لِي *Ya Allah! Please forgive me.* فَإِنَّهُ لَا يَغْفِرُ الذُّنُوبَ إِلَّا أَنْتَ. *Nobody will forgive me. Nobody will forgive my sins except You.*[104] When this is coming sincerely from your heart and you're thinking of all the sins you have done, what do you think Allah ﷻ will do when He ﷻ hears this?

104 Abu Dawud, "Chapter: What to say when waking up," *Sunan Abi Dawud*, Book 43, Hadith 298.

Rasul Allah ﷺ and seeking forgiveness

All the sins of our Prophet ﷺ were already forgiven:

إِنَّا فَتَحْنَا لَكَ فَتْحًا مُّبِينًا

لِّيَغْفِرَ لَكَ ٱللَّهُ مَا تَقَدَّمَ مِن ذَنۢبِكَ وَمَا تَأَخَّرَ وَيُتِمَّ نِعْمَتَهُۥ عَلَيْكَ وَيَهْدِيَكَ صِرَٰطًا مُّسْتَقِيمًا

Indeed, We have given you, [O Muḥammad], a clear conquest. That Allah may forgive for you what preceded of your sin [i.e., errors] and what will follow and complete His favour upon you and guide you to a straight path. (al-Fath 48:1-2)

The *Sahaba* - Companions used to say, we used to count one hundred times[105] and in another narration seventy times[106] that the Prophet daily ﷺ asked Allah ﷻ to forgive him. There is a beautiful *hadith* which gives hope to everyone and is worthy of memorising, particularly for those who say they have made a mistake, done a sin and asked Allah ﷻ for forgiveness, only to go back to it again. This is a common question, seeking what the outcome would be for such a situation. Abu Hurayrah ؓ reported a *hadith Qudsi*, in which *Rasul Allah* ﷺ said, narrating from his Lord:

أَذْنَبَ عَبْدٌ ذَنْبًا فَقَالَ: اللَّهُمَّ اغْفِرْ لِي ذَنْبِي. فَقَالَ تَبَارَكَ وَتَعَالَى: أَذْنَبَ عَبْدِي ذَنْبًا فَعَلِمَ أَنَّ لَهُ رَبًّا يَغْفِرُ الذَّنْبَ وَيَأْخُذُ بِالذَّنْبِ. قَدْ غَفَرْتُ لِعَبْدِي. ثُمَّ

105 Muslim bin Hajjaj, "Chapter: It is recommended to pray for forgiveness a great deal," *Sahih Muslim*, Book 48, Hadith 53.

106 Muhammad bin Ismail al-Bukhari, "Chapter: Seeking Allah's forgiveness by daytime and at night," *Sahih al-Bukhari*, Book 80, Hadith 4.

مَكَثَ مَا شَاءَ اللَّهُ ثُمَّ أَذْنَبَ ذَنْبًا آخَرَ فَقَالَ: رَبِّ اغْفِرْهُ لِي. فَقَالَ تَبَارَكَ وَتَعَالَى: عَلِمَ عَبْدِي أَنَّ لَهُ رَبًّا يَغْفِرُ الذَّنْبَ وَيَأْخُذُ بِالذَّنْبِ. قَدْ غَفَرْتُ لِعَبْدِي. ثُمَّ مَكَثَ مَا شَاءَ اللَّهُ ثُمَّ أَذْنَبَ ذَنْبًا آخَرَ فَقَالَ: رَبِّ اغْفِرْ لِي. فَقَالَ تَبَارَكَ وَتَعَالَى: عَلِمَ عَبْدِي أَنَّ لَهُ رَبًّا يَغْفِرُ الذَّنْبَ وَيَأْخُذُ بِالذَّنْبِ. قَدْ غَفَرْتُ لِعَبْدِي، فَلْيَعْمَلْ مَا شَاءَ

"A servant committed a sin and said: 'O Allah, forgive me my sin.' Allah ﷻ said: 'My servant has committed a sin and then realized that he has a Lord Who forgives sins and Who can punish because of them; so I have forgiven My servant.' Then the servant remained for a while and again committed another sin and said: 'O Lord, forgive me my sin.' Allah ﷻ said: 'My servant has committed a sin, and then realized that he has a Lord Who forgives sins and Who can punish because of them; so I have forgiven My servant.' Then he remained for a while and committed another sin and said: 'O Lord, forgive me my sin.' Allah ﷻ said: 'My servant has committed a sin, and then realized that he has a Lord Who forgives sins and Who can punish because of them; so I have forgiven My servant. Let him do as he wishes.'"
(Bukhari 7507, Muslim 2758)

This *hadith* offers a deeper understanding and hope, keeping in mind the repeated phrase:

عَلِمَ عَبْدِي أَنَّ لَهُ رَبًّا يَغْفِرُ الذَّنْبَ وَيَأْخُذُ بِالذَّنْبِ 'My servant knew that he has a Lord that will forgive and can punish, but I have forgiven him.[107] Similarly we find in *Surah Yusuf*, Prophet Yaqub ﷺ reminding his sons:

يَٰبَنِيَّ ٱذْهَبُواْ فَتَحَسَّسُواْ مِن يُوسُفَ وَأَخِيهِ وَلَا تَاْيْـَٔسُواْ مِن رَّوْحِ ٱللَّهِ إِنَّهُۥ لَا يَاْيْـَٔسُ مِن رَّوْحِ ٱللَّهِ إِلَّا ٱلْقَوْمُ ٱلْكَٰفِرُونَ

O my sons, go and find out about Joseph and his brother and despair not of relief from Allah. Indeed, no one despairs of relief from Allah except the disbelieving people. (Yusuf: 12:87)

So nobody should ever despair from Allah's ﷻ *rahmah* – the loving mercy.

A life-long habit of *istighfar*

When *Sayyidina* Luqman ﷺ was teaching his son, he said:

يَا بُنَيَّ عَوِّدْ لِسَانَكَ اللَّهُمَّ اغْفِرْ لِي فَإِنَّ لِلَّهِ سَاعَاتٍ لَا يَرُدُّ فِيهِنَّ سَائِلًا .[108]

"O my son, accustom your tongue to saying: *'O Allah, forgive me,'* for indeed, Allah ﷻ has hours in which He does not turn away a supplicant." Likewise, we should make this our habit too in the hope that our seeking forgiveness falls in those certain hours where it will be responded to.

Sayyidina al-Hasan's ؓ example is a good one to implement in our homes. أَكْثِرُوا مِنَ الِاسْتِغْفَارِ. 'Ask Allah ﷻ for forgiveness a

107 Muslim ibn Hajjaj, "Chapter: Acceptance of repentance from sin, even if the sin and repentance happen repeatedly," *Sahih Muslim*, Book 50, Hadith 33.

108 Ibn Rajab Al-Hanbali, *Tafseer*, Vol 2, page 653.

lot', in your homes, at your tables as you are eating وَفِي طُرُقِكُمْ *wa fī ṭuruqikum*, on the streets وَفِي أَسْوَاقِكُمْ *wa fī aswāqikum*, in the market, in the gathering *wa fī majālisikum* وَفِي مَجَالِسِكُمْ, wherever you are وَأَيْنَ مَا كُنْتُمْ *wa ayna mā kuntum*, for you do not know when forgiveness will descend'.[109] So, if you're stuck in traffic, ask Allah ﷻ for forgiveness. When you're preparing food, ask Allah ﷻ for forgiveness. When you are in your living room, your bedroom, or you're cleaning the kitchen; driving to *salah* at the *masjid*; driving to work, walking or exercising; in every place practise *istighfar*, until it becomes a habit and becomes a norm.

As with all the methods to purify our dear heart, we connect it back to the Qur'an, as Qatada said, يَدُلُّكُمْ عَلَى دَائِكُمْ وَدَوَائِكُمْ. "This Qur'an guides you to your cure and remedy. Your cure is forgiveness, and your remedy is repentance." The Qur'an teaches us what the disease is – our sins, and the medicine is *al-istighfar*.[110]

رَبَّنَآ ءَامَنَّا فَٱغْفِرْ لَنَا وَٱرْحَمْنَا وَأَنتَ خَيْرُ ٱلرَّٰحِمِينَ

Our Lord, we have believed, so forgive us and have mercy upon us, and You are the best of the merciful. (al-Mu'minoon 23:109)

May Allah ﷻ guide us to repent, do *tawbah* in our heart and seek forgiveness *istighfar* with our tongues, and return to Him ﷻ repeatedly to forgive our sins. *Ya Rabbi Ameen.*

---

109 Ibn Abi Dunya, "When does forgiveness descend?" *At Tawba*, page 125.
110 Nasir ad-Din al-Albani, Kitab *Daif at-Targhib wat-Tarhib*, Vol 1, page 499.

And seek forgiveness of Allah. Indeed, Allah is all Forgiving and Merciful.

(*al-Muzzammil* 73:20)

My Dear Heart

Who are your Enemies?

As much as we try to protect our heart from sin, we know we are going to disobey Allah ﷻ. Just before we commit a sin, there's a voice inside us urging us to give in; *It's okay, it's only once, Allah ﷻ is All-Forgiving; I enjoy it; I'm not doing anyone any harm; what is the big deal?* There's a question that many of us ask ourselves when we have this dialogue going on inside us: who's talking? In this chapter, we are going to answer that by learning about ourselves. There are two factors at play here. One is inside me, and the other one is with me, that will always work to make me disobey Allah ﷻ. The first is *an-nafs* and the second is the *Shaytan*, the devil.

Allah ﷻ mentioned the *Shaytan*, the devil repeatedly in the Qur'an, and He ﷻ clearly said, إِنَّ الشَّيْطَانَ لَكُمْ عَدُوٌّ. *The Shaytan is your enemy*[111]. In more than one place, when the *Shaytan* disobeyed Allah ﷻ he clearly said to Allah ﷻ:

فَبِعِزَّتِكَ لَأُغْوِيَنَّهُمْ أَجْمَعِينَ.

By Your Majesty, I'll lure them, all of them. (*Saad* 38:82)

So, we all need to know that there is an enemy twenty-four seven around me and you. His goal, or his job description is basically to make you and I disobey Him ﷻ. With that, there is another factor inside me called the *nafs*. And Allah ﷻ said in the Qur'an:

وَلَقَدْ خَلَقْنَا ٱلْإِنسَٰنَ وَنَعْلَمُ مَا تُوَسْوِسُ بِهِۦ نَفْسُهُۥ ۖ وَنَحْنُ أَقْرَبُ إِلَيْهِ مِنْ حَبْلِ ٱلْوَرِيدِ

And we have already created man and know what his soul whispers to him, and We are closer to him than [his] jugular vein.
(Qaf 50:16)

Most of the time, the whisper is usually to disobey Allah ﷻ called *hadith al-Nafs*, حَدِيثُ النَّفْسِ the talk of the *nafs* inside us. *Rasul Allah* ﷺ asked Allah ﷻ to protect him and us from the inner talk of the *nafs* with this *du'a*:

اللَّهُمَّ فَاطِرَ السَّمَاوَاتِ وَالْأَرْضِ، عَالِمَ الْغَيْبِ وَالشَّهَادَةِ، رَبَّ كُلِّ شَيْءٍ وَمَلِيكَهُ، أَشْهَدُ أَنْ لَا إِلَهَ إِلَّا أَنْتَ، أَعُوذُ بِكَ مِنْ شَرِّ نَفْسِي، وَمِنْ شَرِّ الشَّيْطَانِ وَشِرْكِهِ، وَأَنْ أَقْتَرِفَ عَلَى نَفْسِي سُوءًا أَوْ أَجُرَّهُ إِلَى مُسْلِمٍ

"O Allah, Creator of the heavens and the earth, Knower of the unseen and the witnessed, Lord and Sovereign of everything, I bear witness that there is

111 Fatir 35: 6.

> no god but You. I seek refuge in You from the evil of my soul, from the evil of *Shayṭān* and his association (with You), and from bringing evil upon myself or dragging it to a Muslim." [112]

With these two factors inside us, *nafs* and the *Shaytan*, how do we know the difference? If the talk inside you is the same and it repeats itself, it's usually your *nafs*. If the tactics have changed, it's usually the *Shaytan*. For example, if our inner talk is 'get up for *fajr*', that's the good *nafs* telling me to get up for *fajr*, I hear it. Then if I hear '*I'm too tired*', and the same phrase is repeated several times, this is my *nafs* telling me this. If it is the *Shaytan*, the reasons will be many; *there's ten minutes left; it's okay, Allah ﷾ is Forgiving, Merciful; it's just this once - these* are different tactics that the *Shaytan* uses.

It is worth noting that they both work together; the *Shaytan* operates on the *nafs* because there is more than one *nafs* inside us. The hopeful side to this is, that from the *Rahmah* (blessing) of Allah ﷾ He ﷾ will not take us to account for what we say inside us. Rather, He ﷾ will take us to account once we act upon the whisperings in our soul. Among the evidence that indicates this is the saying of the Prophet ﷺ, 'Allah has forgiven my nation for what they whisper to themselves and what they say to themselves, as long as they do not act upon it or speak of it.' (Bukhari 6664)

112 Abu Dawood, "Chapter: What to say when waking up," *Sunan Abi Dawood*, Book 43, Hadith 295.

Furthermore, from the great *rahmah* of Allah ﷻ is the way our deeds are recorded, as described to us by *Rasul Allah* ﷺ:

إِنَّ اللَّهَ كَتَبَ الْحَسَنَاتِ وَالسَّيِّئَاتِ، ثُمَّ بَيَّنَ ذَلِكَ، فَمَنْ هَمَّ بِحَسَنَةٍ فَلَمْ يَعْمَلْهَا كَتَبَهَا اللَّهُ عِنْدَهُ حَسَنَةً كَامِلَةً، وَإِنْ هَمَّ بِهَا فَعَمِلَهَا كَتَبَهَا اللَّهُ عَزَّ وَجَلَّ عِنْدَهُ عَشْرَ حَسَنَاتٍ، إِلَى سَبْعِمِائَةِ ضِعْفٍ، إِلَى أَضْعَافٍ كَثِيرَةٍ، وَإِنْ هَمَّ بِسَيِّئَةٍ فَلَمْ يَعْمَلْهَا كَتَبَهَا اللَّهُ عِنْدَهُ حَسَنَةً كَامِلَةً، وَإِنْ هَمَّ بِهَا فَعَمِلَهَا كَتَبَهَا اللَّهُ سَيِّئَةً وَاحِدَةً.

"Allah has recorded the good deeds and the bad deeds and then He made them clear. So whoever intends to do a good deed but does not do it, Allah writes it down with Himself as a complete good deed. If he intends it and then does it, Allah writes it down as ten good deeds, up to seven hundred times, or many more multiples. But if he intends to do a bad deed and does not do it, Allah writes it down as a complete good deed. And if he intends it and then does it, Allah writes it down as only one bad deed."[113]

The battle of the *nafs*

One of the most difficult battles we go through on a daily basis, is going against our *nafs*. جِهَادُ النَّفْسِ, called *jihad al-nafs*. We need to pay special attention to the talk inside us, because this is a combination of the *Shaytan* and our *nafs*

113 Muslim bin Hajjaj, "Chapter: If a person thinks of doing a good deed it will be recorded for him, and if he thinks of doing a bad deed it will not be recorded for him," *Sahih Muslim*, Book 1, Hadith 244.

which leads to actions that may affect our heart. The black dots come when we give in to these whispers and do what they suggest. Every struggle with our *nafs* paves our way to *Jannah*. Allah ﷻ said:

وَأَمَّا مَنْ خَافَ مَقَامَ رَبِّهِۦ وَنَهَى ٱلنَّفْسَ عَنِ ٱلْهَوَىٰ
فَإِنَّ ٱلْجَنَّةَ هِىَ ٱلْمَأْوَىٰ

But as for he who feared the position of his Lord and prevented the soul from [unlawful] inclination, then indeed, Paradise will be [his] refuge. (an-Nazi'at 79: 40-41)

Controlling the *nafs* against the desires is mentioned here because almost all the desires will lead to the disobedience of Allah ﷻ unless it's controlled.

In another *hadith*, which will help us if we keep it close to our heart and in our memory, as we struggle daily to obey Allah ﷻ, it is said:

المجاهد من جاهد نفسه في طاعة الله

"The Mujāhid is the one who strives against his own self in obedience to Allah."[114]

The reality is, it's not easy, because we are usually going against what we love, in order to please Allah ﷻ. Remembering this *hadith* helps us realise that the struggle is equal to being a real warrior battling an internal struggle. Take *Ramadan* for example, when you're fasting and smelling all

114 Jalal al-Din Suyuti, "Chapter on Iman," *Quwwat al-Mughtazi*, Vol 2, Page 650.

the food from bakeries and restaurants, and you want to eat, but you say to yourself '*no, I'm not eating, I'm fasting*' that struggle for the sake of Allah ﷻ is what He ﷻ will reward you for. A well-known saying by the early scholars is "Your greatest enemy is your *nafs* between your two sides."

The *nafs* in the Qur'an

We know from the Qur'an there is one *Shaytan*, but there are three different kinds of *nafs*: the soul at peace; the reproachful soul and the soul that commands to evil. Each one is now explored in more detail.

1. The soul at peace: *Al-Nafs al Mutma'innah* النَّفْسُ الْمُطْمَئِنَّةُ.[115]

Allah ﷻ said at the end of *Surah al-Fajr:*

يَٰٓأَيَّتُهَا ٱلنَّفْسُ ٱلْمُطْمَئِنَّةُ

ٱرْجِعِىٓ إِلَىٰ رَبِّكِ رَاضِيَةً مَّرْضِيَّةً

فَٱدْخُلِى فِى عِبَٰدِى

وَٱدْخُلِى جَنَّتِى

To the righteous [it will be said], "O reassured soul, Return to your Lord, well-pleased and pleasing [to Him], and enter among My [righteous] servants. And enter My Paradise. (al-Fajr: 89:27-30)

The *nafs* is addressed here, Allah ﷻ invites it back to Him ﷻ, and inverts the pleasure, telling the *nafs* it will be 'well-

115 Al-Fajr 89:27-30.

pleased' and then, well pleasing to its Lord. It may seem very difficult to achieve *al-Nafs al-Mutma'innah,* but it's not impossible. We can make our goals high, and aim for the best level we can reach, by the Will of Allah ﷻ. This state of the *nafs* is one in which you are always at peace with Allah ﷻ. يَا الله سَكِّنْةُ النَّفْس – Oh Allah grant tranquillity to the soul – you always feel better when you remember Him ﷻ.

When you sin and disobey Allah ﷻ, you always turn to Him ﷻ right away. Your *nafs* is in peace and you are longing to meet Allah ﷻ. Like *Sayyidina* Bilal ؓ, when he was dying and his wife was crying, he said, "غَدًا نَلْقَى الْأَحِبَّةَ مُحَمَّدًا وَصَحْبَهُ, Why are you crying? I'm going to meet Muhammad ﷺ and the Companions ؓ."[116]

When you are alone, remembering Allah ﷻ on your prayer rug, and you're reading the Qur'an, and you are so content. You don't want anything to happen to disconnect; that state, that's where you're at the point of *Al-nafs al-Mutma'innah* – the soul at peace.

The other qualities of this *nafs* is the belief and certainty that what Allah ﷻ has promised is going to happen in the *akhirah,* and also whatever will happen in this *dunya*, Allah ﷻ has decreed it already. This *nafs* knows there is *khair* in it and accepts it: *It's good for me and I submit to Allah* ﷻ.

116 Abd ar-Ra'uf Muhammad Uthman, "Chapter One: Love for the Messenger," *Kitab Mahabbat ar-Rasool Bayn al-Ittiba' wal-Ibtidaa'*, Page 87.

Another sign that you have *al-nafs al-Mutma'innah* is not only feeling you're at peace, but you will do whatever Allah ﷻ wants you to, the mindset is like this: *Allah ﷻ said do such a thing, so I'm doing it.* As Hasan al-Basri expressed in a beautiful saying, "I have never looked with my eyes or heard with my ears or moved or walked with my legs or used my hand, except that I think: is this in obedience to Allah ﷻ? If it is in obedience, I'll do it. If it is in disobedience, I stop."[117]

2. The reproachful soul, *al-nafs al-Lawwāmah* النفس اللَّوَّامَةُ. This is a good, remorseful soul, and Allah ﷻ made an oath by it in *surah al-Qiyamah*:

لَا أُقْسِمُ بِيَوْمِ الْقِيَامَةِ وَلَا أُقْسِمُ بِالنَّفْسِ اللَّوَّامَةِ

I swear by the Day of resurrection. And I swear by the reproaching soul [to the certainty of resurrection]. (Al-Qiyamah 75:1-2)

The blameworthy *nafs* is the one that will be your internal voice questioning you: *why didn't you wake up for Fajr? Why you are not dressed properly? Why did you say this? Why did you look at that?* If you have this inside you, it's good, because this is what will make you wake up; it's going to push you to repent to Allah ﷻ. It's that reminder which is like somebody who's warning you, and we need warning all the time.

If you keep listening to the reproaches, at some point, you're going to reach النَّفْسُ الْمُطْمَئِنَّةُ, *al-nafs al-Mutma'innah* and

117 Ibn Abi Dunya, "Chapter regarding those who were cautiously pious," *Al-Wara'*, Page 116.

this is something we can supplicate for, and ask Allah ﷻ to give us this before we return to Him ﷻ.

3. The soul that commands to evil: *al-nafs al-Ammarah bi-sū'*, النَّفْسُ الْأَمَّارَةُ بِالسُّوءِ, this is the *nafs* that orders you to do evil and bad deeds. The more your surroundings are full of the disobedience of Allah ﷻ, the more this *nafs* will be encouraged and will lead you to disobey Allah ﷻ. This *nafs* will order you to do wrong. There is a feeling of satisfaction that comes with disobeying, as it's the things your lower self likes and is drawn to. This is because of a synergy between the *nafs* and the *Shaytan* as they work together.

In the Qur'an we find in *Surah Yusuf*, the wife of the Aziz, when she admits to her sin, she doesn't say 'I'm perfect', instead she attributes her action to the influence of *nafs al-Ammarah bi-sū'*:

وَمَآ أُبَرِّئُ نَفْسِيٓ ۚ إِنَّ ٱلنَّفْسَ لَأَمَّارَةٌۢ بِٱلسُّوٓءِ إِلَّا مَا رَحِمَ رَبِّيٓ ۚ إِنَّ رَبِّى غَفُورٌ رَّحِيمٌ

And I do not acquit myself. Indeed, the soul is a persistent enjoiner of evil, except those upon which my Lord has mercy. Indeed, my Lord is Forgiving and Merciful." (Yusuf 12:53)

This *nafs* will keep pushing us with justification: *Do it, it's okay, it's not a big deal,* and together the *Shaytan* and the *nafs* continue to whisper. The battle here is to go against our own *nafs* and protect our heart. We can help ourselves by telling ourselves: *whenever the nafs orders me to do something disobedient to Allah ﷻ, I am going to beg Allah ﷻ to give me the strength not to do it.*

Our goal is to reach the state of *al-nafs al-Mutma'innah*. How we get there is to firstly strive against *al-nafs al-Ammarah bi-sū'* which tells you to do evil and battle against it all the time, as much as we can. If we fail, and we will all fail at some point, then listen to the reproachful soul, *al-nafs al-lawwāmah* the one who is going to question you; *why did you do this*, and *why did you do that?*

We ask *Ya Rabbi*, to give us the soul at peace *al-nafs al-Mutma'innah* النَّفْسُ الْمُطْمَئِنَّةُ. We ask to be pleased with Allah ﷻ and Allah ﷻ be pleased with us. When we achieve this, what will happen? We can hope to be stronger on our journey to *Jannah* and our dear, beautiful heart will be at peace and close to You – *Ya Rabbi Ameen.*

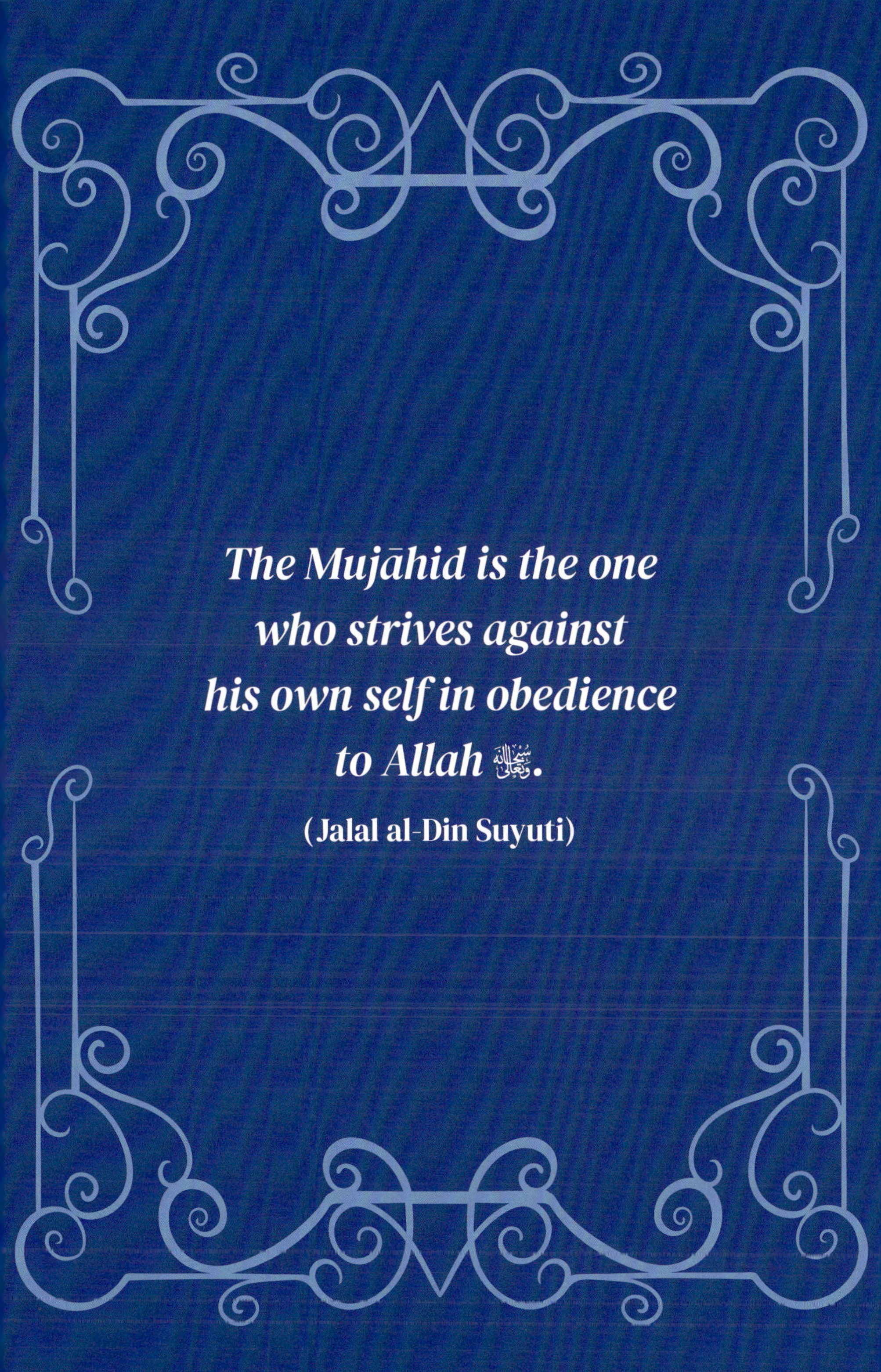
The Mujāhid is the one
who strives against
his own self in obedience
to Allah ﷻ.
(Jalal al-Din Suyuti)

My Dear Heart

What Poisons You?

A righteous man once made an amazing statement. "I am so surprised by people," he said, "They cry and feel sad when someone dies, when in fact it is only their body that leaves this world. Yet they don't cry for someone whose heart dies. And that is worse."

So, my dear heart, are you alive? As we said at the beginning, we're not talking about the physical heart; we're addressing the spiritual heart. What kills the heart gradually are the poisons that lead to disease. You will probably be surprised to learn about the poisons of the heart.

These are things that we normally have in life and need, but they can become poisonous if we have too much of them. The scholars of the heart say that there are four things in life that we need to have less of and there is one thing we need to have more of. The four things we need to have less of are: less talking, less interaction with people, less food and less sleeping. What we need more of is *dhikr*, remembering Allah ﷻ. So, let's look at them one by one and discover what the relationship is to our heart, as we ask it: how are you poisoned?

The four poisons of the heart

1. Talking too much

What is the problem with talking too much? And what counts as talking too much?

This *hadith* makes it clear for us: *Sayyidina* ʿAbdullāh ibn ʿUmar ؓ narrated and it is likely from *Rasul Allah* ﷺ (*Hadith Marfūʿ*)[118] where he ﷺ said:

لاَ تُكْثِرُوا الْكَلاَمَ بِغَيْرِ ذِكْرِ اللَّهِ

"Do not speak too much without the remembrance of Allah." Why?

فَإِنَّ كَثْرَةَ الْكَلاَمِ بِغَيْرِ ذِكْرِ اللَّهِ قَسْوَةٌ لِلْقَلْبِ

"For too much speech without the remembrance of Allah hardens the heart."

118 Abu Isa Muhammad al-Tirmidhi, "Chapter: The prohibition of talking too much without the remembrance of Allah," *Jamiʿ al-Tirmidhi*, Book 36, Hadith 109.

وَإِنَّ أَبْعَدَ النَّاسِ مِنَ اللَّهِ الْقَلْبُ الْقَاسِي

"And indeed, the person furthest from Allah is the one whose heart is hard."

If we talk too much without remembering Allah ﷻ, our spiritual heart will become so hard.

It's common that we often say things and then forget what we said. Who remembers what they said yesterday? The following *hadith* is a caution about our speech:

إِنَّ الرَّجُلَ لَيَتَكَلَّمُ بِالْكَلِمَةِ، لَا يَرَى بِهَا بَأْسًا، يَهْوِي بِهَا فِي النَّارِ سَبْعِينَ خَرِيفًا

'Indeed, a person may utter a word, thinking there is nothing wrong with it, yet because of it he falls into the Fire for seventy years.'[119]

A man or woman can say something, just a word and they don't see anything wrong with it, yet there could be a terrible consequence. Why is that? Sometimes we say things, and it hurts the person we're speaking to. We may not feel it and don't see it as significant, but it hurt the other person. Or sometimes we say something casually to a friend, like 'yesterday I watched this' knowing what you watched wasn't pleasing to Allah ﷻ. This led to somebody else watching the same, they tell someone else and does the same – watching what was displeasing to Allah ﷻ. That one word can lead to severe consequences.

119 Abu Isa Muhammad al-Tirmidhi, "Chapter: What has been related about one who says something to make people laugh," *Jami' al-Tirmidhi*, Book 36, Hadith 11.

Rasul Allah ﷺ predicted signs about the time we are living in now. What did he ﷺ predict? A time of multiple temptations, several trials and a lot of confusion. We've reached a point now, where we don't know what is right or what is wrong, just as was foretold.

عَنْ عُقْبَةَ بْنِ عَامِرٍ قَالَ: قُلْتُ: يَا رَسُولَ اللَّهِ، مَا النَّجَاةُ؟ قَالَ أَمْسِكْ علَيكَ لِسانَكَ، وليسَعْكَ بيتُكَ، وابكِ علَى خطيئتِكَ

'Uqbah ibn 'Āmir ﷺ reported: I said, "O Messenger of Allah, what is the path to salvation?" He ﷺ replied: "Restrain your tongue, let your home suffice you, and weep over your sins."[120]

If we are thinking about our *akhirah*, this is what we should do; talk less and be satisfied with spending time inside our homes. Remembering our sins is where repentance and *istighfār* starts from, to feel remorse sincerely and cry.

A common question is, 'When do I know I'm talking too much? And when do I know I need to talk?' This is answered in a very beautiful parameter set by *Sayyidina* Abu Hurayrah ﷺ who said:

"إِذَا أَعْجَبَكَ الْكَلَامُ فَاسْكُتْ، وَإِذَا أَعْجَبَكَ السُّكُوتُ فَتَكَلَّمْ, If you feel you want to talk, don't talk. And if you feel you don't want to talk, talk.[121]" This means when you're not in the mood to speak

120 Abu Isa Muhammad al-Tirmidhi, "Chapter: What has been related about protecting the tongue," *Jami' al-Tirmidhi*, Book 36, Hadith 104.

121 Abu Hamid al-Ghazali, "Four Things That Lead to Ruin," *Ihya' Uloom ul-Deen*, Vol 3, page 323.

and are usually quiet, then speak, even if it is a little. However, when you have this urge, for example you heard some news and you are restless and want to go and tell everybody: *Did you know? Or, did you hear what happened.* You call your friend and you're trying to get in touch with your mom, or your daughter to tell them – that's the time when you need to stop: don't speak.

Too much talking is going to lead to sins and disobedience of Allah ﷻ because when we talk too much, we're going to make mistakes, and those mistakes, such as exaggeration, or backbiting lead us to sin. And when we sin, the heart is going to be affected. One of the ways to help us speak less and be a benefit to our heart is, part of the advice from this *hadith*; avoiding too much interaction with people.

2. Excessive interaction with people

We need to interact with people, this is part of life. How do we define too much? Take, for example if I were to do the following: in the morning I'm having breakfast with friends. At lunch, I'm meeting someone else; followed by dinner, where I'm invited to another place. A day like this would involve continual interaction with people and talking, which for sure will have an effect on our heart. If we stop to think about why this is a problem, it is the same issue; of talking too much, along with this, there may be things we say or do that upsets or offends another person. This can lead to issues and create problems, sometimes even leading to hatred between people.

Look around your circle and see who you are surrounded by. Something beautiful is said by the scholars of the heart – it is amazing how they made the distinctions. They said people around us are of four kinds: one type is like food and drink, we need them every single day, they are those people who will bring us closer to Allah ﷻ. This could include a scholar, a righteous person and teacher, a dear friend, or our parents or children - those who will remind us if we make mistakes and do something that is not good for our *akhirah*. They teach us what is good, they nourish our heart like food and drink.

The second group of people are like medicine, when we are sick. They are those who help us in different circumstances like in our livelihood, or some other matter of daily life's circumstances.

The third and the fourth group are the ones we need to take an honest look at and see why we are surrounded by them. The third group of people are like a disease and will lead to sickness. When we are with them, we don't get any benefit, they are a waste of time. Usually, their talk is all self-praise, or boasting about what they have; everything is about the *dunya* - this life. These people are the ones you need to keep a distance from.

We have to remember one thing, that some of these people could be our own family. If that's the case, we're not permitted to cut family ties. However, we can reduce the interactions, speak less and listen more. With these relationships, ask Allah ﷻ to protect your heart.

The fourth category are those people who will persuade you to completely disobey Allah ﷻ and beautify every disobedience. They will take you towards all that is *haram*, making you feel good,[122] as your *nafs* and the *Shaytan* encourage this too. So, if we choose to surround ourselves with people like this, it's going to be extremely difficult for us to move away from the disobedience of Allah ﷻ.

Less interaction could look like keeping a day or two every week in which you don't meet people. Even inside your house, if you are with family, especially if it is a large family, give yourself at least half an hour in the morning alone. For our dear sisters, especially mothers, who wear several hats, juggling many roles, at least give yourself an hour in the morning or in the evening, to focus on where you are and where you are going on your path to Allah ﷻ. You deserve to spend this time reflecting. The same applies to brothers who are very busy with work and meeting life's needs; they too should make sure an hour minimum per day is set aside to connect this life with the next one in *akhirah*.

---

122 Ahmad Fareed, "The Four Poisons of the Heart," *Tazkiya tun-Nufoos*, pages 33, 34.

3. Consuming too much food

Food is a necessity for us all and an essential part of life. Yet *Rasul Allah* ﷺ still said many things about the types of food and the quantity we consume. Most notable is:

مَا مَلَأَ ابْنُ آدَمَ وِعَاءً شَرًّا مِنْ بَطْنٍ. 'The son of Adam has not filled any container worse than his stomach.[123] وَإِنْ كَانَ لَا بُدَّ If you have to eat then follow the thirds rule; one third for food, one third for the breath, one third for drink.'

Our eating and drinking should never be to a point that a believer will say they are too full, as this indicates over-eating. One of the scholars even commented saying, 'I wonder if a believer will say "I can't eat anymore."' Here the assumption is a believer would not behave this way in the first place.

What is the relationship between food and religion? Ibrahim ibn Adham, a scholar of hearts said: مَنْ ضَبَطَ بَطْنَهُ ضَبَطَ دِينَه 'Whoever controls their stomach, controls their *deen*.'

وَمَنْ مَلَكَ جُوعَهُ مَلَكَ الْأَخْلَاقَ الصَّالِحَة[124]

And 'Whoever masters their hunger, masters good character.'

If you can control your hunger and don't have to eat as soon as you're hungry, you will develop a good character, as it shows patience and humility.

123 Ibn Hajar al-Asqalani, "Chapter of asceticism and pious restraint: The prohibition of excessive eating," *Bulugh al-Maram*, page 448.

124 Ahmad Fareed, "The Four Poisons of the Heart," *Tazkiya tun-Nufoos*, page 32.

The opposite is true too; there is more disobedience of Allah ﷻ when we are fully satiated and eat to our full. When the month of *Ramadan* comes, it is the ideal opportunity to observe these limits when we eat. When we are hungry, or when we are fasting, we need to practise *not* eating until we are full and stop before this point, to take care of our spiritual heart.

4. Sleeping too much

There is a general agreement that the average person needs eight hours sleep. However, we can be mindful about this as it doesn't need to be in one stretch. The hours we sleep can be divided and it's the *sunnah* to take a *qaylula* قَيْلُولَة, an afternoon nap, if one can. A full eight hours or more in the night can lead to laziness. How will we explain spending one third of our life sleeping when we answer to Allah ﷻ?

To make these changes and curb these four poisons of the heart, has to be a gradual process. To control eating, for example after *Ramadan*, fasting one day a week can help. Over time, this can increase to two days, as well as being mindful of the rule of one third for food, drink and breath. If you normally sleep eight, ten hours or more, cut down an hour at a time and try a short nap in the afternoon. Excessive interacting with people can be reduced, by planning some time alone each week. When we meet fewer people this naturally helps with speaking less too.

Our aim is to live in a way our hearts achieve the best state, free from corruption. The believer's heart gains strength from remembrance of Allah ﷾ – the Exalted, seeking forgiveness, supplication and recitation of the Qur'an. It becomes easier to nourish our hearts when we limit these four poisons that cause us harm.

May Allah ﷾ help us in all the ways that benefit our heart. And may He ﷾ protect us from company and habits that leads us away from Him. *Ya Rabbi Ameen.*

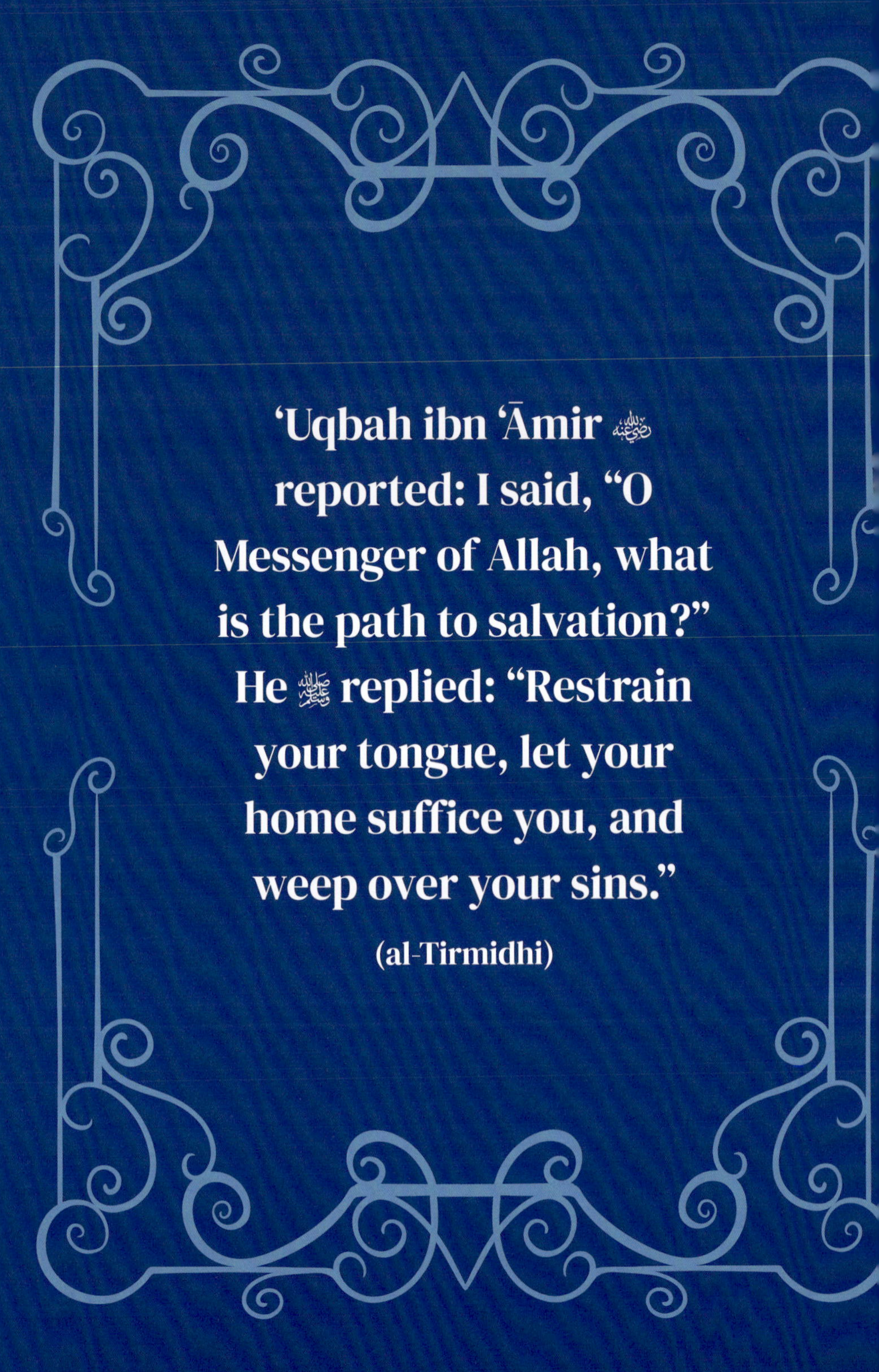

ʻUqbah ibn ʻĀmir رضي الله عنه reported: I said, "O Messenger of Allah, what is the path to salvation?" He ﷺ replied: "Restrain your tongue, let your home suffice you, and weep over your sins."

(al-Tirmidhi)

My Dear Heart

Do you Remember Allah?

In the previous chapters we covered the many issues that affect our heart. Now my dear heart is asking me, 'What should I do?' This is the question for us all: what do we need to do to meet Allah ﷾ with *al-qalb al-saleem* - the sound heart? This sound heart is the one He ﷾ wants us to meet Him ﷾ with. The answer lies in one of the easiest things to do and also the least done, it is called, *dhikrullah* ذِكْرُ اللهِ – remembering Allah ﷾.

Whether we like fishing, eating fish or observing them in the water, have you ever noticed what happens to a fish outside water? It dies, as Allah ﷻ created it this way. The very opposite is true for human beings. If you put a human being under water for a while without oxygen, he or she will die. Why is this? Imam Ibn Taymiyyah رحمه الله has a beautiful parable in which he said, '*al-dhikr*, remembering Allah ﷻ for the heart, is exactly like water for the fish.'[125] This is a profound yet simple thing to always remember. If we look at remembering Allah ﷻ as our oxygen, then it becomes the air I need to breathe without which I won't survive, then we're going to look at *al-dhikr* very differently.

It's human nature to want to know what we're going to get in return for whatever we do or give. Imam Ibn al-Qayyim رحمه الله in a beautiful book called *Al-Wābil al-Ṣayyib*, meaning '*The Heavy Rain that will bring a lot of Fruit*', responds to our instinctive questions. He explains that heavy rain is actually the *dhikr* of Allah ﷻ, which has more than seventy benefits for the one in remembrance. We will look at two of the benefits below.

The benefits of remembrance – *Dhikrullah*
1. A content heart

The first benefit is the heart feels satisfied and fulfilled with *dhikr*. This is similar to the experience in *Ramadan*. We just need to think back to how we felt half an hour before it was

125 Abd al-Razzaq ibn Abd al-Muhsin al-Badr, *Kitab al-Dhikr wa al-Du'a*, page 6.

time to break our fast at *Maghrib*. At that point we're so hungry and thirsty, lacking energy; we just want to eat. Recall how the first sip of water or the first bite of the date tastes. Ibn al-Qayyim likens this feeling of our body being energised after a fast, to how *dhikr* impacts our heart. Just as that food gives life to the body, he said, إِنَّهُ قُوَّةُ ٱلْقَلْبِ وَٱلرُّوحِ, "For indeed, *dhikr* is the strength of the heart and the soul."[126] This is something those who experience that moment of breaking fast can truly appreciate more.

Whenever you feel empty, or bored, or feel lost about this life, just stop for a second and do any *dhikr*, say *Astaghfir-ullah*, *Subhan Allah*, *Alhamdulillah* or any other remembrance of Allah ﷻ, or *salawat* on *Rasul Allah* اَلصَّلَاةُ عَلَى ٱلنَّبِيِّ. Repeating *dhikr* slowly, taking your time will surely have a good effect on your heart.

2. Defeating the *Shaytan*

Our persistent enemy we struggle to get rid of, and who often defeats us, is the *Shaytan*. The best way to battle the *Shaytan*, and reduce his influence over us, is *al-dhikr*. Allah ﷻ taught us the words:

قُلْ أَعُوذُ بِرَبِّ ٱلنَّاسِ مَلِكِ ٱلنَّاسِ إِلَٰهِ ٱلنَّاسِ مِن شَرِّ ٱلْوَسْوَاسِ ٱلْخَنَّاسِ

I seek refuge in the Lord of men, King of men, The god of men, from the evils of the lurking whisperer (the Shaytan). (al-Nas 30:1-4)

126 Ibn al-Qayyim, "Remembrance of Allah and its benefits," *Al-Wabil al-Sayyib*, page 42.

Who is *al-waswas*? The one who whispers is the *Shaytan*. Whenever we want to do something good and then inside us we get the whispers: *I'm too tired, let's do it tomorrow, maybe this is not the best, let me just think about it;* all these thoughts to distract us are his whispering.

The way to overcome this is to get up for *salah* and remember Allah ﷻ. Once we remember Allah ﷻ, the *Shaytan*'s whisper becomes ' خَنَّاسُ *khannās*'. In Arabic *khannās* means when something becomes much smaller, decreases and then disappears. The effect of the *Shaytan* will diminish.

Another tool is *Ḥiṣn al-Muslim* which means '*The Fortress of the Muslim*' and is literally a fortress for us. This popular small book found in multiple languages is all about *dhikr*. The *dhikr* in this book of *du'a's* is our protecting fortress – *Ḥiṣn*, because the believer is surrounded by the whispers of Satan, and needs this protection.

3. Feeling serene through the day

In our world today, being anxious and suffering from anxiety and general worries about the future are very common. Not knowing what will happen about our jobs and livelihood; or an exam tomorrow; or worrying about our children's education and schooling are just a few of the many things we are preoccupied with. Each and every one of us wants to live in peace. The statement in *Surah al-Ra'd*, is where Allah ﷻ gives us the remedy:

ٱلَّذِينَ ءَامَنُواْ وَتَطْمَئِنُّ قُلُوبُهُم بِذِكْرِ ٱللَّهِۗ أَلَا بِذِكْرِ ٱللَّهِ تَطْمَئِنُّ ٱلْقُلُوبُ

Those who have believed and whose hearts are assured by the remembrance of Allah. Unquestionably, by the remembrance of Allah hearts are assured. (al-Ra'd 13:28)

And the opposite is true too. In *Surah Taha* Allah ﷻ says:

وَمَنْ أَعْرَضَ عَن ذِكْرِى فَإِنَّ لَهُۥ مَعِيشَةً ضَنكًا وَنَحْشُرُهُۥ يَوْمَ ٱلْقِيَٰمَةِ أَعْمَىٰ

And whoever turns away from My remembrance – indeed, he will have a depressed [i.e., difficult] life, and We will gather [i.e., raise] him on the Day of Resurrection blind. (Ta-Ha 20:124)

The choice is ours, whether we turn to Allah ﷻ or turn away from Him. A person's livelihood being constricted doesn't mean they don't have money or resources. So many people have everything, yet still, they don't feel happy. They don't feel relaxed or serene because they turned away from the remembrance of Allah ﷻ. If we turn inwards and examine ourselves for the past twenty-four hours, how many of these hours were spent in the remembrance of Allah ﷻ?

This doesn't mean we stop living our life and not do anything else. We need to do several things as part of our daily life and there are many opportunities for *dhikr* throughout the day too. In the morning, for example, when we get into the car, do we say the *du'a* for travel? This is *al-dhikr*.

اللَّهُ أَكْبَرُ، اللَّهُ أَكْبَرُ، اللَّهُ أَكْبَرُ،

سُبْحَانَ الَّذِي سَخَّرَ لَنَا هَذَا وَمَا كُنَّا لَهُ مُقْرِنِينَ، وَإِنَّا إِلَىٰ رَبِّنَا لَمُنقَلِبُونَ

[Allah is the Greatest, Allah is the Greatest,
Allah is the Greatest].

Exalted is He who has subjected this to us, and we could not have [otherwise] subdued it [on our own]. And indeed we, to our Lord, will [surely] return. (al-Zukhruf 43:13)

When we enter the house; when we put our shoes on. Do we remember to say these *du'as*? They take very little time, thirty seconds, but they give us the happiness and serenity we're looking for.

4. Allah ﷻ is remembering us

Do you want Allah ﷻ to remember you? Is this something we really spend time thinking about. It seems unbelievable, that you and I, ordinary people who sin, can be remembered by Allah ﷻ Most High. However, this is something He ﷻ said: فَٱذْكُرُونِيٓ أَذْكُرْكُمْ, '*You remember me, I will remember you.*'[127] So yes, Allah ﷻ will remember each and every one of us who remembers Him ﷻ. We should take advantage of this reality and keep doing *dhikr.* For this you don't need *wudu*, you don't need time or to face in a particular direction. For women, you don't need to be covered. The only thing you need is your heart and tongue. Even if your tongue is not moving, your heart can say it:

لَآ إِلَٰهَ إِلَّا ٱللَّهُ وَحْدَهُۥ لَا شَرِيكَ لَهُ

127 Al-Baqarah 2:152.

Lā ilāha illallāhū waḥdahu lā sharīka lah. There is no god except Allah, alone, without any partner.

We are living in transactional times and someone may think *what am I going to get out of repeating dhikr ?* If you say:

لَآ إِلَٰهَ إِلَّا ٱللَّهُ وَحْدَهُۥ لَا شَرِيكَ لَهُۥ لَهُ ٱلْمُلْكُ وَلَهُ ٱلْحَمْدُ

Lā ilāha illallāhu waḥdahū lā sharīka lah,
lahu 'l-mulku wa lahu 'l-ḥamd.

There is no god except Allah, alone, without any partner. To Him belongs the dominion, and to Him belongs all praise.

For saying this one hundred times throughout the day, what will happen? You will get one hundred good deeds and a hundred bad deeds will be removed[128] and it's going to be a complete protection from the *Shaytan* until the evening. If you say it again in the evening it will be the same until morning. Just reflect on this!

How many of us really want to have a tree in *Jannah*?

مَنْ قَالَ سُبْحَانَ اللَّهِ الْعَظِيمِ وَبِحَمْدِهِ

"Whoever says: *Subḥānallāhi 'l-'aẓīmi wa bi-ḥamdih* (Glory be to Allah, the Magnificent, and with His praise), a palm tree will be planted for him in Paradise." [129]

---

128 Muhammad bin Ismail al-Bukhari, "Chapter: The characteristics of Iblis and his soldiers," *Sahih al-Bukhari*, Book 59, Hadith 102.

129 Abu Isa Muhammad al-Tirmidhi, "Chapter. Concerning the virtues of 'Glory is to Allah, and with His Praise'," *Jami' al-Tirmidhi*, Book 48, Hadith 95.

How long would it take us to say this, just one breath. Many of the *Sahaba* ﷺ said doing *dhikr* was way more beloved to them than any other act (apart from the obligatory).

فَٱذْكُرُونِيٓ أَذْكُرْكُمْ وَٱشْكُرُوا۟ لِي وَلَا تَكْفُرُونِ.

Remember Me; I will remember you. And thank Me, and never be ungrateful. (al-Baqarah 2:152)

The best cleanser for the heart is the *dhikr* of Allah ﷻ:

أَلَا إِنَّ لِكُلِّ شَيْءٍ صَقَالَةً وَصَقَالَةُ ٱلْقُلُوبِ ذِكْرُ ٱللَّهِ

Everything has a cleansing agent, and the best cleansing agent is *dhikr* of Allah ﷻ. [130]

Allah ﷻ said in the Qur'an:

ٱتْلُ مَآ أُوحِىَ إِلَيْكَ مِنَ ٱلْكِتَـٰبِ وَأَقِمِ ٱلصَّلَوٰةَ ۖ إِنَّ ٱلصَّلَوٰةَ تَنْهَىٰ عَنِ ٱلْفَحْشَآءِ وَٱلْمُنكَرِ ۗ وَلَذِكْرُ ٱللَّهِ أَكْبَرُ ۗ وَٱللَّهُ يَعْلَمُ مَا تَصْنَعُونَ

Recite, [O Muḥammad], what has been revealed to you of the Book and establish prayer. Indeed, prayer prohibits immorality and wrong-doing, and the remembrance of Allah is greater. And Allah knows that which you do. (al-Ankabut, 29:45)

Finally, we should ask Allah ﷻ frequently in the words of this *du'a*:

130 Muhammad bin Abdullah al-Khatib, "Chapter: Remembrance of God and drawing near to Him," *Mishkat al-Masabih*, Book 9, Hadith 60.

ٱللَّهُمَّ أَعِنِّي عَلَىٰ ذِكْرِكَ وَشُكْرِكَ وَحُسْنِ عِبَادَتِكَ.[١٣١]

'Ya Allah! Help me to remember You and to give thanks to You, and to worship You in the best manner.'

May Allah ﷻ make us from those who remember Him ﷻ plentifully and fulfil the instruction to do lots of *dhikrullah* – the only thing in the Qur'an we are encouraged to do abundantly. May He ﷻ protect our hearts from forgetting and grant us the guidance to be amongst the believing men and women who remember Allah ﷻ often. *Ya Rabbi Ameen.*

إِنَّ ٱلْمُسْلِمِينَ وَٱلْمُسْلِمَٰتِ وَٱلْمُؤْمِنِينَ وَٱلْمُؤْمِنَٰتِ وَٱلْقَٰنِتِينَ وَٱلْقَٰنِتَٰتِ وَٱلصَّٰدِقِينَ
وَٱلصَّٰدِقَٰتِ وَٱلصَّٰبِرِينَ وَٱلصَّٰبِرَٰتِ وَٱلْخَٰشِعِينَ وَٱلْخَٰشِعَٰتِ وَٱلْمُتَصَدِّقِينَ وَٱلْمُتَصَدِّقَٰتِ
وَٱلصَّٰٓئِمِينَ وَٱلصَّٰٓئِمَٰتِ وَٱلْحَٰفِظِينَ فُرُوجَهُمْ وَٱلْحَٰفِظَٰتِ وَٱلذَّٰكِرِينَ ٱللَّهَ كَثِيرًا وَٱلذَّٰكِرَٰتِ
أَعَدَّ ٱللَّهُ لَهُم مَّغْفِرَةً وَأَجْرًا عَظِيمًا

Indeed, the Muslim men and Muslim women, the believing men and believing women, the obedient men and obedient women, the truthful men and truthful women, the patient men and patient women, the humble men and humble women, the charitable men and charitable women, the fasting men and fasting women, the men who guard their chastity and the women who do so, and the men who remember Allah often and the women who do so – for them Allah has prepared forgiveness and a great reward. (al-Ahzab 33:35)

131 Muhammad bin Abdullah al-Khatib, "Chapter: The supplication of the tashahhud," *Mishkat al-Masabih*, Book 4, Hadith 372.

Remember Me; I will remember you. And thank Me, and never be ungrateful.

(al-Baqarah 2:152)

My Dear Heart

Do you read Allah's Words?

As we are on this journey to Allah ﷻ – *Ya Rabbi* – we hope to end with a pure heart, just as we began with a pure heart. One of the essentials we need to carry with us is something that keeps the heart clean and purifies it whenever needed. Surely you can guess what it is? It is the words of Allah ﷻ, the Qur'an.

The words of my Lord

هَذَا كَلَامُ رَبِّي

'This is the speech of my Lord'

When I looked at the Qur'an in this way, and reflected that these are His ﷻ words *kalāmullāh* – كَلَامُ اللهِ, my relationship with the Qur'an changed. I was taught, when you pick up the Qur'an and open it, put your finger on the page and say, هَٰذَا كَلَامُ رَبِّي. 'This is the word of my Lord.' If you do this, your feeling towards the Qur'an will change too. Whilst you may be memorizing and reviewing certain *ayaat* or simply reading and reciting it – the one thing we must recall is: the Qur'an is directly our Lord's speech and should not be treated like any other 'book.' The month of *Ramadan* is a good opportunity, when it's beautiful how Qur'an reading increases, as the very month is called 'The month of the Qur'an.' The most important focus to benefit from is that all the time we spend listening, reciting and learning in *Ramadan*, we should remember that this is not an ordinary book in our hands.

In the time of Imam Ahmed, a huge *fitna* – a trial and test for him was the widespread opinion that the Qur'an is a creation of Allah.[132] Imam Ahmed clarified that this was not correct, and in fact the Qur'an is the words of Allah ﷻ that He ﷻ said Himself.

Apart from using the name 'The Qur'an,' we can use and connect by saying these are 'the words of my Lord.' Beside this, there are many names Allah ﷻ uses for the Qur'an for this amazing book.

---

132 Ahmad ibn Hanbal, *Al-Jami' Li Uloom Al-Imam Ahmad,* Vol 3, page 517.

The names of the Qur'an

When something has many beautiful characteristics, it usually has more names related to these qualities. Such are the names of the Qur'an. Knowing these different names will inspire and help us to have a deeper relationship with the 'words of my Lord' *kalāmullāh.* When we pick up the Qur'an, these different names should come to mind.

Al-Qur'an

We all know this is what Allah ﷻ named His words, which means: 'the one that you read' Allah ﷻ said to *Rasul Allah* ﷺ:

وَإِنَّكَ لَتُلَقَّى ٱلْقُرْءَانَ مِن لَّدُنْ حَكِيمٍ عَلِيمٍ

And Indeed, [O Muhammad], you receive the Qur'an from one Wise and Knowing. (al-Naml 27:6)

Al-Kitāb – the Book, this is the common name when used in the Arabic language, 'the Book', is usually understood to mean Al-Qur'an. But in English, when we say 'the book,' it is more general and could be *any* book. Allah ﷻ also said:

ٱلْحَمْدُ لِلَّهِ ٱلَّذِىٓ أَنزَلَ عَلَىٰ عَبْدِهِ ٱلْكِتَٰبَ وَلَمْ يَجْعَل لَّهُۥ عِوَجَا ۜ

[All] praise is [due] to Allah, who has sent down upon His servant [Muhammad] the Book and has not made therein any deviance. (al-Kahf 18:1)

And in turn, *Rasul Allah* ﷺ made our relationship between Our *Rabb*, himself and the Qur'an very clear when he ﷺ said: "Whoever loves Allah and His Messenger should read the Qur'an."

Al-Furqān – The Criterion. Allah ﷻ also uses this name for the Qur'an. It's the distinction between truth and falsehood. It is what divides truth from falsehood. What is the benefit of us knowing this? When Allah ﷻ said in the Qur'an, this is *haram*, then this means it is forbidden. If He ﷻ even alludes to it, and tells us to stay away from it, then we stay away from it, because this is the truth. Likewise, is the case for falsehood. Allah said, تَبَارَكَ ٱلَّذِى نَزَّلَ ٱلْفُرْقَانَ عَلَىٰ عَبْدِهِۦ لِيَكُونَ لِلْعَـٰلَمِينَ نَذِيرًا. *Blessed is He who sent down the Criterion [Furqān] upon His servant that he may be to the worlds, a Warner.*[133] So why is *Rasul Allah* ﷺ نَذِيرًا a Warner? Knowing the meaning of the name *al-Furqān* means that we need to understand what we are reading is the truth, and not open to any argument. The Creator of everything, these are His words; He knows what's right and what is wrong.

An-Nūr – In *surah al-Nisa*, Allah says: وَأَنزَلْنَا إِلَيْكَ نُورًا مُّبِينًا. *And we have sent to you a clear light.* (*al-Nisa* 7:174) Let's think about when we need light – *Nūr*? When do we use a torch? It's when we are in darkness or lost, and need to see our way and use a light as a guide so we don't fall, or trip. Such is the *al-Nūr*, lighting the path ahead for us.

133 Al-Furqan 25:1.

Al-Mawʿiẓah – an admonition or counsel مَوْعِظَةٌ Allah ﷻ said:

يَٰٓأَيُّهَا ٱلنَّاسُ قَدْ جَآءَتْكُم مَّوْعِظَةٌ مِّن رَّبِّكُمْ وَشِفَآءٌ لِّمَا فِى ٱلصُّدُورِ وَهُدًى وَرَحْمَةٌ لِّلْمُؤْمِنِينَ

O mankind, there has come to you instruction from your Lord and healing for what is in the hearts and guidance and mercy for the believers. (Yunus 10:57)

In this *ayah* we are given four names for the Qur'an and four descriptions. يَا أَيُّهَا النَّاسُ, people, قَدْ جَاءَتْكُم, I have sent to you, *mawʿiẓah* مَوْعِظَةٌ, admonition. What is an admonition? This is when He ﷻ reminds me what the reality of this *dunya* is; the reality of where I am living. This counsel is one in which He ﷻ reminds me where I'm going; the Day of Judgement.

Ash-Shifāʿ – a cure; the *ayah* from *Surah Yunus* tells us the Qur'an is a cure to what's in the hearts. What's in our hearts? The diseases of the heart covered in the previous chapters, such as jealousy; anger; envy; arrogance – all the diseases of the heart have their cure in the Qur'an. شِفَاءٌ لِّمَا فِي الصُّدُور, Even mental illnesses when we feel down, or anxious, and for physical illnesses we perform رُقيَةٌ *Ruqyah*, using words from the Qur'an as a protection and cure. When we want to be guided and we don't know where we're going, or what we should do, we need to study the Qur'an which will be a guidance for our hearts and a mercy – a *Raḥmah*.

It is true we will find things difficult at times because we're not used to them, but it is a *raḥmah* from Allah ﷻ. He's called it *Raḥmah* and the Qur'an is the best *dhikr*. Whether during *Ramadan* or beyond during the rest of the year, the best *dhikr*, the best form of remembrance is actually reciting the Qur'an, the Book of Allah ﷻ in *salah*.

Whether we can go to the masjid in *Ramadan*, or not, and for those who pray at home, begin a special habit of two units of *salah* alone, making time for yourself and Allah ﷻ. Place the Qur'an in front of you and keep reading, making the reading longer and longer. Why should you do this? Firstly, Allah ﷻ loves the *salah*, Allah ﷻ loves His words, and now you are making time for both. The best part is to experience what will happen to you after you do start doing this. See what will happen to you after you spend longer time in prayer. During this special *nafl salah* try to read at least half a page or ideally one or two pages. Even if you don't know Arabic, you can still do this using the transliteration.

In *surah al Naml* – 'the Ant' Allah ﷻ tells *Rasul Allah* ﷺ:

وَإِنَّكَ لَتُلَقَّى ٱلْقُرْءَانَ مِن لَّدُنْ حَكِيمٍ عَلِيمٍ

And indeed, [O Muhammad], you receive the Qur'an from One who is Wise and All-Knowing (al-Naml 27:6).

Furthermore, in *Surah al-Qamar* Allah ﷻ uses a strong word of admonition.

وَلَقَدْ جَآءَهُم مِّنَ ٱلْأَنۢبَآءِ مَا فِيهِ مُزْدَجَرٌ
حِكْمَةٌۢ بَٰلِغَةٌۖ فَمَا تُغْنِ ٱلنُّذُرُ

And there has already come to them of information that in which there is deterrence. Extensive wisdom - but warning does not avail [them]. (al-Qamar 54:4-5)

حَبْلُ اللَّهِ ***Ḥablullāh*** – **The rope of Allah** The scholars agree, the 'rope of Allah' in this *ayah* is the Qur'an: وَاعْتَصِمُوا بِحَبْلِ اللَّهِ جَمِيع.[134] When do we use a rope? If you do hiking, or mountain climbing, you use a rope because it holds you and protects you from falling. This is what the Qur'an should do for us; saving us from falling into sin, or drifting away from Allah ﷻ into all the desires and distractions of this *dunya*.

Hence our role as believers is to hold firmly to the Qur'an. If we think back to *Ramadan*, and our relationship with reading the Qur'an; was our reading just for that special month? What happens after *Ramadan*, should we be having a vacation? O Allah, may we not be of those who only focus on the words of our Lord during that month. After *Ramadan* there is no 'time-off' from the Qur'an, there is only continuation.

134 Ibn Jarir al-Tabari, "Chapter: Āl-Imran," *Kitab Tafsir al Tabari*, Vol 5, page 646.

Al-Ṣirāṭ al-Mustaqeem – The Qur'an is the straight path. We ask Allah ﷻ every day for *Al-Ṣirāṭ al-Mustaqeem*. We ask Him ﷻ to guide us and make it easy to stay on the straight path. In *Surah al-An'am*, we are told:

وَأَنَّ هَٰذَا صِرَٰطِى مُسْتَقِيمًا فَٱتَّبِعُوهُ

Indeed, this is My straight path, follow it. (al-An'am 6:153)

Here this is referring to the Qur'an. And on the Day of Judgement, the Messenger of Allah ﷺ said in his final sermon: اللَّهُمَّ هَلْ بَلَّغْتُ؟ اللَّهُمَّ فَاشْهَدْ *Ya Allah*, did I deliver the message? *Ya Allah*, You are my witness. [135]

Another characteristic of the Qur'an is *Balāgh* – communication بَلَاغٌ. It is a communication that announces the words from Allah ﷻ that should admonish us. We will be asked by Allah ﷻ if we received the message? And the answer is yes, we did receive this communication and caution.

The following advice in the words of *Sayyidina* Uthman رضي الله عنه helps us to examine our relationship with the words of our Lord. He said: 'لَوْ طَهُرَتْ قُلُوبُنَا مَا شَبِعَتْ مِنْ كَلَامِ رَبِّنَا.[136] If our hearts are pure, we will never have enough from the Qur'an', meaning we will never be satisfied. When we don't feel we want to read Qur'an, we need to clean our heart. If it is truly pure, we will never have enough of reading it. Another beautiful saying is from Khabbab ibn al-Aratt رضي الله عنه, who said to a man:

135 Abu Dawud, "Chapter: Regarding the abolition of riba," *Sunan Abi Dawud*, Book 23, Hadith 9.

136 Abu Nuaeem al-Asbahani, *Hilyat-ul-Awliya*, Vol 7, page 272.

"Draw close to Allah ﷻ as much as you can, and know that you will not draw closer to Him ﷻ with anything more beloved to Him ﷻ than His ﷻ words."

The *du'a* of *Rasul Allah* ﷺ is what we supplicate with for our hearts:

اِجْعَلِ ٱلْقُرْآنَ رَبِيعَ قُلُوبِنَا، وَجِلَاءَ هُمُومِنَا، وَشِفَاءَ أَحْزَانِنَا، وَذَهَابَ أَحْزَانِنَا

> *Ya Allah*! Make the Qur'an the spring of our hearts, the reason that all our disease and sickness to be cured and all our worries be removed.[137]
>
> *Ameen*!

137 Sulayman bin Hamd, "The second sermon: The story of Dhun-noon," *Shua' min al Mihrab*, Vol 6, page 165.

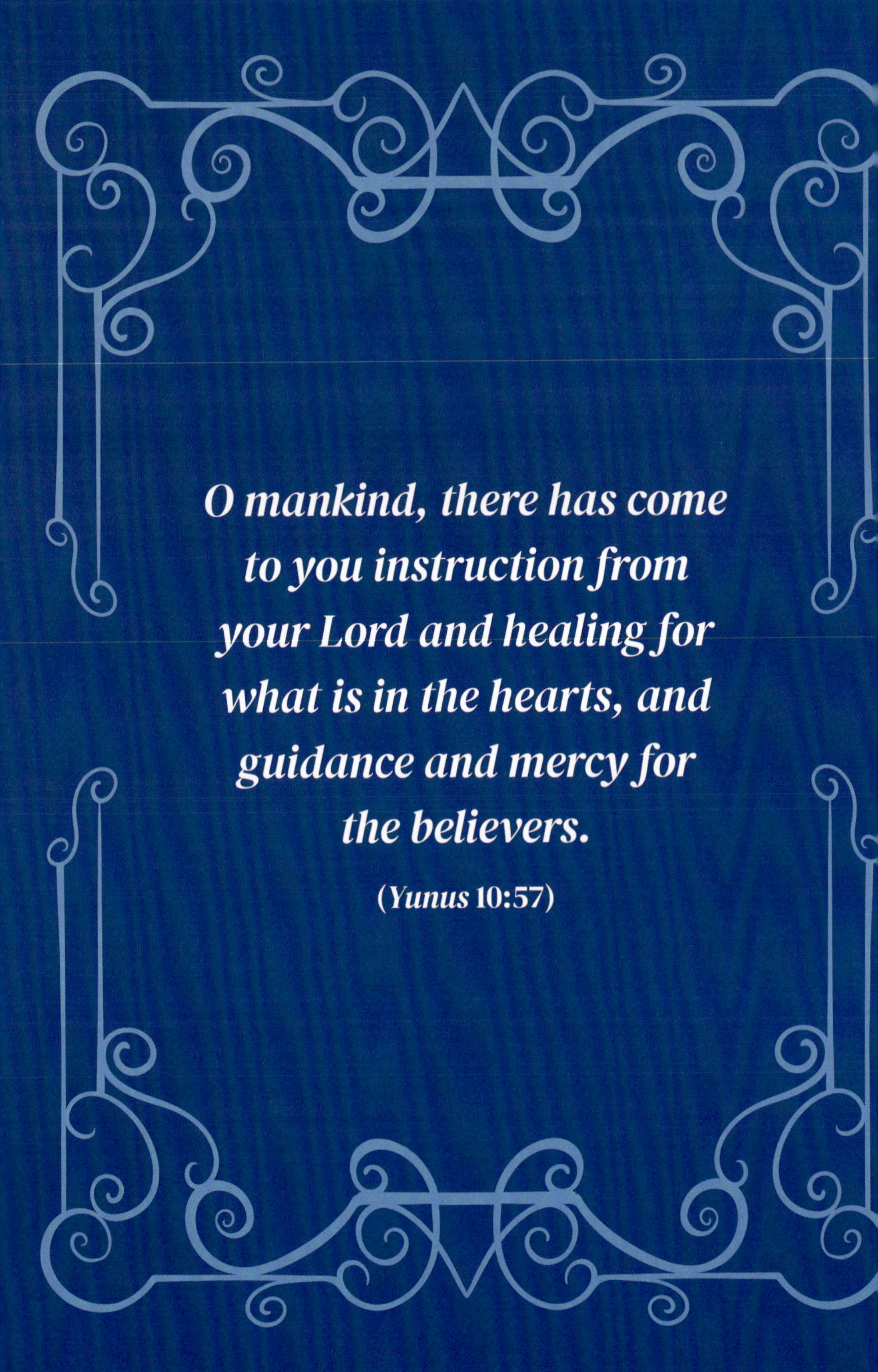
O mankind, there has come to you instruction from your Lord and healing for what is in the hearts, and guidance and mercy for the believers.
(Yunus 10:57)

My Dear Heart

Do you love the Prophet ﷺ?

In the previous chapter we explored the benefit of the words of our Lord – *Kalāmullāh* has on purifying our dear heart. It is from Allah's ﷻ words that we find another way to purify our heart in one of the most frequently repeated verses in the Qur'an that is often heard at *Jumu'ah* (Friday) *salah*:

إِنَّ ٱللَّهَ وَمَلَٰٓئِكَتَهُۥ يُصَلُّونَ عَلَى ٱلنَّبِيِّ ۚ يَٰٓأَيُّهَا ٱلَّذِينَ ءَامَنُوا۟ صَلُّوا۟ عَلَيْهِ وَسَلِّمُوا۟ تَسْلِيمًا

Indeed, Allah confers blessing upon the Prophet, and His angels [ask Him to do so]. O you who have believed, ask [Allah to

confer] blessing upon him and ask [Allah to grant him] peace. (al-Ahzab 33:56)

This is a practise that we need to include in our daily life, if we want to clear our heart and return it to the pure state we started off with. Imam Ibn al-Qayyim wrote a book called *Jala'ul Afhaam* in which he listed more than forty benefits of sending *salawat* on *Rasul Allah* صَلَوَاتُ عَلَى النَّبِيِّ عَلَيْهِ الصَّلَاةُ وَالسَّلَامُ: *Ṣalawāt ʿalā an-Nabī ʿalayhi aṣ-ṣalātu wa-s-salām* "Blessings upon the Prophet, peace and blessings be upon him."

Before we look into some of these, each one of us needs to ask ourselves this question: When was the last time you sent blessings (*ṣalawat*) upon the Prophet ﷺ, or said O Allah, send blessings upon Muhammad ﷺ اللَّهُمَّ صَلِّ عَلَى مُحَمَّدٍ ﷺ?

There's no need to make it complicated. The easiest way to send *ṣalawat* upon the Prophet ﷺ is simply to say: "Allāhumma ṣalli ʿalā Muḥammad" — don't overcomplicate it. For the full, traditional wording, the Prophet ﷺ explained when asked: *"Allāhumma ṣalli ʿalā Muḥammad wa ʿalā āli Muḥammad, kamā ṣallayta ʿalā Ibrāhīm wa ʿalā āli Ibrāhīm."* This means: "O Allah, send blessings upon Muhammad ﷺ and upon his family, as You sent blessings upon Ibrāhīm and his family." [138]

It takes one second, maybe two seconds to remember these few words. Yet, our human nature will always want to know

138 Abu Dawud, "Chapter: Sending salat upon the Prophet ﷺ after the tashah-hud," Sunan Abi Dawud, Book 2, Hadith 589.

what benefit this is going to bring; what will we gain from doing this? Hence below we go into the benefits in more detail.

Benefits of sending Salawat on *Rasul Allah* ﷺ

1. An act of worship – *Ibadah*

Sending *salawat* is an act of obedience to Allah ﷻ. When we say it, we are doing the same as the angels, as detailed in the verse above from *Surah al-Ahzab*.

In answer to what we gain if we send prayers (blessings) upon the Prophet ﷺ, I'll share a true story with you. I was travelling on an international flight when I fell very sick with fever. I took Tylenol and reached a point where the Tylenol was no longer working and there was still ten more hours of the flight left. So, I called the flight attendant and asked if they have any ibuprofen, which I know I needed. She looked at me and said she was sorry, but she couldn't give it to me due to regulations. So, I said, okay, I'm a physician and I know that I need it, but I also know that we need to follow rules.

Then I remembered sending prayers upon the Prophet – peace and blessings be upon him صَلَاةٌ عَلَى النَّبِيِّ عَلَيْهِ الصَّلَاةُ وَالسَّلَامُ, and I kept doing it for the next two hours with full *yaqeen* – full certainty that this is going to work. I didn't get better instantly, but noticed how Allah ﷻ operates. After two hours, I was still very sick and another flight attendant came to me and said, you look very sick, do you need anything? I replied yes and asked 'Do you have ibuprofen?' She said, I do, generally I'm not supposed to give it to you, but as you are a physician, I'll give it to you. I took the tablets and Allah ﷻ permitted a temporary cure, and I was able to sleep the rest of the flight.

The reason I'm sharing this is because it shows one of the ways sending prayers on the Prophet ﷺ can help us. There's a long *hadith* when Ubay ibn Ka'b رضي الله عنه was with *Rasul Allah* ﷺ. He said, '*Ya Rasulullah*! I normally send *salawat* on you. How much should I do? One fourth?', he said, 'that's great. Can you do more?' He said, 'one third', *Rasul Allah* ﷺ said, 'that's great. Can you do more?' He said, 'half.' He said, 'that's great. Can you do more?' And then he said, 'okay, then I'm going to do all of it.' Then he ﷺ responded with two things, إِذًا تُكْفَى هَمَّكَ وَيُغْفَرُ لَكَ ذَنْبُكَ 'you will have nothing to worry about, and your sins will be forgiven.'[139]

Whenever we say the *salawat*, we really have to have *yaqeen*, certainty, that it works. There is a general principle in our *deen* not to 'test' things out and think to ourselves: *let's see, maybe it will work, maybe it will not.* This is not the right way to go about this. Instead, we should have hope in the best

139 Abu Isa Muhammad al-Tirmidhi, "Chapter: The exhortation for remembrance of Allah and remembrance of death at the end of the night, and the virtue of increased salat upon the Prophet ﷺ," *Jami' al-Tirmidhi*, Book 37, Hadith 43.

outcome: '*Ya Allah! You taught me through Rasul Allah* ﷺ *that this is going to work, and I'm saying it and I know it works.*' Doing *Salawat* is obeying Allah ﷻ and following the example of the angels. When you do this constantly and with certainty, you will find many worries are removed by the Will of Allah ﷻ.

2. Multiple rewards

Abū Hurayrah رضي الله عنه reported that the Messenger of Allah ﷺ said: "Whoever sends one blessing upon me, Allah will send ten blessings upon him."[140] Allah ﷻ will send ten *salawat*, ten *du'a* for us when we send blessing on our *Rasul* ﷺ. This is like someone telling you to give them one dollar, and they will return ten dollars to you – a transaction everyone will be willing to do. When sending prayers (blessings) upon the Prophet ﷺ how much more reward there is than a financial transaction!

3. A higher degree

How many of us want our levels to be higher? We all want this. We regret that we have so many sins, and want Allah ﷻ to forgive us. Abū Ṭalḥah al-Anṣārī reported that the Messenger of Allah ﷺ said:

140 Muslim bin Hajjaj, "Chapter: Sending salat upon the Prophet ﷺ after the tashahhud," *Sahih Muslim*, Book 4, Hadith 74.

عَنْ أَبِي طَلْحَةَ الْأَنْصَارِيِّ، قَالَ: قَالَ رَسُولُ اللَّهِ ﷺ

مَنْ صَلَّى عَلَيَّ صَلَاةً، صَلَّى اللَّهُ عَلَيْهِ بِهَا عَشْرًا، وَحُطَّتْ عَنْهُ عَشْرُ سَيِّئَاتٍ، وَرُفِعَتْ لَهُ عَشْرُ دَرَجَاتٍ

"Whoever sends one prayer (blessings) upon me, Allah will send ten upon him, ten sins will be erased from him, and ten degrees will be raised for him."[141] Imagine if you send one hundred blessings a day, that would multiply into thousands.

4. Etiquettes of *du'a*

Whenever we make *du'a*, raising our hands to Allah ﷺ and asking Him, one of the etiquettes is, after you praise Allah ﷺ, you send صَلَوَاتُ عَلَى النَّبِيِّ عَلَيْهِ الصَّلَاةُ وَالسَّلَامُ on the Prophet and then continue with the rest of your *du'a*. The scholars taught us that this *salawat* causes our *du'a* to be granted.

5. Closeness to the Messenger of Allah ﷺ

Everyone will, for sure, want to be close to *Rasul Allah* ﷺ on the Day of Judgement. If we want him to be our neighbour, then we need to do a lot of prayers (*salawat*). *Rasul Allah* ﷺ said, أَوْلَى النَّاسِ بِي يَوْمَ الْقِيَامَةِ أَكْثَرُهُمْ عَلَيَّ صَلَاةً, 'The closest and who has the highest right upon me, (upon the *Rasul* ﷺ) is the one who sends a lot of *salah* on me.'[142]

141 Jāmiʿ al-Tirmidhi, Hadith 485, Hasan Ṣaḥīḥ

142 Abu Isa Muhammad al-Tirmidhi, "Chapter: What has been related about the virtues of sending salat upon the Prophet," *Jami'al-Tirmidhi*, Book 3, Hadith 32.

We can apply this to our real-life situation. If there is someone who always remembers you; always asks about you, texts you; checks in on you, wouldn't you love them more and give them more priority? This is what closeness to the *Rasul* ﷺ is about. Another benefit listed by Imam Ibn al-Qayyim is receiving the reply of *Rasul Allah* ﷺ.[143] Who would not want to talk to *Rasul Allah* ﷺ ? Of course we all want to, but how are we going to do that? By sending *salawat.*

Abū Hurayrah ﵁ reported that the Messenger of Allah ﷺ said: "Do not make your houses like graves. Do not make my grave a place of celebration. And send *ṣalawat* (blessings) upon me, for your *ṣalawat* reaches me wherever you may be." [144]

6. Purification

We have covered ways to purify the heart in every chapter. What we are covering is how our life can be purified as a result of our heart being cleansed. It's a common feeling to think: *I want my life to be pure. I want my house to be pure, my children to be pure. I don't need anything else if Allah* ﷻ *gives me these.* Ibn al-Qayyim explains that sending *ṣalawat* upon the Prophet ﷺ is a *zakāh* for the one who does it and a purification for his life.

143 Ibn al Qayyim, *Jala' al Afham fi Fadl al Salah wa al Salam 'ala Khayr al Anam.*
144 Abū Dāwūd, Hadith 1047; also in An-Nasā'ī and others, ḥasan

The Prophet ﷺ instructed us: "Send blessings upon me, for your blessings upon me are a purification for you."[145] This means that when we send *ṣalawat* upon the Prophet ﷺ, it cleanses us, increases us in goodness, and even brings *barakah* (blessing) in our time and efforts. The one hour that we might spend doing one thing, where there are blessings, we actually achieve ten things in the same amount of time, by Allah's ﷻ permission.

عَنْ أَوْسِ بْنِ أَوْسٍ، قَالَ: قَالَ رَسُولُ اللَّهِ ﷺ:

إِنَّ مِنْ أَفْضَلِ أَيَّامِكُمْ يَوْمُ الْجُمُعَةِ، فِيهِ خُلِقَ آدَمُ، وَفِيهِ قُبِضَ، وَفِيهِ النَّفْخَةُ، وَفِيهِ الصَّعْقَةُ، فَأَكْثِرُوا عَلَيَّ مِنَ الصَّلَاةِ فِيهِ، فَإِنَّ صَلَاتَكُمْ مَعْرُوضَةٌ عَلَيَّ.

قَالُوا: يَا رَسُولَ اللَّهِ، وَكَيْفَ تُعْرَضُ صَلَاتُنَا عَلَيْكَ وَقَدْ أَرِمْتَ؟ يَعْنُونَ الْمَوْتَ قَالَ: إِنَّ اللَّهَ عَزَّ وَجَلَّ حَرَّمَ عَلَى الْأَرْضِ أَنْ تَأْكُلَ أَجْسَادَ الْأَنْبِيَاءِ.

Aws ibn Aws reported that the Messenger of Allah ﷺ said: "Indeed, among the best of your days is Friday. On it Adam was created, on it he died, on it the Trumpet will be blown, and on it the Blast will strike. So increase in sending prayers (*ṣalawat*) upon me on that day, for your prayers are presented to me." They said: "O Messenger of Allah, how will our prayers be presented to you when you have decayed?" He ﷺ replied: "Allah, Mighty and Majestic, has forbidden the earth from consuming the bodies of the Prophets."

I will respond.[146]

---

145 Musnad Aḥmad (22960); Shuʿab al-Īmān by al-Bayhaqī. Authenticated as ḥasan by al-Albānī.

146 Abu Dawud, "Chapter: Visiting Graves," *Sunan Abi Dawud*, Book 11, Hadith 322.

In another *hadith*, the Prophet ﷺ said: "There is no one who sends greetings (*salam*) upon me except that Allah ﷻ returns my soul to me so that I may return his *salam*."[147] How little time it takes to say: *"Allāhumma ṣalli 'alā Muḥammad"* and we are assured Allah ﷻ returns his soul to him ﷺ so that he can respond to our greeting. When we say *salam* on the Prophet ﷺ, we receive blessings and purification. When we send *salam*, he ﷺ is spiritually returned to respond to our greeting. Both are easy acts with great reward.

There are blessed times of the year where we increase in all our *ibadah*, such as in *Ramadan*, when we can send more blessings, and particular days such as Friday – *Jumu'ah*. Friday is one of the most blessed days as the above *hadith* mentioned, hence we are told: 'Send abundant blessings on me' فَأَكْثِرُوا عَلَيَّ مِنَ الصَّلَاةِ.[148]

Salawat – a part of life

Whenever you are free and unoccupied say: "O Allah, send blessings upon Muhammad ﷺ" اللَّهُمَّ صَلِّ عَلَى مُحَمَّدٍ When you are cooking, purify the cooking, make it better by sending blessings upon the Prophet صَلَوَاتٌ عَلَى النَّبِيِّ عَلَيْهِ الصَّلَاةُ وَالسَّلَامُ ﷺ. If you're not feeling good, things aren't working out and you feel down, say:

147 Abū Dāwūd, *Sunan Abī Dāwūd*, Hadith 2041; Musnad Aḥmad 3712. Graded ṣaḥīḥ by al-Albānī (*Ṣaḥīḥ Abī Dāwūd*, no. 2041).

148 Abu Dawud, "Chapter: About seeking forgiveness," *Sunan Abi Dawud*, Book 8, Hadith 116.

اللَّهُمَّ صَلِّ عَلَى مُحَمَّدٍ وَعَلَى آلِ مُحَمَّدٍ

Last but not least, there is a *hadith* that teaches us the importance of *salawat* on the Prophet ﷺ along with other vital advice. The Companions saw *Rasul Allah* ﷺ getting up on the minbar and he said, "*Ameen*" They asked, "*Ya Rasul Allah*! Why did you say *Ameen*?" He ﷺ replied, "Jibril (عليه السلام) came to me and said: 'May he be humiliated, may he be humiliated, may he be humiliated – the one who:

- lives through *Ramadan* and is not forgiven,
- the one in whose presence I am mentioned, and he does not send *salawat* (blessings) upon me,
- and the one who has one or both of his parents reach old age, yet he does not enter *Jannah* because of them.

The Prophet ﷺ said "*Ameen*" after each one of the points mentioned above. [149]

May Allah ﷻ make us always remember *Rasul Allah* ﷺ. May Allah ﷻ beautify our tongues with الصلاة عَلَيْهِ الصَّلَاةُ وَالسَّلَامُ.

اللَّهُمَّ صَلِّ عَلَى مُحَمَّدٍ وَعَلَى آلِ مُحَمَّدٍ، كَمَا صَلَّيْتَ عَلَى إِبْرَاهِيمَ وَعَلَى آلِ إِبْرَاهِيمَ

149 Muhammad bin Abdullah al-Khatib, "Chapter: Blessing on the Prophet, and its excellence," *Mishkat al-Masabih*, Book 4, Hadith 350.

Rasul Allah ﷺ said:
"Whoever sends one prayer (blessings) upon me, Allah will send ten upon him, ten sins will be erased from him, and ten degrees will be raised for him."
(al-Tirmidhi)

My Dear Heart

Do you Pray at Night?

We have learned a great deal about what makes our heart impure and the ways to keep it pure. There are times when we are actively cleansing our heart for a long period, such as during *Ramadan*. However, what happens for the rest of the year? The spiritual health of our heart is just like exercising and diet which needs to be consistent if we want to build muscles and stay healthy. What else can we do to make sure our heart is cleansed and stays clean?

One of the best things that needs to be done consistently, not only in *Ramadan*, is *qiyām al-layl* قِيَامُ اللَّيْلِ the night *salah*. Many people do it in *Ramadan* when all the mosques are full. However, after *Ramadan* this habit may gradually be lost.

The Night Prayer *qiyām al-layl* and *Rasul Allah* ﷺ

When *Rasul Allah* ﷺ first received revelation and returned to his beloved wife *Sayyida* Khadijah رضي الله عنها, he said *zammilooni, zammilooni* زَمِّلُونِي زَمِّلُونِي,[150] meaning 'Cover me, cover me.' *Sayyida* Khadija رضي الله عنها covered *Rasul Allah* ﷺ with a cloak or blanket. *Surah al-Muzzammil* meaning 'The One Wrapped in a Cloak' refers to this experience. For the Messenger of Allah ﷺ *qiyām al-layl* was an obligation:

يَا أَيُّهَا الْمُزَّمِّلُ قُمِ اللَّيْلَ إِلَّا قَلِيلًا

O You [Prophet], enfolded in your cloak!

Arise [to pray] the night, except for a little.
(al-Muzzammil 73:1-2)

To stand in prayer for most of the night was an obligation for *Rasul Allah* ﷺ. This is not an obligation for us, however, it's an amazing virtue and one of the defining characteristics of a believer to observe some night prayer.

And our Prophet ﷺ said, 'قِيَامُ اللَّيْلِ شَرَفُ الْمُؤْمِنِ.[151] The honour of the believer is the night *salah.*' And Allah سبحانه وتعالى praises those who perform night *salah*. When He سبحانه وتعالى mentions His servants – the عِبَادُ الرَّحْمَٰنِ, the special elite servants, one of their criteria is, وَالَّذِينَ يَبِيتُونَ لِرَبِّهِمْ سُجَّدًا وَقِيَامًا *And those who spend*

150 Muhammad bin Ismail al-Bukhari, "Prophetic commentary on the Qur'an: Who has taught (the writing) by the pen," *Sahih al Bukhari*, Book 65, Hadith 479.

151 Ibn 'Uthaymin, *Kitab Liqa' al-Bab al-Maftuh*, Vol 119, page 15.

[part of] the night to their Lord prostrating and standing [in prayer]. (*al-Furqan* 25:64)

Allah ﷻ also said:

تَتَجَافَىٰ جُنُوبُهُمْ عَنِ ٱلْمَضَاجِعِ يَدْعُونَ رَبَّهُمْ خَوْفًا وَطَمَعًا وَمِمَّا رَزَقْنَٰهُمْ يُنفِقُونَ

Their sides part [i.e., they arise] from their [beds]; they supplicate their Lord in fear and aspiration, and from what We have provided them, they spend. (As-Sajdah 32:16)

This verse is one to remember and to ask Allah ﷻ to help you to reject the bed so you can stand up in the last third of the night, even thirty minutes before *Fajr,* in front of Him ﷻ. In the state of being so tired, this verse is an incentive to be of those who reject their bed, in favour of their Lord.

The best *salah*

Abū Hurayrah ﷺ reported that the Messenger of Allah ﷺ said: The best prayer after the obligatory prayers is the night prayer *Qiyām al-Layl.* [152]

Sayyida Aisha ﷺ described how *Rasul Allah* ﷺ, used to do a minimum eleven *rakah*[153] daily between *Isha* and *Fajr* (there's a different opinion about how many *rakat*). Whether he did it in the beginning of the night or towards the end of the night or all the night, he used to stand up in *salah* till

152 Muslim bin Hajjaj, "Chapter: The virtue of fasting in Muharram," *Sahih Muslim*, Book 13, Hadith 261.

153 Muhammad bin Ismail al-Bukhari, "Chapter: The eyes of the Prophet ﷺ used to sleep, but his heart used not to sleep," *Sahih al-Bukhari*, Book 61, Hadith 78.

his feet were cracked, and in another account, almost bleeding. When Aisha ﵂ asked him, 'Why are you doing this, *Ya Rasulullah*? all your sins were forgiven.' He replied: 'أَفَلاَ أُحِبُّ أَنْ أَكُونَ عَبْدًا شَكُورًا, Shouldn't I be a grateful servant to Allah ﵎?'[154]

In *Surah Muzzammil*, Allah ﵎ confirms *Rasul Allah's* ﷺ *qiyām:*

إِنَّ رَبَّكَ يَعْلَمُ أَنَّكَ تَقُومُ أَدْنَىٰ مِن ثُلُثَيِ ٱلَّيْلِ وَنِصْفَهُۥ وَثُلُثَهُۥ وَطَآئِفَةٌ مِّنَ ٱلَّذِينَ
مَعَكَ ۚ وَٱللَّهُ يُقَدِّرُ ٱلَّيْلَ وَٱلنَّهَارَ ۚ عَلِمَ أَن لَّن تُحْصُوهُ فَتَابَ عَلَيْكُمْ ۖ فَٱقْرَءُوا۟ مَا تَيَسَّرَ
مِنَ ٱلْقُرْءَانِ ۚ عَلِمَ أَن سَيَكُونُ مِنكُم مَّرْضَىٰ ۙ وَءَاخَرُونَ يَضْرِبُونَ فِى ٱلْأَرْضِ يَبْتَغُونَ
مِن فَضْلِ ٱللَّهِ ۙ وَءَاخَرُونَ يُقَـٰتِلُونَ فِى سَبِيلِ ٱللَّهِ ۖ فَٱقْرَءُوا۟ مَا تَيَسَّرَ مِنْهُ ۚ وَأَقِيمُوا۟
ٱلصَّلَوٰةَ وَءَاتُوا۟ ٱلزَّكَوٰةَ وَأَقْرِضُوا۟ ٱللَّهَ قَرْضًا حَسَنًا ۚ وَمَا تُقَدِّمُوا۟ لِأَنفُسِكُم مِّنْ خَيْرٍ
تَجِدُوهُ عِندَ ٱللَّهِ هُوَ خَيْرًا وَأَعْظَمَ أَجْرًا ۚ وَٱسْتَغْفِرُوا۟ ٱللَّهَ ۖ إِنَّ ٱللَّهَ غَفُورٌ رَّحِيمٌۢ

Indeed, your Lord knows, [O Muḥammad], that you stand [in prayer] almost two thirds of the night or half of it or a third of it, and [so do] a group of those with you. And Allah determines [the extent of] the night and the day. He has known that you [Muslims] will not be able to do it and has turned to you in forgiveness, so recite what is easy [for you] of the Qur'ān. He has known that there will be among you those who are ill and others traveling throughout the land seeking [something] of the bounty of Allah and others fighting for the cause of Allah. So recite what is easy from it and establish prayer and give zakah and loan Allah a goodly loan. And whatever

154 Muhammad bin Ismail al-Bukhari, "The statement of Allah the Exalted: That Allah may forgive you your sins of the past and the future," *Sahih al Bukhari*, Book 65, Hadith 358.

good you put forward for yourselves - you will find it with Allah. It is better and greater in reward. And seek forgiveness of Allah. Indeed, Allah is Forgiving and Merciful. (al-Muzzammil 73:20)

Standing up in the night means you are giving up the comfort of your bed and rest, especially after being tired throughout the day. In the night when you are standing up for *salah*, it means Allah ﷻ is more important to you than your comfort and rest. This is one of the things the *Shaytan* works diligently to make us avoid and not perform.

The Messenger of Allah ﷺ said: "When one of you sleeps, *Shayṭan* ties three knots at the back of his head. With every knot he says: 'You have a long night ahead of you, so sleep.' If the person wakes up and remembers Allah ﷻ, one knot is undone. If he performs *wuḍu*', a second knot is undone. And if he prays, the third knot is undone. Then he wakes up energetic and with a good heart. Otherwise, he wakes up lazy and with a foul heart." The *Shaytan*'s work is to make us sleep longer and miss the blessings of *qiyām*. However, when you start your day with this *nafl Salah* before *Fajr*, even two *rakah*, you will see how active you feel; how the day is full of blessings and you feel good. The opposite is also very true, as it says in the *hadith* that missing our *Fajr salah* will make us feel bad and lazy.[155]

You may have seen some people who have a brightness, a *nur* coming from their face. Have you ever wondered why?

---

155 Muslim bin Hajjaj, "Chapter: Encouragement to pray at night even if it is little," *Sahih Muslim*, Book 6, Hadith 247.

Al-Hasan al-Basri ﷺ was asked: 'Why are those who pray at night the most beautiful people? He said: Because they left themselves to the Most Merciful, so He ﷻ clothed them in light from His ﷻ light.[156] What is Allah's ﷻ *nur* – light? He ﷻ tells us in *Surah al-Nur*:

ٱللَّهُ نُورُ ٱلسَّمَٰوَٰتِ وَٱلْأَرْضِ ۚ مَثَلُ نُورِهِۦ كَمِشْكَوٰةٍ فِيهَا مِصْبَاحٌ ۖ ٱلْمِصْبَاحُ فِى زُجَاجَةٍ ۖ ٱلزُّجَاجَةُ كَأَنَّهَا كَوْكَبٌ دُرِّىٌّ يُوقَدُ مِن شَجَرَةٍ مُّبَٰرَكَةٍ زَيْتُونَةٍ لَّا شَرْقِيَّةٍ وَلَا غَرْبِيَّةٍ يَكَادُ زَيْتُهَا يُضِىٓءُ وَلَوْ لَمْ تَمْسَسْهُ نَارٌ ۚ نُّورٌ عَلَىٰ نُورٍ ۗ يَهْدِى ٱللَّهُ لِنُورِهِۦ مَن يَشَآءُ ۚ وَيَضْرِبُ ٱللَّهُ ٱلْأَمْثَٰلَ لِلنَّاسِ ۗ وَٱللَّهُ بِكُلِّ شَىْءٍ عَلِيمٌ

'Allah is the Light of the heavens and the earth. The example of His light is like a niche within which is a lamp; the lamp is within glass, the glass as if it were a pearly [white] star lit from [the oil of] a blessed olive tree, neither of the east nor of the west, whose oil would almost glow even if untouched by fire. Light upon light. Allah guides to His light whom He wills. And Allah presents examples for the people, and Allah is Knowing of all things.' (al-Nur 24:35)

For those who do *qiyām al-layl* Allah ﷻ gives them part of His ﷻ light. A frequent question that comes up is: it's just too hard for me to get up, I try my best, but still can't wake up for *qiyām*? This statement gives us some clarity as the Prophet ﷺ said: إِنَّ الرَّجُلَ لَيُذْنِبُ الذَّنْبَ فَيُحْرَمُ بِهِ قِيَامَ اللَّيْلِ. "A man may commit a sin, and because of it he is deprived of standing (in prayer) at night."[157]

---

156 Ibn al-Jawzi, "Chapter 98," *Al-Mudhish*, page 523.

157 Reported by Ibn Mājah (Hadith 4022)Classified as ḥasan (good) by al-Albani in Ṣaḥiḥ Ibn Mājah.

A man queried a righteous man, saying he could not get up for the *qiyām al-layl*, so he asked him what he needs to do. And he said: لَا تَعْصِهِ بِالنَّهَارِ وَهُوَ يُقِيمُكَ بَيْنَ يَدَيْهِ بِاللَّيْلِ. "Do not disobey Him during the day while He is the One who makes you stand before Him at night."[158] In other words, it is Allah ﷻ Who will allow us to sleep and He ﷻ will permit us to wake up in the night.

Sufyan al-Thawri ﵀, a famous follower, said: 'I was deprived of the night *salah* for five months because of one sin.'[159] This is a point for all of us to ponder upon: sins have consequences. One of the consequences of sins is the removal of a good deed from us. So anytime you find yourself being permitted to do something good, which then ceases, the first question to ask yourself is, *what did I do wrong*?

A beautiful statement from Abu Sulayman describes the attachment to the night prayer, where he said: "The people of *qiyām al-layl*, the people of the night are enjoying their night more than the people of amusement are in their amusement, and if it were not for the night, I would not love to remain in this world." What he was stating is that those who spend their night occupied in the *dunya*, whether they are with people talking, or on their phone, or watching something, they don't experience the joy that comes from *qiyām al-layl*. When anyone performs the night prayer, they will truly understand this.

---

158 *Ahmad Farid*, "Causes of the heart's life and its beneficial nourishment: Qiyam al-Layl," *Tazkiyat al-Nufus*, page 50.

159 Ibid, 51.

The best time for *qiyām al-layl*

In the global north and the global south there are long winter nights at opposite times of the year. In contrast, countries in the Middle East and around the equator, have nights and days that stay almost the same length throughout the year. The experience of the night prayer is therefore different depending on the time of year and location. The winter nights are a blessing because they are long. Ḥasan al-Baṣrī is reported to have said, "The best season for a believer is winter. Its nights are long for those who wish to pray, and its days are short for those who wish to fast."[160]

During the winter nights, it's easier to get six hours sleep or more if needed before waking up for the night prayer. This helps to wake up full of energy to stand in *salah* and talk to Him ﷾, and ask from Him ﷾. The best time to ask Allah ﷾ for what you want, including forgiveness, is actually just before *Fajr.*

In the *hadith al-Qudsi,*[161] we are informed that Allah ﷾ comes down in the way that befits Him ﷾ in the last third of the night. Abū Hurayrah ؓ reported that the Messenger of Allah ﷺ said: "Our Lord, Blessed and Exalted, descends every night to the lowest heaven during the last third of the night and says: 'Who is calling upon Me so that I may answer him? Who is asking Me so that I may give him?

160 Ibn Rajab al-Ḥanbalī, *Laṭā'if al-Ma'ārif.*
161 Ṣaḥiḥ al-Bukhari 1145, Ṣaḥiḥ Muslim 758

Who is seeking My forgiveness so that I may forgive him?'[162]

One of the righteous people Ibn al-Munkadir said, 'There is nothing left from the joy of this *dunya* except the night *salah*, meeting and knowing righteous brothers and sisters, and *salah* in congregation.'[163]

We can take advantage of the blessed month of *Ramadan* to gain the habit of *qiyām*, by offering two or four *rakah qiyām al-layl* before *Fajr*, before going back to bed. A common question is whether one should do this night *salah* after *Isha* or only before *Fajr*? It is better to plan to do it before the *Fajr salah*. However, if one cannot and is worried they will not wake up in time, then it is better to do it before going to bed. This can be one *rakah*, three, or five, but at the very least make sure that there is one extra *salah* you do every night for Allah ﷻ. By His permission, we will experience the benefits as we develop this habit.

May Allah ﷻ make it easy for all of us, and may Allah ﷻ help us be regular in *qiyām al-layl*. We ask Allah ﷻ for His permission to purify our hearts in the last third of the night, and forgive us our sins that are a barrier to this *ibadah*. *Ya Rabbi Ameen.*

---

162 Muhammad bin Ismail al-Bukhari, "Chapter: Supplication in the last third of the night," *Al-Adab Al-Mufrad*, Book 32, Hadith 8.

163 Ruqayyah al-Muharib, "Chapter on what the Muslim gains from the night prayer in this world and the hereafter," *Kitab al-Ibanah an Asbab al-I'anah ala Salat al-Fajr wa Qiyam al-Layl*, page 22.

Abu Hurayrah ؓ reported that the Messenger of Allah ﷺ said: The best prayer after the obligatory prayers is the night prayer *Qiyam al-Layl*.

(Muslim)

My Dear Heart

Are you Asking Allah?

We found in chapter twenty-five that our hearts find rest in the remembrance of Allah ﷻ. One of the ways we find this peace and satisfaction is through an act of worship that brings us closest to our *Rabb*. It is one of the unique things that Allah ﷻ tells us to do repeatedly: making *du'a* – supplicate to Him ﷻ for all our needs. The beauty of it is, it's not an extra form of *ibadah*, it's an order from Allah ﷻ. So when we raise our hands, that action by itself, before we even use our voice, is actually an act of worship we will be rewarded for. In *Surah Ghafir* He ﷻ says in the imperative, urging us to call on Him:

وَقَالَ رَبُّكُمُ ٱدْعُونِىٓ أَسْتَجِبْ لَكُمْ ۚ إِنَّ ٱلَّذِينَ يَسْتَكْبِرُونَ عَنْ عِبَادَتِى سَيَدْخُلُونَ جَهَنَّمَ دَاخِرِينَ

And your Lord says, "Call upon Me; I will respond to you." Indeed, those who disdain My worship will enter Hell [rendered] contemptible. (Ghafir 40:60)

We need to reflect on ourselves, are we making the most of this invitation? When we finish *salah*, with *Assalaamu Alaikum* to our right and left, what do we usually do next? Most people, not everybody, but most leave the *salah* immediately to do the next thing on their mind, whether it is necessary or not. Or, another instinct is to immediately reach out for our phone and look at it instead of raising our hands and asking Allah ﷻ. *Rasul Allah* ﷺ saw a *sahabi* doing this and he looked at him and said 'has this man nothing to ask of Allah ﷻ? [164] In other words, does he not need Allah ﷻ anymore?

A powerful verse which comes between the verses about fasting in *Ramadan* in *Surah al-Baqarah* makes the closeness of Allah ﷻ to us clear. A *Sahabi* asked *Rasul Allah* ﷺ about Allah ﷻ, and He responded:

وَإِذَا سَأَلَكَ عِبَادِى عَنِّى فَإِنِّى قَرِيبٌ ۖ أُجِيبُ دَعْوَةَ ٱلدَّاعِ إِذَا دَعَانِ ۖ فَلْيَسْتَجِيبُوا۟ لِى وَلْيُؤْمِنُوا۟ بِى لَعَلَّهُمْ يَرْشُدُونَ

164 Muhammad bin Ismail al-Bukhari, "Chapter: Recitation of the Qur'an," *Sahih al-Bukhari*, Book 10, Hadith 151.

And when My servants ask you, [O Muḥammad], concerning Me – indeed I am near. I respond to the invocation of the supplicant when he calls upon Me. So let them respond to Me [by obedience] and believe in Me that they may be [rightly] guided.
(al-Baqarah 2:186)

Our *Rabb* didn't even say 'tell them I am near.' He ﷻ said 'I am very near':فَإِنِّي قَرِيبٌ meaning very close. أُجِيبُ دَعْوَةَ ٱلدَّاعِ, and the *ayah* continues with Allah ﷻ assuring those who call on Him ﷻ will be responded to.

Rasul Allah ﷺ said: إِنَّ اللَّهَ حَيِيٌّ كَرِيمٌ يَسْتَحِي إِذَا رَفَعَ الرَّجُلُ إِلَيْهِ يَدَيْهِ أَنْ يَرُدَّهُمَا صِفْرًا خَائِبَتَيْنِ. Allah ﷻ is حَيِيٌّ shy, in the way that befits Allah ﷻ and generous. He ﷻ feels shy if a servant of His raises his or her hand and He ﷻ lets him or her head back empty handed.[165] Meaning, no way He ﷻ will not respond.

There are two things to remember when asking Allah ﷻ: the first, even if you have nothing to ask Allah ﷻ, raising your hand and saying, *Ya Allah! Ya Allah! Ya Rabbi! How glorified You are*. That by itself is an act of worship. الدُّعَاءُ هُوَ الْعِبَادَةُ. *Du'a*, supplication, by itself is the essence of acts of worship.[166] Secondly, we can and should ask repeatedly. If I were to ask you for something, the first time, you may agree to it, then the second and third time you would probably be fine too, but by the fifth time? Surely anyone

165 Abu Isa Muhammad al-Tirmidhi, "Chapter: Indeed, Allah is Hayy, Generous," *Jami' al-Tirmidhi*, Book 48, Hadith 187.

166 Abu Dawud, "Chapter: Regarding Supplication," Sunan *Abi Dawud*, Book 8, Hadith 64.

would lose their patience. However, not Allah ﷻ. *Rasul Allah* ﷺ said:

مَنْ لَمْ يَسْأَلِ اللَّهَ يَغْضَبْ عَلَيْهِ

"Whoever does not ask Allah, He becomes angry with him."[167]

Similarly, Allah ﷻ said in *Surah Ghafir*:

إِنَّ ٱلَّذِينَ يَسْتَكْبِرُونَ عَنْ عِبَادَتِى سَيَدْخُلُونَ جَهَنَّمَ دَاخِرِينَ

Indeed, those who disdain My worship will enter Hell [rendered] comtemptible. (Ghafir 40:60)

When we don't ask Allah ﷻ, it's an act of arrogance and we should rest assured not to fall into the trap that the *Shaytan* lays with thoughts such as: *I asked and He did not answer.* There is no truth in this as we learn what happens to *du'as* from a *hadith* of *Rasul Allah* ﷺ where he said when a Muslim raises his hands asking Allah ﷻ, as long as what he is asking Allah ﷻ is not a sin, or to sever the kinship relationship, then one of three outcomes will happen.[168] This is a very important concept for everyone because many people say, I asked, I asked, but nothing happened. From this *hadith* we learn that:

1. Either He ﷻ is going to give you what you asked for, and every one of us has had this experience.

167 Abu Isa Muhammad al-Tirmidhi, "Chapter: From It: Whoever does not ask Allah, He gets angry with him," *Jami' al-Tirmidhi*, Book 48, Hadith 4.

168 Abu Isa Muhammad al Tirmidhi, "Chapter: About waiting for relief and other than that," *Jami' al-Tirmidhi*, Book 48, Hadith 204.

We have had this where, you asked Allah ﷻ and He ﷻ gave you what you asked for.

2. He's ﷻ not going to give it to you now, He's ﷻ going to give it to you on the Day of Judgement, and at that point you will be extremely happy. This is because, when He ﷻ grants me there, where my needs will be way more than here in this life, it will be even more valuable.

3. Instead He ﷻ is going to remove a harm from our life. How many times did you say, *I almost was in an accident. This almost happened to me and it didn't happen*, why? It's the *du'a* that you asked for, and the answer came in the form of a removal of something harmful.

Etiquettes of *du'a*

So when we ask Allah ﷻ, let us come with the following etiquettes. We should try our best to be in *ṭahārah* - the state of *wudu*. It's not a requirement, but it's better to be in a state of *wudu* if we can be. Also, if we can face the *qibla* it is good, and saying the *du'a* at least three times is best.

Ibn Masʿūd ﵁ said:

"When the Prophet ﷺ made *du'a*, he would supplicate three times, and when he asked (Allah for some-

> thing), he would ask three times."[169] Allah ﷾ loves those who are consistent and persistent in a state of *du'a*. When making *du'a*, we start with praising Allah ﷾ such as: "Glory is to You, O Allah, and praise and blessed is Your Name, and exalted is Your Majesty." The Prophet ﷺ heard a man making *du'a* without praising Allah ﷾ or sending blessings on the Prophet ﷺ. He said: "When one of you prays, let him begin by praising and glorifying his Lord, then send blessings upon the Prophet ﷺ, then let him supplicate for whatever he wishes."[170]

Second, remember when we talked about صَلَاةٌ عَلَى النَّبِيِّ. It's one of the keys for my *du'a* to be answered. Ask Allah ﷾ for forgiveness. لَا إِلٰهَ إِلَّا أَنْتَ سُبْحَانَكَ إِنِّي كُنْتُ مِنَ الظَّالِمِينَ. And then ask Allah ﷾ anything you want. Nothing is small for Allah ﷾. Don't say I'm shy to ask Allah ﷾. Who else is going to give you?

Preparing our mindset is just as important as the outward preparation. Firstly, we are beggars, and Allah ﷾ is the One Who has everything. He ﷾ says in *Surah Fatir*:

يَٰٓأَيُّهَا ٱلنَّاسُ أَنتُمُ ٱلْفُقَرَآءُ إِلَى ٱللَّهِ ۖ وَٱللَّهُ هُوَ ٱلْغَنِىُّ ٱلْحَمِيدُ

O mankind, you are those in need of Allah, while Allah is Free of need, the Praiseworthy. (Fatir 35:15)

---

169 Ṣaḥīḥ Muslim, Kitāb al-Dhikr wa'l-Du'ā' wa'l-Tawbah, ḥadīth no. 2734

170 Sunan Abī Dāwūd, ḥadīth 1481

The words in this *ayah*: *Fuqarāʾilā Allāh*, means those totally dependent on Allah ﷻ as beggars, in need. It comes from the noun *al-faqīr* (singular) which is used for someone with little to sustain themselves – this is not just in the material sense, but its our human weakness and need for Allah ﷻ in every moment. [171]

Secondly, I need to ask Allah ﷻ knowing with certainty that He ﷻ is listening to me. Part of a beautiful *du'a* by the companion Abdullah ibn Mas'ud رضي الله عنه includes the following:

اللَّهُمَّ إِنَّكَ تَرَى مَكَانِي، وَتَسْمَعُ كَلَامِي، وَتَعْلَمُ سِرِّي وَعَلَانِيَتِي

> "*Ya Allah!* Indeed You see my place, You hear my speech, and You know my hidden and my open state." [172]

We need this closeness to Allah ﷻ in our heart when we supplicate. In another *hadith*, reported by Abu Hurayrah رضي الله عنه, *Rasul Allah* ﷺ said: "None of you should say, 'O Allah, forgive me if You wish, o Allah, have mercy on me if You wish,' but rather be decisive in your request, for there is no reproach for that." (Bukhari)

Thirdly, I need to supplicate with proper manners. As *Sayyidina* Omar رضي الله عنه always used to say, 'I'm not worried that Allah ﷻ will answer my *du'a*, I am worried that I do not fulfil the requirement of the *du'a*, or 'I carry the concern about [how to make] *du'a*.'[173]

171 Ibn Kathīr, Tafsir Ibn Kathir (Abridged), trans. Safi-ur-Rahman al-Mubarakpuri (Riyadh: Darussalam, 2000), vol. 8, p. 103.

172 Sulayman ibn Ahmad al-Tabarani, "Chapter: Al-A'een," *Al-Mu'jam aṣ-Ṣaghīr*, Vol 2, page 15.

173 bn Qayyim, "Chapter: Supplication is among the most beneficial of remedies," *Ad-Da' wa Dua'*, page 29.

If we imagine the situation where you are talking to someone and that person is looking at their phone, their thoughts are somewhere else, their mind is not taking in what you're saying. You're going to feel like neither you or what you're saying is important to this person. Imagine this with Allah ﷻ. We're raising our hands, our brain is somewhere else, we might even be distracted by something else nearby that catches our eyes or ears, all while we're making *du'a*. We don't want to find ourselves asking *Rabb al-'ālameen* like this.

Instead, make *du'a* in the best way possible so that it is answered, which in summary, is keeping three things in mind. One, is to remember the three ways that *du'as* are certainly answered, which includes answers which come in a way we were not expecting. Two, be sure within yourself that Allah ﷻ will respond. Three, choose the best times to make *du'a*.

So, as we said, for the *du'a* and the supplication to be granted, choose the right time, choose the right place, be in the right state, be sure and have certainty Allah ﷻ is listening and Allah ﷻ will respond.

The most blessed places and times for *du'a*

There are special places and times for supplication. Some of these may come once in a lifetime like the pilgrimage of *Hajj* or *Umrah*, where the pilgrim can make the most of the opportunity. Entering *Masjid al-Haram* offers a blessed opportunity as one looks at the Ka'ba, to make heartfelt *du'as*. When a pilgrim is at al-*Safa* and *al-Marwah*, standing on these small hills, this is a special time for *du'a* too. In *Arafah*, the main day of *Hajj*, this is the height of blessed times to supplicate to Allah ﷻ for everything. Just like we looked at the etiquettes of *du'a* above, and how to prepare ourselves mentally, so too is the preparation for the best times and places to make *du'a*, and making the most of these opportunities important. It's like the way we all look out for the retail 'sales' when we can make the most of the offers. So too with Allah ﷻ are these special times and places of *du'a*, where He ﷻ multiplies the blessings for us.

Amongst the best times to make supplication during the year, is of course *Ramadan*. The Prophet ﷺ said: "There are three whose supplication is not rejected: the fasting person until he breaks his fast, the just leader, and the supplication of the one who has been wronged."[174] Therefore, all day when you are fasting, just as you're going about your usual routine keep asking: *Ya Allah! Please forgive me. Ya Allah! Bless my children. Ya Allah! Make my children righteous. Ya Allah! Give me health. Ya Allah! Give me more life and make my deeds good. Ya Allah! Bring Muslims back to Your beautiful religion. Ya Allah! Lift all these calamities that are surrounding us.* There is so much we need to ask Allah ﷻ for. The time

174 Abu Isa Muhammad al-Tirmidhi, "Chapter: The *Mufarridun* have preceded," *Jami' al-Tirmidhi, Book* 48, Hadith 229.

just before breaking fast is special too and another opportunity for *du'a*.

Another specific blessed time for *du'a* which is often missed is between the *adhan* and *iqamah.* For example, when you are in the *masjid*, after the *adhan* is called, and especially at *Maghrib adhan*, followed by roughly five minutes until the *iqamah*. These few minutes are a blessed time as stated by *Rasul Allah* ﷺ: 'Supplication between the *adhan* and the *iqamah* is not rejected.'

During this time, it's better not to interact with anyone, but raise your hands in prayer. Just like this blessed time before *Maghrib* is important, so too is the time before *Fajr* which we discussed in depth in the previous chapter. Our supplication before *Fajr adhan,* is a huge opportunity for everyone, every dawn, right there in our homes.

When we are performing *salah*, we should supplicate as much as possible in *sujood*. The Prophet ﷺ said: "The closest a servant is to his Lord is while he is in prostration, so increase in supplication therein." [175] So, when in *sujood*, we should keep asking Him ﷻ, keep begging Him ﷻ. Another time for *du'as* to be granted by the permission of Allah ﷻ, is when it rains.

There is a beautiful *hadith* which makes an important point about our own condition when we are asking from Allah ﷻ. When *Rasul Allah* ﷺ, said "O people, Allah is good

175 Muslim bin Hajjaj, "Chapter: What is to be said while bowing and prostrating," *Sahih Muslim*, Book 4, Hadith 245.

and accepts only what is good...” Then he mentioned the man who travels a long distance, dishevelled and dusty, stretching his hands towards the sky, saying, “O Lord, my Lord”, and his food is unlawful, and his drink is unlawful, and his clothing is unlawful. He was raised on forbidden things, so how can he be answered?

Our attention in this *hadith* is focused on that state a person is in; that he is eating, drinking, or dressed in what is unlawful – *haram* or the sources of all these are *haram*. It could be the money that he is fulfilling his needs from comes from a prohibited source. In response to this *Rasul Allah* ﷺ asked how he will be given what he is asking for?

For us this means as we beg for our needs from Allah ﷿, let us all make sure that we live in a way pleasing to Allah ﷿ throughout the year. Often an effort to eat only *halal*, for example is made in *Ramadan*, but then forgotten afterwards. When we want our *du‘as* answered, we need to strive to continue to do this.

Finally, whatever we are doing, it is worthwhile to remember the noble example of *Sayyidina* Ibrahim ﵇, as he was building the Ka‘ba with *Sayyidina* Ismail ﵇ and prayed:

وَإِذْ يَرْفَعُ إِبْرَٰهِـۧمُ ٱلْقَوَاعِدَ مِنَ ٱلْبَيْتِ وَإِسْمَـٰعِيلُ رَبَّنَا تَقَبَّلْ مِنَّآ ۖ إِنَّكَ أَنتَ ٱلسَّمِيعُ ٱلْعَلِيمُ

رَبَّنَا وَٱجْعَلْنَا مُسْلِمَيْنِ لَكَ وَمِن ذُرِّيَّتِنَآ أُمَّةً مُّسْلِمَةً لَّكَ وَأَرِنَا مَنَاسِكَنَا وَتُبْ عَلَيْنَآ ۖ إِنَّكَ أَنتَ ٱلتَّوَّابُ ٱلرَّحِيمُ

And [mention] when Abraham was raising the foundations of the House and [with him] Ishmael, [saying], "Our Lord, accept [this] from us. Indeed, You are the Hearing, the Knowing. Our Lord, and make us Muslims [in submission] to You and from our descendants a Muslim nation [in submission] to You. And show us our rites [of worship] and accept our repentance. Indeed, You are the Accepting of Repentance, the Merciful. (al-Baqarah 2:127-128)

Sayyidina Ibrahim ﷺ and *Sayyidina* Ismail ﷺ were building the Ka'ba, but we are striving through our acts of *ibadah*; our fasting in *Ramadan*, our *salah* and our charity; plus our daily activities; our reading and understanding of the Book of Allah; our service to our family and community, everything we do should be accompanied with '*Ya Allah! Taqabbal minnā* تَقَبَّلْ مِنَّا, Accept it from us.' And if we didn't do things in the best way, if we have sinned, if we have disobeyed, we ask Allah ﷻ to accept our repentance, *Ya Rabbi Ameen.*

May Allah ﷻ accept our supplications. May He ﷻ give us the ability to turn to Him ﷻ frequently in *du'a* with a pure heart, in obedience to Him ﷻ. *Ya Rabbi Ameen.*

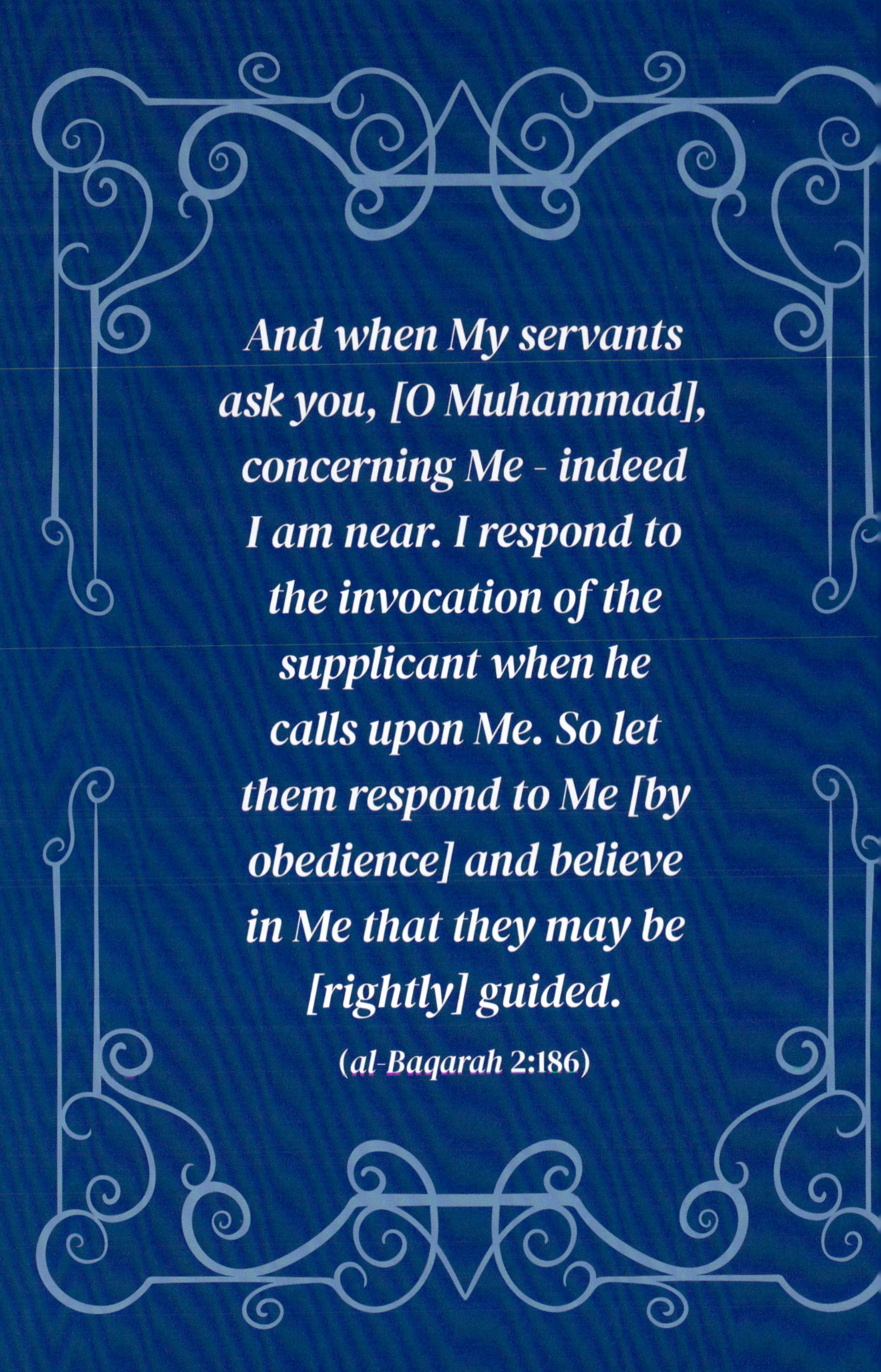
And when My servants ask you, [O Muhammad], concerning Me - indeed I am near. I respond to the invocation of the supplicant when he calls upon Me. So let them respond to Me [by obedience] and believe in Me that they may be [rightly] guided.
(al-Baqarah 2:186)

My Dear Heart

Are you Pure?

اَلْحَمْدُ لِلَّهِ رَبِّ الْعٰلَمِينَ

Praise be to Allah Lord of the Worlds.

Everything comes to an end. *Rasul Allah* ﷺ said in a beautiful *hadith*[176]:

"Jibrīl came to me and said: Love whomever you wish, for you will one day be separated from them. Live as long as you wish, for you will one day die. Do whatever you wish, for you will be recompensed for it. Know that the honour

176 Ibn Hamdun, "Chapter 13: On intellect, prudence, experience, foolishness, and ignorance," *Kitab at-Tadhkira al-Hamduniyya*, Vol 3, page 240.

[Full hadith in Reported by al-Ṭabarānī in al-Muʿjam al-Kabīr (3296), al-Bayhaqī in Shuʿab al-Īmān (9522), and others. Authenticated as ḥasan by al-Albānī in Ṣaḥīḥ al-Jāmiʿ, no. 2742.]

of the believer is his standing in prayer at night, and his dignity is his being independent of people."

At the end of our journey to purify our dear heart, we started with acknowledging the pure, crystal clear heart Allah ﷾ gives every newborn. As we go through life, that crystal can get dirty because of our surroundings; what we see, what we hear, who we interact with, and the desires we give in to. One by one, dot by dot, we add impurities to our heart. At the same time, Allah ﷾ gave us the remedies, the cleansing agents to keep our heart unpolluted by going back immediately and removing impurities, because our goal is to purify the heart Allah ﷾ gave us.

Looking back over the chapters, what is it that will help us return to Allah ﷾ with a clean heart? The first thing is paying attention to what we say, by having a filter for our tongue. Let's make sure most of what we say is pleasing to Allah ﷾.

Secondly, what do we look at and what do we listen to? If there are non-permissible *haram* things we are looking at, remove them and ask for Allah's ﷾ help to do this. Ask Allah ﷾ to put *barakah* in your time. Time is the same as the tongue; if we don't use it in Allah's ﷾ pleasure, we're going to use it in displeasing ways.

Let us look within us and see what feelings we have towards others: *do I think I'm better than everybody else? Do I look down at people? Do I have anger in me? And why am I angry? Is it because I think I'm better and I am entitled to certain things? Do I lie? And why do I lie?* All these thoughts and emotions, once we recognise them, and pay close attention to them, then we can apply the cure for each one.

Thirdly, look at our lifestyle and surroundings. Are we consuming too much food? Are we indulging in excessive talking, too much interaction with people? Are we looking at *haram*, or even looking too much at *halal*? All these corrupt our heart. The heart is very easily corrupted, but also just as easily cleaned and restored. That's the mercy - *rahmah* of Allah ﷻ.

If we take the blessed month of *Ramadan* as a 'model month', we can use it as a benchmark for the rest of the year. It's a month when we make extra effort; we fast, perform *taraweeh* and *qiyām al-layl*, we read and study the Qur'an – in the 'month of the Qur'an'; we stay away from sin with extra caution, and we guard our tongue. During *Ramadan*, it's easier for our hearts to be pure when we are taking all these steps towards Allah ﷻ. And may He ﷻ accept everything we did. What happens the day after *Eid al-Fitr*? Let's think back to last *Ramadan*, did we plan and make resolutions to keep after *Ramadan*?

There are two things we can do from one *Ramadan* to the next to help ourselves. The first is the selfie of my heart; what black spots did I allow to gather, and secondly have I used any remedies to clean them? The checklist of remedies are: *Did I remember Allah ﷻ with regular dhikr? Did I read the*

Qur'an? Did I ask Allah سبحانه وتعالى for forgiveness? Did I send regular salah and salam on the Prophet ﷺ? What about my obligatory salah? Am I the same as I was in Ramadan? Did I do qiyām al-layl? What is my relationship with the sunnah? How is my relationship with the Book of Allah سبحانه وتعالى? Am I being forgiving and generous? All these are good deeds and every good deed, once we do it, will remove a bad deed. When we do a bad deed, it's best to make it a habit to follow it up immediately with a good deed. He ﷺ said, 'Follow a bad deed with a good deed, it will be erased completely.'[177]

When we think back to *Ramadan*, we can see it as a training camp. Allah سبحانه وتعالى sends us training camps throughout the year but *Ramadan* is the biggest one for thirty days. Every day we were blessed to fast, we are grateful for it, and if we weren't able to for a reason like ill health, travel or pregnancy, then we substituted through giving *fidya* – or we planned to fast after the month and make the fasts up. What this proves to us is we have the resolve to obey Allah سبحانه وتعالى. If we can do it in *Ramadan*, we can do it after that by the permission of Allah سبحانه وتعالى.

In the year that passes from one *Ramadan* to the next, if we don't attempt to fast, our hearts will need a greater amount of cleansing, so it benefits us to keep up fasting, even if it is one day a week. Or we can try the three 'white' days a month (the Islamic months, 13th, 14th and 15th) and gradu-

177 Abu Isa Muhammad al-Tirmidhi, "Chapter: What has been related about having amicable relations with people," *Jami' al-Tirmidhi*, Book 27, Hadith 93.

ally form a habit. We can move on to two days a week, then every other day, especially in the short winter days for those of us who have this advantage.

Next, we look to the best cleansing agent for our heart: the Qur'an and our relationship with it. We need to make the best effort to keep our connection with it alive and beg Allah ﷻ that He ﷻ does not take us away from the Qur'an. Whether reading or learning how to read, whether understanding, memorizing, reviewing, whatever we are doing, we need to continue our efforts. It's understandable we will not be able to do exactly what we did in *Ramadan*, but we can do at least fifty percent and avoid becoming someone who worships *only* in *Ramadan*. Let's make sure our *masajid* stay full, remembering that every step we take to the *masjid*, as we put one foot in front of the other, a sin is removed.

With this *du'a* frequently on our tongue, we strive to do all we can to meet our *Rabb* with *Qalbun Saleem* – The sound heart.

اللَّهُمَّ آتِ نُفُوسَنَا تَقْوَاهَا، وَزَكِّهَا أَنْتَ خَيْرُ مَنْ زَكَّاهَا، أَنْتَ وَلِيُّهَا وَمَوْلَاهَا

"O Allah, grant our souls their taqwā, and purify them, for You are the best to purify them. You are their Guardian and Master."[178]

I ask Allah ﷻ to accept our efforts to purify our hearts. I ask Him ﷻ to forgive our shortcomings and increase us in obedience to Him ﷻ alone. *Ya Allah* give us more time,

178 Muslim bin Hajjaj, "Chapter: Supplications," *Sahih Muslim*, Book 48, Hadith 99.

prolong our lives and give us the ability to do righteous deeds. *Ameen.*

رَبَّنَا لَا تُزِغْ قُلُوبَنَا بَعْدَ إِذْ هَدَيْتَنَا وَهَبْ لَنَا مِن لَّدُنكَ رَحْمَةً ۚ إِنَّكَ أَنتَ ٱلْوَهَّابُ

Our Lord, let not our hearts deviate after You have guided us,
and grant us from Yourself mercy. Indeed, You are the Bestower.
(Āl-Imran 3:8)

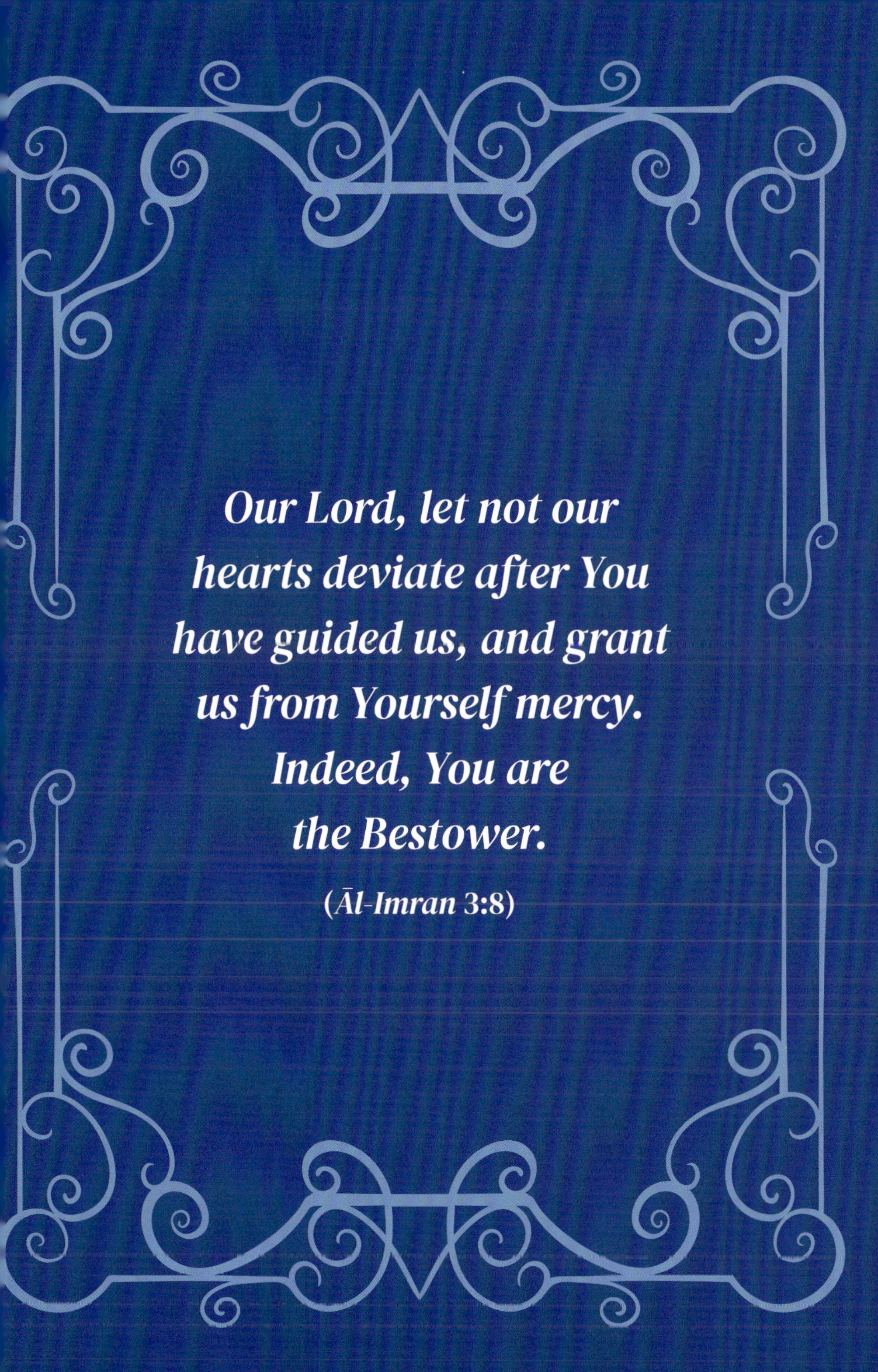
Our Lord, let not our hearts deviate after You have guided us, and grant us from Yourself mercy. Indeed, You are the Bestower.
(Āl-Imran 3:8)